PROVINCETOWN

Two women on Provincetown's back shore. Photograph courtesy of the
Pilgrim Monument and Provincetown Museum.

KAREN CHRISTEL KRAHULIK

PROVINCETOWN

From Pilgrim Landing to Gay Resort

New York University Press • *New York and London*

NEW YORK UNIVERSITY PRESS
New York and London
www.nyupress.org

Library of Congress Cataloging-in-Publication Data
Krahulik, Karen Christel.
Provincetown : from Pilgrim landing to gay resort / Karen Christel Krahulik.
p. cm. — (American history and culture (New York University Press)
Includes bibliographical references (p.   ) and index.
ISBN 0–8147–4761–2 (cloth : alk. paper)
1. Provincetown (Mass.)—History.   2. Provincetown (Mass.)—Social conditions.
I. Title.   II. Series.
F74.P96K73   2005
974.4'92—dc22   2005001779

New York University Press books are printed on acid-free paper,
and their binding materials are chosen for strength and durability.

Manufactured in the United States of America

10 9 8 7 6 5 4 3 2 1

For Robin A. Moscato and Lesley R. Matheson

Contents

Acknowledgments

TO THE MORE than seventy Provincetown townspeople who shared their stories with me in oral history interviews, I owe my deepest respect and appreciation. I know that my book will please some of you some of the time, and I hope that each of you sees how our conversations about Provincetown's past have brought this book to life. I am especially grateful for the day I met Gaby Kleykamp. An artist and volunteer at the Provincetown Public Library, Gaby took an interest in the Provincetown Oral History Project that I began in 1996, and she ended up scheduling and videotaping most of my interviews. Two other people in Provincetown deserve special recognition: Debbie DeJonker-Berry, the director of the Provincetown Public Library, supported me the entire way as a colleague and a friend; and Jeffory Morris, the curator of the Pilgrim Monument and Provincetown Museum, and also a friend, spent countless hours locating and scanning most of the images that this book now contains.

I incurred many debts during my three-year stay in Provincetown. I am grateful to current and past residents Stephen Borkowski, Gabriel Brooke, Helen Caddie-Larcenia, Diane Corbo, Napi Van Derek, and Jim Zimmerman for locating photographs and offering to share their stories in greater depth. Dan Scroggins and Kathleen Scroggins went out of their way to help me re-create the memory of Amelia Carlos, Kathleen's mother and Dan's grandmother. Marilyn Bean, Laurel Guadazno, and Chuck Turley from the Pilgrim Monument and Provincetown Museum; Luitgard "Lu" Hefland, Rene Gibbs-Brady, Jean Jarret, Laine Quinn, and Priscilla Randall from the Provincetown Public Library; and Dale Fanning, director of the former Provincetown Heritage Museum, all were quick to lend a helping hand. Ruth O'Donnell and Marguerite Beata Cook never missed an opportunity to offer me a happy-hour cocktail and to entertain me with stories about growing up in Provincetown. David Gleason, a doctoral candidate, was a delightful colleague. And the poet Sarah Messer, a fellow at the Provincetown Fine Arts Work Center, enchanted and soothed me with her clever yet warm prose. New York University, Harvard University, and the Bay

State Historical League provided financial assistance while I was conducting fieldwork and writing in Provincetown. The Massachusetts Foundation for the Humanities supported the Provincetown Oral History Project.

My academic advisors provided the most instructive form of mentorship: they led by example more than by direction. Lizabeth Cohen believed in me before I did, and she believed in this project from the start. She taught me how to shape a research project and an argument. Lisa Duggan helped me imagine the possibilities of a queer historical project, and she taught me how to think about a politics of pleasure. The first thing that impressed me about Martha Hodes was her unflinching command of African American history. She taught me the value of historiographic interventions and the contours of race in nineteenth-century America. In 1992 Susan Ware introduced me to the complexities of women's history and worked with me as a friend and mentor until I completed my work in 2000. Daniel Walkowitz introduced me to the politics of working-class histories and insisted that I become a better historian and writer.

I would also like to thank Penelope Johnson for being one of the most insightful and gracious teachers that I have ever had. In my own classes I have tried to follow her cue and am confident that my students have benefited as a result. And I thank Richard Hull for introducing me to the NYU history department. Lizabeth Cohen's graduate students at NYU read and commented on several chapters of my dissertation. I'd like to thank Katy Berry, Cindy Derrow, Kirsten Fermaglich, Michael Lerner, Neil Maher, Louise Maxwell, Debra Michals, Joan Saab, and Rona Wilk for their thoughtful analyses and warm friendships.

Duke University provided a talented network of colleagues and friends. I'd like to thank Francisco Hernández-Adrián, Zoila Airall, Leon Dunkley, Eric Estes, Carlisle Harvard, Juanita Johnson, Roger Kaplan, Beth Kivel, Felicia Kornbluh, Anna Krylova, Ian Lekus, Donna Lisker, Elaine Madison, Larry Moneta, Diane Nelson, Jean Fox O'Barr, Jolie Olcott, and Sue Wasiolek. I am lucky to have two families that care for my dog, Mabel, when I am out of town: Priscilla Wald, Joe Donahue, and their children Evan and Nathaniel will always have a special place in our heart; and Ray and Jennifer Caldwell will always be our favorite "keepers." I am especially indebted to Kerry Poynter, the program coordinator of the LGBT Center. He has been a delightful and talented colleague of mine for more than five years. Two competent and enthusiastic Duke students, Maddie Dewar and Adam Paige Hall, stepped in at the end to draw maps, locate missing sources, and review the manuscript. Patricia Allee and Emil R. Krahulik were excellent proofreaders. Eric Zinner has always had high hopes for this project, and he, Emily Park, and Despina Papazoglou Gimbel at NYU Press did their best to keep me on track.

I owe my sanity to an extended coterie of friends: Robin Burhke, Susan Culligan, Donna Flax, Denise Gaylord, Sue Anne Morrow, Robert Porter, Tracey Price, Donna Szeker, Liz Wheeler, and my Monday evening discussion group in Provincetown kept my spirits up and my head clear when the fogs of Cape Cod and North Carolina enveloped me. Robin Moscato, my butch mentor and best buddy for nearly two decades, taught me how to maintain my integrity despite the comings and goings of friends, lovers, and family members. Her partner, Michelle Goffe, accepted me as a part of their family. Her daughter and my namesake, Karen Leslie Moscato, reminded me how to live young again. Lesley R. Matheson, my other closest friend and longtime swimming partner, has always been there with a gem of advice and a warm smile.

A special note about Emil R. Krahulik, my father: he has sent me a brief, handwritten note (often using stationery from upscale hotels in distant lands) and at least one newspaper clipping every week since I left home at the age of fifteen. I look forward to each one. Christel J. Krahulik, my mother, has complemented Emil's letters with postcards and birthday cards. We've been working on a new "understanding" for as long as I've been working on this book. I am grateful that both projects have received the love and attention that they deserve.

Finally, I want to thank Susan Allee for her breadth of knowledge, passion, and integrity. We met in Provincetown at the moment I ceased looking for the love of my life, and there she was.

I was fortunate to have colleagues at Duke and elsewhere read the manuscript in its entirety. John Howard, Leisa Meyer, Leila Rupp, Marc Schachter, and Micol Seigel read early drafts of the manuscript and provided encouragement and guidance. During the final stages of revision, Marc Stein offered observations that enhanced the narrative considerably.

Introduction

"PROVINCETOWN IS a caring town. And I'm proud of it," Portuguese native Amelia Carlos declared in February 1998, just months before her lifelong tenure as a Provincetown resident came to an unexpected but peaceful end.[1] Amelia had the kind of Provincetown charm that caught the attention of visitors from afar and made them want to spend as much time and money as possible at this place called Land's End. Born on August 1, 1910, just four days before the dedication ceremonies for the Provincetown Pilgrim Monument, Amelia enjoyed nearly a century of change at the tip of Cape Cod.

Amelia's parents, Mary Joseph and Antone Rego, immigrated to Provincetown from St. Michael in the Azores and lived in the west end of town, the Portuguese end, at 48 Franklin Street. Like most Portuguese women in Provincetown, Amelia Carlos had strong ties to the fishing industry: her father worked the sea rather than the land, as did her husband, Frank. After marrying on October 13, 1931, Amelia and Frank Carlos spent most of their lives in the west end, at 52 Creek Road, where they raised two children, Kathleen and Frank, born in 1932 and 1941.

Amelia's husband, Frank, the son of Frank Carlos Sr. and Jennifer Randall, was the offspring of a "mixed" Portuguese–Nova Scotian marriage, a more common combination than either side cared to admit. Frank Carlos Jr. started fishing at an early age after being pulled from school to help support the family when his father died unexpectedly. Frank's new stepfather also was a fisherman but had lost his eyesight and needed Frank to captain his boat. The romance and excitement of fishing were lost on Frank, but with few other options, he found himself bound to the industry, working on various boats before entering Provincetown's cold-storage freezers, also called "fish factories," for much of his adult life. When the freezers closed, Frank took a job as the janitor of the Provincetown High School and, later, as the night clerk at the Moors Hotel.

As did most Portuguese women and girls in Provincetown, Amelia Carlos worked alongside male friends and relatives. She picked and sold blueberries in order to buy clothes for school, and when she was fourteen, she washed glasses and silverware at the Pilgrim House. Later, Amelia waited on tables at the Provincetown Inn; was a clerk for Malchman's, one of the few clothing stores in town; worked at the Patrician convenience store; cleaned houses; catered dinner parties, including one for Truman Capote; and took over at the Moors when her husband died in 1978. Two enterprising ventures also occupied a good part of her time: selling homemade beach-plum jam out of her kitchen and through local stores and renting three small cottages that Frank had built in the 1940s directly behind their house. Amelia supplemented and eventually replaced Frank's income with money from the tourists and seasonal residents that she welcomed into her cottages and home on Creek Road.

Amelia Carlos grew up during a tumultuous but exciting time in Provincetown, when Portuguese immigrants were displacing Anglo-European "Yankees"; artists were making Provincetown the "summer art capital of the world"; and tourists were flocking to Land's End in unprecedented numbers to watch the artists and Portuguese laborers at work and to visit the Pilgrim Monument, the new 252-foot reminder of Provincetown's colonial legacy. Spending most of her life in the west end of town, Amelia socialized infrequently with Yankee residents, most of whom lived in the east end. Portuguese west enders seldom traveled to the Yankee east end and vice versa, even though it was a distance of two miles or less away. Amelia's vivid memory illuminates the tension that existed between the two cultures: "I remember my daughter going to school here and we had a girl in her class who was always saying that her ancestors came over on the *Mayflower,* so therefore she was better than any of the other girls," Amelia explained. "So I said, 'you go back and tell that girl that if the *Mayflower* brought all the people that it was supposed to, it would have sunk before it got around the Cape.' That girl never said that again."

Amelia was one of many Portuguese residents who interacted often with Provincetown's artists. Besides being on friendly terms with resident artists like Harvey Dodd, she mingled with artists in town and allowed at least two of them to paint portraits of her. Both painters and writers thought of Portuguese working-class residents as especially "picturesque." Amelia also rented her affordable cottages to artists. Provincetown had its share of both Yankee and Portuguese natives that were gay, but it was also home to a disproportionate number of gay people who either were artists or were attracted to artists' communities —the arts having long-standing affiliations with unconventional identities and behaviors of a wide variety.

Many of Provincetown's natives accepted and were fond of gay and lesbian visitors and residents, and in this regard Amelia's relationships were emblematic. "We've lived with them all [our] lives," Amelia explained in 1998, "so I don't think anything about it. Really." Amelia, who, in her own words, "could spot a homosexual ten miles away," was, according to her gay grandson, Dan Scroggins, "deeply interested [in] enjoying and cultivating friendships with men," an affinity that worked well with the hundreds of gay men arriving in Provincetown with money to spare and seeking accommodations.[2] Many gay men rented Amelia's cottages, with some referring to her affectionately as "Madame Carlos" or "Mother Superior."

John Carbone's memories of his first summer at Land's End illustrate the importance of including Portuguese entrepreneurs like Amelia in the story of Provincetown's development into a gay resort. After enduring a couple of early-summer days in chilly New England, John, a dancer from New York who was visiting the artists Romano and Grace Rizk, was not convinced that Provincetown was the place for him. Soon, however, he "fell right in with it," and as he reminisced in 1997, "there was Amelia Carlos who was such a wonderful person. She said that she had a cottage that I could have and rent, and I said well anything [other than] what I was already staying in. And so that was the beginning, and we became fast friends, always exchanging blueberry muffins or whatever . . . and that was the beginning of my staying here from 1954 to this day."[3] During the 1960s John worked with Catherine Huntington at the Provincetown Playhouse and at Ciro & Sal's Restaurant. And after renting one of Amelia's cottages, he bought a house in North Truro (adjacent to Provincetown) with his "friend." Amelia's daughter Kathleen Scroggins remembered John Carbone and Amelia's other favorite tenants, whom her mother visited off-Cape in both good times and bad: "They were like family," Kathleen explained in 2004.[4]

While husbands, brothers, and fathers were out fishing or, increasingly, taking tourists out to find fish, Portuguese women engaged in a number of income-generating enterprises. Some left their homes to bait hooks, work in the cold-storage freezers, or wait on tourists in restaurants and shops. Others, like Amelia, had some of these jobs and also turned their spare rooms, kitchens, and parlors into boardinghouses. Through these boardinghouses, Portuguese women built trusting relationships with gay men and women and helped facilitate Provincetown's twentieth-century transformation from a fishing seaport to a vacation destination.

People often imagine Provincetown, a narrow strip of sand located at the outermost curve of Cape Cod, Massachusetts, as a bustling, gay—meaning both homosexual and lively—summer resort. Also called "Land's End," "Cape Tip," "Cape End," and, to some, "Queersville, U.S.A," Provincetown has meant different things to different people.[5] In 1916 the *Provincetown Advocate* captured the invigorating energy that continues to charge Provincetown's lavish summer seasons: "Provincetown is full. Provincetown is intoxicated: full of people, intoxicated with pleasure. As never before, perhaps, inland people have been coming to this old Pilgrim town seeking and obtaining beneficial climactic and scenic change." The paper then confessed, "What there is about Provincetown that exerts a charm we dwellers of a lifetime may not know, but that Provincetown does allure is obvious— . . . And that the charm is becoming more potent is revealed by the ever increasing number of persons and sales."[6]

This single portrait nicely weaves the fabric that has made Provincetown such a textured and colorful destination: its fame as the landfall of the *Mayflower* Pilgrims, its charm as an eccentric artists' colony, and its allure as a Dionysian playground.[7] It also hints at one of the town's most dramatic economic changes: its transformation from a fishing village into a resort town. Like Nantucket, Provincetown handled the decline of its lucrative nineteenth-century seaport by turning its rotting wharves, narrow dirt roads, and scenic beaches into tourist attractions. Provincetown was one of many northeastern villages caught up during the late 1800s in a regional movement to "capture the colonial," as the historian Dona Brown describes it.[8] Following the lead of its colonial counterparts, Provincetown enticed tourists by billing itself as a charming seaport and a key American landmark. In contrast to more demure colonial towns, however, Provincetown also featured its growing population of Portuguese immigrants and its famous art

colony, which eventually became one of the East Coast's most popular gay vacation destinations. In these and other ways, Provincetown stood out as an outlandish outback.

At the same time, Provincetown's history reveals a larger story about community, citizenship, and leisure. It is a story that illuminates American hopes and dreams, particularly those of past and recent immigrants. It chronicles local and international relationships that changed a remote spit of sand and quiet seaport into a bustling resort town. And it traces the rise and fall of specific groups and the economic changes they brought to a small New England village. Above all, Provincetown's history follows lives grounded in hope and skepticism as it exposes both the romance and failure of community.[9] As Katherine Dos Passos implied in her 1936 travelogue *Down Cape Cod*, the history of Provincetown is like "the history of the United States in little."[10]

Nearly an island, Provincetown has geographic dimensions that have been critical to its economic and demographic changes over time. Extending outward into the Atlantic Ocean, the Cape Cod peninsula poses as the flexed arm of southeastern Massachusetts, while Provincetown takes the shape of both a powerful fist keeping the mainland at bay and a hooked finger beckoning visitors from afar. Provincetown might best be described as a modern-day hamlet. It is a provincial New England village with prominent church steeples, "Cape Cod" and "salt box" homes, quaint side streets, and a breath-taking, steel-blue harbor. Land's End is hemmed in on three sides by water—the Atlantic Ocean to the north, Cape Cod Bay to the west, and Provincetown Harbor to the south—and it is bordered by only one town, Truro, an unassuming village roughly ten miles "up-Cape," as Cape Codders like to say. Leaning up against more than one thousand acres of Sahara-like sand dunes, Provincetown is nearly four miles long and barely more than two streets wide. Provincetown's 8.35 square miles of land area includes 21.3 miles of tidal shoreline. It is 290 miles from New York City, 117 miles from Boston, and 78 miles from Plymouth, Massachusetts. While Provincetown's population peaked in 1890 with 4,642 full-time residents, during the twentieth century its average year-round population dipped slightly and hovered near 3,500. During the summer, some 20,000 additional visitors and part-time residents might, on any given day, find themselves taking up space at Land's End.[11]

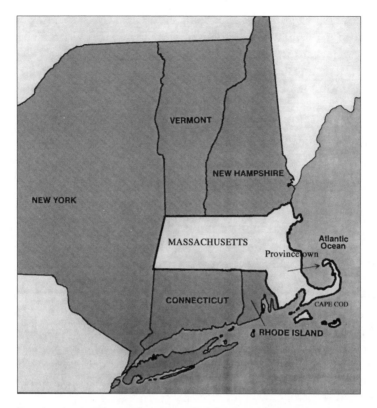

Provincetown is located at the end of the Cape Cod peninsula, which extends outward from the East Coast into the Atlantic Ocean.

Provincetown's main promenade, lined with guesthouses, restaurants, retail boutiques, and bars, is now known appropriately as Commercial Street, although in earlier years when the townspeople looked to the sea rather than to tourists for financial gain, residents called it Front Street. Commercial Street anchors Provincetown along the water from its east to its west end. Its primary thoroughfare, Bradford Street, once known as Back Street, parallels Commercial and is one block to the north toward the sand dunes and the award-winning beaches of the Cape Cod National Seashore. Connecting Bradford and Commercial Streets are numerous narrow side streets that form a ladder hugging the inner shore. At the far west end of town a strip of sand called Long Point hooks outward to frame Provincetown Harbor, which is one of the

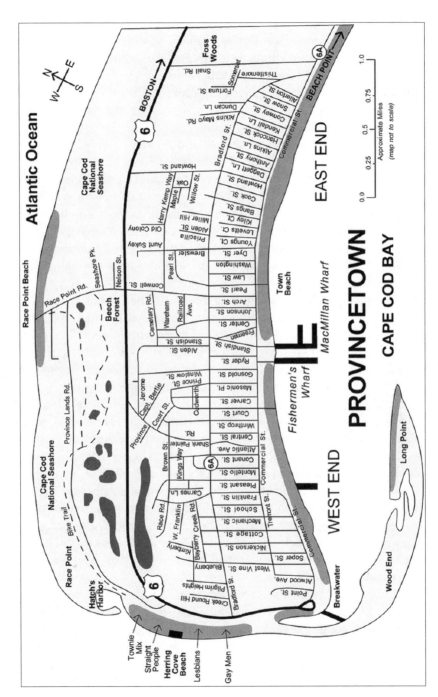

Overview map of Provincetown. Design by Adam Paige Hall.

7

largest natural harbors on the East Coast and was home to the U.S. Navy's North Atlantic Fleet during both world wars.

For at least a century, both residents and guests have seen Province-town as having two tiers. Most visitors enter by what residents call the "East End," once the home of wealthy Yankees, summer residents, and established artists. They then pass through the "Center" of town, where the railroad tracks once were and where MacMillan Pier now stands, to the "West End," where Amelia Carlos and Provincetown's Portuguese residents and their tenants lived. Provincetown recently put up East End and West End road signs along Bradford and Commercial Streets, thus reviving its historic ethnic-class divisions so that visitors, and not just residents, could participate in the nostalgia of Provincetown's less gentrified past. Although extensive gentrification has altered the demographics of the town and has spruced up neglected buildings and houses, the streets and basic layout remained the same throughout the twentieth century, with minor exceptions.[12]

Provincetown's size and remote location at the apex of a long, narrow peninsula reaching sixty miles out into the Atlantic Ocean limited the economic options and labor pools of those who chose to live there. Like island dwellers elsewhere, from the seventeenth to the twentieth century, Provincetown residents used the sea as an asset. They manufactured salt and concentrated on whaling, fishing, trading, and smuggling, all requiring residents to import both foreign and native-born laborers. Leading up to the turn of the twentieth century, however, a number of factors—notably the discovery of petroleum oil in 1859, which made whale oil obsolete, and the Portland Gale that struck New England in 1898, decimating Provincetown's shoreline of wharves—threw Cape Tip's once lucrative seaport economy into jeopardy.[13] By the mid-1930s, even while the whistles and conveyer belts of its five cold-storage freezers were reminding residents and visitors with a cacophonous ring that Provincetown was still a fishing village, many townsfolk began looking to tourists rather than to fish to supplement the withering seaside economy.

To compound Provincetown's financial and geographic limitations, people of varying races, classes, ethnicities, genders, and sexual orientations have sought to make this near island of sand their home. Although precolonial and colonial travelers, including the Pamet Indians and *Mayflower* Pilgrims, found shelter in Provincetown's harbor, they chose to reside elsewhere. The first to make Provincetown their home were Anglo-European settlers, later known collectively as Yankees, who arrived just before the 1700s. In the early and mid-1800s these Yankees began importing laborers from Portugal and the Azores, who also found Provincetown to be a congenial New World home. Throughout the nineteenth century, the families and friends of Portuguese sailors established a tight-knit neighborhood in the West End of town. Beginning in 1899, several well-known artists flocked to Land's End, and an assortment of sexual and gender nonconformists, many of whom doubled as artists, migrated there from as early as 1914.

Throughout the twentieth century, these groups jockeyed for control over Cape Tip's limited space and economic resources. In the 1920s, for instance, some Yankees reacted to their waning power and the growing influence of their Portuguese neighbors by organizing Ku Klux Klan chapters.[14] Later, in the 1950s, when white gay men transmogrified many of Provincetown's once neutral sites into gay spaces, Provincetown's Portuguese and Yankee officials responded by closing down one of Cape Tip's most popular gay nightclubs. After that action failed to "clean house," as one journalist put it, town leaders appealed to "all decent people in Provincetown" to rid its streets and establishments of homosexuals. In these ways, debates about morality and difference have been crucial to change and the formation of community at Land's End.

These tensions emerged in part from Provincetown's reputation as a liberated community that doubled as the perfect hometown or resort town. In *Hometowns: Gay Men Write about Where They Belong*, Reed Woodhouse pens several pages in honor of Land's End:

> To such an extent that Provincetown is, for anything, known for us, known for being one of the two or three places on the continent where gay people can be seen in something like their native habitat. It is one of our hometowns. . . . In Provincetown I've had the chance to get "family" right, and if not go home *again*, to go there happily, for the first time.[15]

Woodhouse's romance with Provincetown is intriguing not only because it addresses the importance of hometowns to many gay men and lesbians but also because it speaks to a broader condition: the disappearance of traditional hometowns across the United States during the twentieth century and the anxiety some people felt over the loss of these provincial settings. Small towns across the United States have been in states of economic and cultural atrophy since World War II, some since the Great Depression.[16] Only those small towns with creative municipal leaderships able to market their natural, historic, or work-related surroundings as tourist destinations have survived what the historian Richard O. Davies calls the "main street blues."[17]

Provincetown's popularity and success as a hometown facilitated its demographic and economic turns and illustrates the first main paradox of its history: that while creating an ideal home and a lucrative economy, immigrants of all backgrounds ended up losing their homes to the laborers and consumers they were determined to attract. Yankee migrants were the first to settle permanently at Land's End. They brought with them Portuguese sailors, who sent for families and friends and eventually prompted Yankees to depart. Portuguese immigrants were soon renting rooms in their homes to gay men and lesbians, who quickly established Provincetown as their home away from home. Over time, gay men and lesbians helped make Provincetown prohibitively expensive, which, in turn, facilitated the departure of the very people who first housed them. Some of the Portuguese residents moved to Truro or farther up-Cape; others moved to different sections of the United States; and a few returned to Portugal or the Azores.

Questions of ethnicity and the need for labor further complicated Provincetown's cycles of immigration. Yankees were the first to import foreign-born laborers in order to bridge a working-class gap in the fisheries. These laborers, so-called dark-skinned Portuguese and Azorean immigrants, eventually took hold of the fishing industry and new service economy, in the process becoming white and American. In turn, Portuguese residents joined white gay men and lesbians to import another group of foreign-born laborers, black seasonal workers from Jamaica. Eastern European student workers later joined Jamaicans to fill the working-class void that had resulted from Provincetown's shift in the late twentieth century from a popular vacation destination into an exclusive resort.

Increasingly, Provincetown has become a destination for the privileged, even among the gay men and lesbians who in 1997 called Provincetown "*Our* Town."[18] Although many working-class gay men and lesbians spend a day or week in Provincetown, the high cost of getting to and staying at Land's End excludes far more visitors than it includes. This phenomenon raises the second main paradox of this book, that places like Provincetown, which people envision as communities of freedom, can end up reproducing inequality. Yankees, Portuguese immigrants, and gay men and lesbians all sought liberation in Provincetown, yet once there, they all, in turn, ended up creating new forms of discrimination.

Finally, even though Provincetown often fulfilled the complicated desire for hometown familiarity, it also is a tourist destination, a place to which people have traveled in order to escape their actual hometowns, families, jobs, and mundane or hectic lives. A central component of Provincetown's appeal has been the way in which it has allowed certain outcasts—religious, sexual, and otherwise—to behave and appear in ways they would not on their own main streets or in front of their own neighbors, relatives, or coworkers. In this way, Provincetown reflects the nature of vacationing in the sense, as the historian Cindy Aron explains, that "vacations disclose what people choose to do rather than what they are required to do."[19] Thousands of vacationers have chosen Provincetown because, even if they couldn't reside there—and many could—they could at least sample the kind of liberation it has offered. Thus Provincetown's success has rested partly on what it offered—a space of possibility rather than limitation—and on what other places lacked. One might think of it as a safety valve to a number of pressure cookers its visitors and residents stewed in elsewhere.

In Provincetown immigrants of all backgrounds tapped into previously unattainable forms of citizenship and belonging.[20] The possibilities of citizenship commenced as early as the seventeenth century when European explorers, seafarers, and "pilgrims" left their homelands for wealth and freedom in the New World. And they continued into the twenty-first century as gay men and lesbians started holding "official" weddings and honeymoons at Land's End, just months after the Massachusetts Supreme Court permitted them official access to the coveted institution of marriage.

Anglo-European Yankees bolstered their claims to citizenship in the United States and to Land's End by holding fast to Provincetown's role as the place that first gave shelter to their religiously persecuted ancestors, the *Mayflower* Pilgrims. For many of them, Provincetown symbolized their birthright to own rather than work and to rule rather than follow. Portuguese immigrants shared a similar patriotic allegiance. In Provincetown they escaped forced military service, extreme poverty, and other socioeconomic hardships in the Azores and on the Portuguese mainland. But Portuguese immigrants arrived in the United States and in Provincetown with no citizenship rights and with the "wrong" color of skin. For them, becoming American meant easing closer to the prevailing Yankee community by emphasizing their independence and by becoming white.

Gay men and lesbians found Provincetown's semi-isolated location, which offered a measure of anonymity, protection, and romance, similarly liberating. By the mid-twentieth century, trips to Provincetown began to function as a way, both literally and symbolically, to come out of the closet and into a gay world. (In the 1990s, Cape Air Airlines cleverly picked up on this by advertising its service from Boston to Provincetown as the fastest way to "come out.") By the late twentieth century, gay men and lesbians extended their claims to freedom at Land's End by linking their financial investments to their rights as citizens.

These examples illustrate how race, sexual orientation, and class each played a role in determining who did and did not gain citizenship rights at Land's End. At times citizenship took on legal connotations— the right to vote, hold office, serve on juries, get married—however it often referred to cultural and economic compatibility as well. Provincetown's visitors and residents negotiated the terms of citizenship—of belonging—by recognizing the importance of diversity as well as the value in likeness or sameness.[21] As a community of likeness with a high threshold for deviation, Provincetown set out clear but permeable boundaries of citizenship that included and excluded different people at different times.

The story told in the forthcoming pages navigates Provincetown's past, particularly its political, cultural, and economic legacies. The first section, "Inventing Provincetown, 1859–1928," charts Provincetown's concurrent development from a whaling seaport into a "colonial" village, Portuguese enclave, and artists' workshop. After an overview of Provincetown's precolonial and colonial past, chapter 1 examines how Yankees, still smarting from the demise of the whaling industry, learned that Provincetown needed something more than salty air and a snail-like train in order to flourish as a popular summer resort. Chapters 2 and 3 look at how writers enticed visitors to Land's End by racializing Portuguese townsfolk and romanticizing the presence of resident artists. Chapter 2 examines early-twentieth-century Portuguese immigration strategies and cultural adaptations, and chapter 3 traces the members of Provincetown's art colony who arrived in the 1910s and facilitated its turn into a gay mecca. This chapter also introduces gay artists and residents, known as "our queers," who came of age or who migrated to Provincetown in the 1920s and 1930s.

Provincetown's economic strategies during the Great Depression and cold war set the stage for part II: "Surviving Provincetown, 1929–1969." Chapter 4 details how the financial strains of the Depression prompted residents to rely on an economic system of "swapping" and to welcome an increasing number of outsiders. Chapter 5 focuses on how Portuguese and Yankee residents responded to the postwar influx of gay men and lesbians.

The third and final section, "Gentrifying Provincetown, 1970–2000," looks at Provincetown's final turn into a gay and lesbian resort. Chapter 6 illustrates how women challenged Provincetown's change into a resort for gay men. Chapter 7 assesses the tensions and effects of living in an internationally renowned gay mecca.

The names used to describe a people's race or sexuality or to indicate a class position that are accepted today were not necessarily recognized in years past. For instance, sources emanating from Provincetown during the early twentieth century made only obscure or coded references to "homosexuals."[22] Because terms like "gay" and "lesbian" do not appear in the literature on early Provincetown until the 1930s, I use the terms that do appear, including nouns like "artist" and "bachelor" and adjectives like "tender" and "affected," to designate homoerotically inclined or differently gendered men. Residents also used "maiden ladies," "singular women," "independent women," and "spinster" to mark homoerotically inclined or differently gendered women. From the early 1930s on, words like "lesbian," "bulldagger," "sissy-boy," "belle," "faggot," "gay," and "trade" appear in both written and oral sources. Where appropriate, I use these terms to illustrate how a shift in labels hinted at a shift in the class position, sensibilities, and citizenship status of Provincetown's guests.

A number of other useful terms will appear. Despite its history as a homophobic slur, I use the term "queer" as an analytic tool because it describes a wide range of sexual and gender iconoclasts, most of whom engaged in homosexual sex and all of whom engaged in some form of unconventional erotic or gender behavior.[23] The term "queer" appears at times in the sources I cite, and in these instances carries both its original meaning as generally unconventional as well as its later meaning as sexually unconventional.

The attitudes toward race in Provincetown have been as nuanced as attitudes toward sexual orientation. To untangle the ways in which residents understood race, I point to times when Portuguese residents identified themselves as white while others identified them as ranging from "black" to "creamy olive." I explore Provincetown's relationship to immigration and ethnic tourism in order to highlight tensions regarding race and ethnicity. I also consider how residents' ideas about ethnic and class differences changed over time, finding that in Provincetown, race and class mattered as much as, and often more than, sexual orientation.

Divisions between residents and visitors, hosts and guests, insiders and outsiders, and, critically, natives versus all others continue to determine those who do and do not "belong" at Land's End. "Washashore" is a quirky but valuable term that Provincetown natives invented to describe those who came to Provincetown for a brief vacation but stayed on as residents. Similarly, the meaning of the term "native" changed in Provincetown at least three times during the twentieth century. At the beginning of the century, it usually referred to white Yankees born in Provincetown. By the 1930s, promoters used "native" to denote what they called "dark-skinned" Portuguese residents and to market Provincetown as an exotic fishing village. Near the middle of the century, as vacationers inundated Land's End, townsfolk used "native" to distinguish residents from visitors, and accordingly, it became a term for any person born in Provincetown, regardless of race, class, ethnicity, or sexual orientation.

Finally, I separate Yankees from Portuguese residents and Portuguese residents from artists not because these were discrete categories. The boundaries separating them were permeable—people moved among communities by interacting sexually, reproductively, socially, and professionally. There were Portuguese artists, half-Yankee and half-Portuguese natives, and white Irish, Scottish, and Nova Scotian townsfolk that did not fit neatly into the categories I map out. But these groups did, nonetheless, think of themselves as distinct communities. In other words, despite mobility between groups and despite the changing characteristics of Portuguese and Yankee communities, residents held fast to racial, class, and cultural distinctions.

The questions guiding this history have been as influential as the approach. I began a decade ago with a few obvious queries: How did a small New England town blossom from a Yankee seaport, artists' workshop, and Portuguese fishing village, into what some now call "a gay Disneyland?"[24] And how did this transformation affect the residents of and visitors to Provincetown? My later interrogations reflect the ways in which I have come to see Provincetown's past as more complicated and far-reaching: How has Provincetown been involved in an international exchange of laborers? And how have the intertwined processes of consumerism and citizenship contributed to the making of present-day Provincetown? Instead of asking why Provincetown is still a white town, I see more clearly now that Provincetown has never been completely white. Most of Provincetown's visitors, landholders, and business owners have been white or have become white, but a large proportion of its workers, those invisible to outsiders, have not been white.

These questions led me to examine three facets of Provincetown's history. The first focuses on how Provincetown's past illuminates the local fallout of larger events, like the bohemian rebellion of the Progressive Era, the migration patterns of the first and second world wars, and the arrival of the second wave of feminism. What impact has global capitalism had on the residents of a small fishing village and resort town at the far end of Cape Cod? The second facet examines how Provincetown's history contributes to an understanding of larger processes such as discrimination, immigration, and economic mobility. How and why did townsfolk welcome some migrants, like famous white artists and wealthy gay men, while discouraging others, like black visitors and working-class vacationers, from spending time at Land's End? The third part explores the unanticipated outcomes of residents' successes in marketing Provincetown as a landfall of freedom. How did Provincetown's fame as a birthplace of liberation contribute to or hinder its development into a colonial outback, Portuguese fishing village, and gay resort?

Like gay and lesbian communities in urban centers, such as San Francisco, New York City, Boston, and Philadelphia, or in smaller cities like Buffalo, a combination of personal, political, and economic relationships launched Provincetown's gay world.[25] Yet still, it did not originate in gay and lesbian private key parties or nightclubs that were run and managed by the mafia, nor did it spring from gay and lesbian political organizations like the Daughters of Bilitis or the Mattachine Society. And unlike the development of queer cultures in gay resort areas such as Cherry Grove on Fire Island, Provincetown's gay world did not take root because of its proximity to a large urban center or its long-standing connections to a gay-dominated theater group. Urban enclaves, to be sure, were critical to Provincetown's conversion into a gay resort, but so too was its unusual blend of inhabitants and economies.

Similarly, although Provincetown's reputation as an art colony influenced the migration of gays and lesbians from places of intolerance to Provincetown because it was rumored to be "artsy"—meaning tolerant of difference in the name of creativity—this reputation alone did not make Provincetown into a gay haven. Although a similar phenomenon took place in Greenwich Village, gay resort areas do not spring automatically from art colonies, nor do all art colonies develop naturally into gay meccas. Rehoboth Beach, Delaware, and South Beach, Florida, are two examples of gay vacation destinations that were not first thriving art colonies. At the same time, art colonies such as Taos, New Mexico, East Hampton, New York, and New Hope, Pennsylvania, although rumored to be gay friendly, never did and do not now share Provincetown's esteem or market as an internationally renowned gay mecca. And although most of Provincetown's townspeople insist that the Portuguese residents were beyond reproach in welcoming gays and lesbians, theirs was still a conservative, Catholic culture that did not condone homosexuality. Indeed, neither the artistic freedoms of the art colony nor the open-mindedness of the Portuguese residents—alone or together—accounts for Provincetown's evolution into a gay mecca. What or, more likely, what combination of people, economies, and prejudices made Provincetown what it is today?

PART I

INVENTING PROVINCETOWN, 1859–1928

> Provincetown is different from all the rest of the Cape: different from all the rest of the world—although all "land's end" places have a certain haunting odor and resemblance.
>
> —Agnes Edwards, *Cape Cod: New and Old*, 1918

IN 1873, Provincetown resident James Gifford joined Yankee businessmen from numerous northeastern seaports in an attempt to place Provincetown in its proper "colonial" context. Fourteen years earlier the discovery of petroleum oil had sent the whaling industry into a dismal downward spiral, and people along the Atlantic's northeastern seaboard were struggling to ignite replacement industries. Some towns, like New Bedford, Massachusetts, joined the Industrial Revolution and built textile mills and factories. More isolated enclaves, like the island of Nantucket, looked to tourists. On the outskirts of the newly created region called "Old New England" sat Provincetown, a village with neither the space to build large factories nor the means to transport visitors to Cape Cod's hinterland.

This changed in 1873 when the Old Colony Railroad completed its final extension from Wellfleet to Provincetown. With an eye on the profits to be made from the nation's budding tourist industry, James Gifford offered a glimmer of hope at the railroad's opening ceremonies: "We gladly welcome all, of whatever station or pursuit, from whatever part of our common heritage they may have made their pilgrimage here today." He admitted that in contrast to places like Plymouth, Massachusetts, which in 1850 had built a monument commemorating the *Mayflower* Pilgrims, Provincetown had "neither ancient monument to

GIFFORD HOUSE, PROVINCETOWN, MASS.

Photograph of New Central House at high tide ca. 1900 (above). Postcard of The Gifford House ca. 1910 (below). Courtesy of the Pilgrim Monument and Provincetown Museum.

excite curiosity nor cultivated landscape nor fine architecture to delight the eye." Yet Provincetown's harbor, he boasted, was an exceptional historic landmark worth visiting because it had provided "refuge to fleets and navies and . . . more than two hundred and fifty two [sic] years ago was the first haven this side of the ocean to shelter the bewildered *Mayflower* in whose cabin . . . was signed the famous compact that proved the progenitor of constitutional freedom in America."[1]

Gifford, who owned two of Provincetown's few grand hotels, the Gifford House and the Pilgrim House, was one of several Yankees who hoped the railroad and Provincetown's reputation as a healthy "watering place" would bolster its weakened seaport economy by luring visitors to Land's End. The railroad had helped spread markets in New England and beyond, so why not, he surely imagined, expand them to the very tip of Cape Cod.[2] One of the railroad's greatest proponents, Dr. John M. Crocker, agreed. In 1869, the same year he bought Provincetown's weekly newspaper, the *Provincetown Advocate*, Crocker noted, "'[Henry David] Thoreau declared that it was the destiny of Cape Cod to become one of the greatest 'watering places' in New England. It only remains to make these towns of easy access by rail to turn the outside world toward them for a summer resort.'"[3]

The Old Colony Railroad became Provincetown's most expedient link to the "outside world." Speed had become crucial to the fishing industry as the demand for "fresh" (meaning frozen) rather than salted fish escalated. Now, by rail, fishermen could take their catch to New York or Boston more rapidly, and merchants could buy goods, also in New York, more easily. But the owners and workers of packet boats (sloops transporting mail, cargo, and passengers) resented the railroad because it made their mode of transportation nearly obsolete. In addition, the railroad, which reached Hyannis in 1854, Orleans in 1865, and Wellfleet in 1870, also forced stagecoach owners like Samuel Knowles to reconfigure their routes. Knowles once enjoyed a lucrative business carrying passengers the distances not yet covered by rail, for example, from Orleans to Wellfleet or from Wellfleet to Provincetown. Rather than meeting visitors at the railroad terminus and taking them to the next town or village, Knowles and other stagecoach owners carried them from railroad depots to nearby hotels or boardinghouses.[4]

During the nineteenth century, the railroad transported urban residents wanting to escape the supposedly harmful effects of living in smoggy, industrial centers to "watering places"—ocean, lake, and riverside destinations that offered sunbathing, fresh air, swimming, seafood, and a salubrious mode of living. By the 1830s doctors and health reformers were prescribing these conditions as cures for such urban illnesses as respiratory difficulties and skin ailments.[5] Accordingly, places like Newport, Rhode Island, and Provincetown became known as desirable seashore destinations. An advertisement for Provincetown's Union House in 1856 urged "sick people and well ones" to come to this great "WATERING PLACE" for sea bathing and healthful living.[6] Provincetown's "climate is unequaled," its board of trade announced in 1897. "It is one of the healthiest towns in the country . . . free from any prevailing sickness or epidemics of serious character. The death rate is low. There are no extreme excesses of heat or cold."[7] In addition to claiming that Provincetown was "a mecca of pilgrimage from every part of the United States," it concluded, adding, "Those who come from places enervated with the heat, oppressed with overwork and the strenuousness of modern existence, return home recuperated and refreshed."[8]

Provincetown offered the benefits of an oceanside climate as well as the infrastructure to support its status as a popular resort. By the early 1900s, a number of hotels and boardinghouses were promising "beneficial and climatic change," including Provincetown's turn-of-the-century health "spa," the Ocean View Sanitarium, located at 378 Commercial Street and run by Dr. Ella F. Birge and her husband, Dr. William Birge.[9] In all, Provincetown assembled an appealing package. As Edmund Carpenter noted in 1900, "Those who go once to Provincetown go many times, for the great salt sea has its odors to the nostrils, its sights to the eyes, its songs to the ears, its breath upon the cheek, and its kiss upon the lips, fascinating, enthralling, satisfying."[10]

But despite the help of the railroad, steamers, and packets that moved travelers and markets to the tip of Cape Cod, boosters failed to turn Provincetown into a crowded summer resort. By the start of the twentieth century, Provincetown needed something more. Specifically, it needed to tap into the desires of America's new touring and vacationing classes. As rural villages nationwide dwindled economically and demographically, Provincetown struggled to escape a similar future of despair.

Provincetown's eventual transformation into a summer resort reflects the changes in leisure options and desires during the nineteenth and early twentieth centuries. According to historian Cindy Aron, in the early and mid-1800s travelers sought out the temperate climates and re-laxation offered by seaside resorts. This form of vacationing coincided with the new pastime known as touring: traveling that focused on vis-iting as many famous sights as possible over a brief period. At least two kinds of travelers emerged during this time, vacationers seeking rest and relaxation and tourists interested in historic or cultural improve-ment. As opposed to vacationers, tourists were looking for educational excursions that contained some form of personal enrichment. Linking their time to middle- and upper-class ethics, tourists aimed, even when not at work, to be productive rather than idle or wasteful.[11]

During the nineteenth century, vacationing expanded to include rigorous physical activity instead of or at least in addition to restful re-generation. And touring branched out to include secular, patriotic pil-grimages to America's historic or scenic treasures; relaxing trips to eth-nic workplaces; and romantic excursions to art colonies. Concurrently, white middle- and upper-class Americans began formulating a stable and honorable national identity. In the absence of ancient ruins or me-dieval structures, they made scenic treasures, like Niagara Falls and the Hudson River Valley, and historic landmarks, like Mount Vernon and Bunker Hill, emblematic of their young nation. These places celebrated the individuals, communities, and landscapes that symbolized Amer-ica's democratic past and its future as a powerful nation.[12] As Aron notes, "touring historic sights and monuments served obvious patriotic functions . . . people on touring vacations often sought to visit spots where Americans had been courageous, strong and 'plucky,' or where famous people had been born or laid to rest."[13]

In addition to feeling proud and productive by making secular pil-grimages that helped create and celebrate America's history, white mid-dle- and upper-class tourists emphasized their own racial and socioe-conomic privilege by visiting, indeed touring, workplaces run by im-migrants. Coined "alienated leisure" by sociologist Dean MacCannell, visits to such workplaces meant sightseers could get closer to society's more physical, serious side of work.[14] Witnessing dangerous or thrilling "labor" simultaneously reinforced the class, race, and ethnic distinc-tions between those with the means to watch others at work and those being watched while at work. Beginning in the 1820s, tourists visited coalfields, ironworks, stockyards, and fishing villages. Like trips to his-toric monuments, visiting workplaces also fulfilled patriotic functions. It allowed privileged Americans to stand at a distance from immigrant workers and working-class laborers while taking pride in their country's technological advancements, ingenuity, and methods of exploitation.

Finally, white middle- and upper-class tourists made tracks for scenic destinations that promised stunning views and chances to rub elbows with artists at work. In the mid-1800s, tourists and others in New England envisioned artists as especially gifted, and as a result, their occupations acquired a lofty, even patriotic, significance. Some tourists believed that by watching painters, sculptors, or poets at work, they would be able to identify with them and might even become enlightened or more talented beings themselves.[15] Together, artists and those admiring them made otherwise empty images of seashores and sunsets into romantic and potentially liberating features of American life.

After the booms and busts of the nineteenth century, Provincetown remade itself in the twentieth century into a unique vacation destination. Indeed, Land's End promised to satisfy all three aspects of the perfect American tour: the patriotic pilgrimage to significant historic sites, the fascination with the cultures of working-class and immigrant laborers, and the attraction to the creativity of art. Specifically, Provincetown offered a trip to the site of the *Mayflower* Pilgrims' landing, an opportunity for "alienated leisure" provided by working-class Portuguese fishermen and women, and a romantic encounter with writers and artists. By embracing both touring and vacationing, Provincetown turned itself into a popular destination that would prosper rather than perish. In this way, about a half-century before Provincetown became a haven for gay men and lesbians, it evolved from a declining whaling center and preindustrial outback into a "quaint," "exotic," and "artsy" resort.

I

Colonial Outpost

Provincetown has a right to be proud of itself. It has charm, flavor, distinction. It has a historical background, unexcelled in New England, and it has a record for the producing of noble men and women that is wholly in excess of its mere size. The state hails old Provincetown with heartiness and trusts that it will never permit itself to lose its own particular charm.

—*Boston Post*, August 4, 1927

AT THE TURN of the twentieth century, when Portuguese and artistic communities were becoming increasingly visible in Provincetown, Yankees set out to clarify that they were the best citizens and the rightful owners of Land's End. They did this by highlighting the town's significance in what came to be known as the "Age of Discovery," when Europeans first found the New World. In particular, they emphasized the *Mayflower* Pilgrims' arrival in 1620, even though both Native Americans and sixteenth-century European explorers had "discovered" Provincetown before the Pilgrims' fortuitous landfall.

Indeed, Yankees' claims to Provincetown as their hard-won home were far more tenuous than they put forth. Some New England historians and archeologists believe it is possible and even probable that the Late Archaic Native Americans were the first to forage for food and shelter at the tip end of the Cape some 2,000 years ago (Provincetown having taken shape geographically only 3,500 years ago). Most historians agree that the Pamet (Payomet) Indians, a group affiliated with the Nauset tribe, lived in Truro and farther west on Cape Cod but hunted and fished in Provincetown, which they called Chequoket (or Chequokette). Although their numbers dwindled as Europeans exposed them to smallpox, bubonic plague, and other diseases, the Pamet

Indians were well acquainted with Provincetown before the *Mayflower* Pilgrims arrived.[1]

In addition to Native American inhabitants, European explorers are believed to have landed in or near Provincetown before 1620. In 1853, while building the house at 7 Cottage Street, known now as the Norse Wall Guesthouse, workers unearthed remnants of supposedly ancient masonry. Coincidentally, sixteen years earlier the Danish historian Carl Christian Rafn had published a translation of Norse expedition records, which referred to a possible voyage near Cape Cod made by Thorwald Eriksson—brother of the famous Leif Eriksson—around 1004 C.E. According to Rafn, Thorwald damaged the ship's keel and repaired it onshore, possibly in Provincetown. Although the evidence is inconclusive, the Norse Wall Guesthouse exemplifies how history and legend have helped Provincetown turn its bland, sandy canvas into a technicolor landscape worthy of visits from tourists near and far: "We think Thorwald picked this beautiful spot in the West End. We hope you do too," its current innkeepers declare.[2]

The European explorers who predated the *Mayflower*'s arrival include the Italian John Cabot, born as Giovanni Caboto, who piloted the British-backed *Matthew* (possibly with his son Sebastian) near Cape Cod on his way to Virginia in 1498. Giovanni da Verrazano sailed the *Dauphine* in 1524 along a good portion of the northeastern seaboard and described Cape Cod in a letter, dated July 8, 1524, to King Francis I of France. In 1602 Bartholomew Gosnold led the *Concord* along a similar route from the coast of present-day Maine to Narragansett Bay, naming Cape Cod and several islands en route. In 1605 Samuel de Champlain sailed around Cape Cod, and four years later Henry Hudson, representing the Dutch East India Company, did the same in the eighty-ton ship *Half Moon*. Captain John Smith had the dubious honor of introducing Captain Thomas Hunt to the area. In 1614 Hunt imprisoned twenty-four Nauset and Patuxet Native Americans. Later, in 1616, in *A Description of New England*, which included a map showing Stuards Bay (Cape Cod Bay) and Cape James (Cape Cod), Smith wrote that Hunt, "most dishonestly, and inhumanely, for their kind usage of me and all our men, carried [the Native Americans] with him to Malaga, and there for a little private gain sold those silly savages for rials of eight."[3]

Yet when promoters held Provincetown high by reviving its past, the nostalgia for these explorers paled in comparison to that garnered for two other groups of early visitors: the "original" New England pilgrims—the *Mayflower* passengers—and the bands of smugglers and traders that established Provincetown early on as a lawless oasis. After several failed attempts, the *Mayflower* Pilgrims finally left Plymouth, England, on September 6, 1620. On November 11, nine days before reaching land, forty-one men signed the *"Mayflower* Compact," a "covenant" between them and their God. The compact bound its signers together,

> into a civill body politick, for our better ordering and preservation and furtherance of ye ends aforesaid, and by vertue hearof to enacte, constitute and frame such just and equall lawes, ordinances, acts, constitutions and offices, from time to time, as shall be thought most meete and convenient for ye generall good of ye colonie, unto which we promise all due submission and obedience.[4]

Provincetown boosters later hailed this document as "the first charter of a true democratic country known in human history" and "the prolific parent of constitutional freedom in America."[5] Or as another writer explained in 1886, "Then and there, in that little cabin, the idea of a 'government of the people, by the people, for the people,' first sprang into being and began its beneficial work."[6]

The *Mayflower* Pilgrims planned to drop anchor off the coast of Virginia but landed in Provincetown Harbor by accident on November 20. One Pilgrim enthusiastically described "sand hills, much like the downs of Holland, but much better; the crust of earth a spit's [spade's] depth [of] excellent black earth" and "oaks, pines, sassafras, juniper, birch holly . . . ash, [and] walnut." But most seemed to agree with Captain John Smith, who found Provincetown in 1614 to be rather desolate, consisting mostly of sand dunes and shrub "trash."[7] The *Mayflower* Pilgrims stayed a snappy five weeks, long enough to wade ashore, survey the land, try to replenish their supplies, and steal from the local Native Americans. On December 15, they set sail again for the more promising shores of what eventually became Plimouth Plantation. Outside its peaceful harbor and rolling sand hills, Provincetown had little to recommend it, and pleased as they were to reach land, the *Mayflower* Pilgrims held out hope for finding a more fertile New World home.

Not wanting to lose such a splendid opportunity, those seeking to bolster Provincetown's reputation during the nineteenth and twentieth centuries found in the *Mayflower*'s brief layover a seemingly endless supply of historic charm. H. H. Sylvester was one of the first writers, in 1882, to invoke the Pilgrims: "It was at Provincetown that the Pilgrims first landed. . . . Here the storm-tossed, weather-worn *Mayflower,* with her precious freight found her first safe anchorage."[8] Provincetown, boosters would insist, is a classic "Pilgrim town" and a place of liberation that has welcomed outcasts for centuries. In *Saints and Strangers,* historian George F. Willison paints a flattering portrait of these early renegades: "The Pilgrims were not nineteenth century pietists, or quietists. They were not pale plaster saints, hollow and bloodless. They were men—and women, too—of courage and conviction, strong and positive in their attitudes, prepared to sacrifice much for their principles, even their very lives."[9] Some of the *Mayflower* Pilgrims, Willison's "saints," were also known as Separatists, who were seeking refuge from religious persecution in England. But the majority, including Myles Standish and John Alden, were "strangers," orthodox members of the Anglican Church who were seeking economic opportunity rather than religious safety. True to its past, Provincetown has harbored both "saints" fleeing persecution and "strangers" seeking economic advantage from the seventeenth century to today. Even so, those invoking the *Mayflower* Pilgrims to highlight Provincetown's noteworthy past have focused exclusively on its saints rather than its strangers.

But the *Mayflower* Pilgrims did not forget what they referred to as Cape Cod or "Cape Land." According to a document by Thomas Smyth, three colonists—Thomas Prence, Captain Myles Standish, and William Padd—were given permission to fish and use Cape Land in any way they saw fit for three years, beginning on June 9, 1651. At the end of this period, Samson (or Sampson), a chief of the Nauset tribe, exchanged the land with the Plymouth colony's Governor Thomas Prence for one box, two brass kettles, six coats, and twelve hoes, axes, and knives. Seven years later an act decreed that Cape Land, which was useless for most agricultural purposes, would be held in common for the colony but that fishing gains would be taxed at the rate of one shilling and six pence per barrel of fish. In 1692 Plymouth became part of the Massachusetts Bay Colony, and under its jurisdiction, Cape Land was renamed the Province Lands. Two hundred years later, in 1890, these transfers of land and rights resurfaced as residents tried to determine "who own[ed] the Province Lands?"[10] Although this question dates back to Provincetown's earliest years, it continues to divide residents and tourists at Land's End.

In addition to highlighting its Pilgrim heritage, writers often billed Provincetown as an "anything goes" oasis by invoking its early history of lawless disorder. Throughout the seventeenth and into the eighteenth century, Provincetown remained a semirestricted refuge frequented by Native Americans and foreign-born explorers, fishermen, and traders who devised their own regulations to keep the peace in Provincetown's harbor. Yet from time to time, officials from Plymouth patrolled the area, bringing Provincetown its first taste of institutionalized discipline and punishment, as is evidenced by the 1667 arrest and whipping of three Pamet Indians apparently caught stealing liquor from a boat moored in Provincetown Harbor.[11] Still, this incident failed to bring order to what had become known as a playground for outlaws. In 1705 William Clap notified Governor Dudley of the Massachusetts Bay Colony that "very often hear is opportunity to seas vessels, and goods which are upon a smoglen acompt." Furthermore, he continued, "most of thar men . . . were outlandish men I judge porteges."[12] On July 13 of the same year, another eyewitness lodged a similar complaint against "Cap Cod": "'I have liveed hear at the Cap this 4 year and I have very often every year sien that her maiesty has been very much wronged of har dues [by people that] taks up drift whals.'"[13]

Apparently the Massachusetts Bay Colony attempted to "clean up" the Province Lands, or at least give visitors there proper religious guidance, by assigning the Reverend Jeremiah Cushing to the end of the Cape at some point before 1700. Unfortunately, all that is known about Cushing is that his wife gave birth to a son, Ezekiel, in Provincetown in 1698.[14] Colonialists made more earnest and binding efforts in 1714 when the General Court decreed an act, entitled The Precinct of Cape Cod, to "preserv[e] the harbor at Cape Cod and regulat[e] the inhabitants and sojourners there."[15] This act placed the Province Lands under the jurisdiction of Truro, which officials had incorporated five years earlier, and stipulated that "the inhabitants there are obliged to procure and support a learned orthodox minister of good conversation."[16] The General Court demanded that the fishermen support the minister, and it levied a weekly tax on each seafarer.

In relation to Truro, Provincetown earned its reputation as an unruly and unwanted stepsibling long ago. Indeed, it did not take long for Truro to begin grumbling about its attachment to and, even worse, responsibility for the unwieldy territory known as the Province Lands. One year after the General Court's ruling, Truro's residents requested clarification of its obligations toward the Province Lands so that it could better determine "how to act in regard to some persons."[17]

Maritime and New England historians estimate that the residents of Truro and other parts of the Cape may have established seasonal dwellings during the late 1600s and early 1700s in what is now known as the West End of Provincetown, an area sheltered by Long Point to the east and a series of hills to the west. These dwellings probably became permanent ones, with "squatters" carving out small, family-centered neighborhoods. Whether these residents wanted their own town rights or whether Truro decided to sever ties with the Province Lands is unclear. What is certain is that on June 14, 1727, the Massachusetts Bay General Court incorporated Provincetown (a last-minute name change from Herrington) as a town and shared province. One of the most interesting aspects of Provincetown in light of late-twentieth-century territorial disputes is its history of, technically, common ground. The incorporation of Provincetown reads as follows:

> Be it enacted, etc. that all the lands on said Cape (being Provincelands) be and hereby are constituted a township by the name of Provincetown, and that the inhabitants thereof be invested with the powers and privileges and immunities that any of the inhabitants of any of the towns within the Province by law, are, or ought to be invested with, saving always the right of this Province [Massachusetts Bay] to said land, which is to be in no wise prejudiced, and provided that no person or person be hindered and obstructed in building such wharves, stages [fishing shanties], work houses, and flakes [to dry fish] and other things as shall be necessary for the salting, keeping, and packing their fish or in cutting down and taking such trees and other materials growing on said Provincelands as shall be needful for that purpose, or in any sort of fishing, whaling or getting of bait at the said Cape; but that the same be held as common as heretofore with all the privileges and advantages thereunto in any wise belonging.[18]

Ironically, just as Provincetown established itself as a shared province, its inhabitants decided to abandon ship. Town records indicate that in 1741 the Reverend Spear departed because Provincetown no longer had enough inhabitants to make his presence there worthwhile. By 1748 only two or three families still lived there, and by 1755 three houses remained, but no people.

As the *Mayflower* Pilgrims and others quickly learned, Province-town's soil was sandy and, for the most part, infertile. But more important, its location at the end of one of the East Coast's longest peninsulas made it susceptible to repeated attack and seizure. For decades its vulnerability to enemy ships remained unchecked. Although French brigades had been raiding Provincetown's defenseless harbor since the early 1700s, it was the French and Indian War (1755–1763) that depleted Provincetown of its human and commercial resources. In the final year of the war, however, the General Court gave Provincetown its first house of worship, and two years later the town hired a full-time minister. This need for a meeting house and spiritual instruction indicates that a fair number of settlers had now taken up residence at Land's End.[19]

In the years before the American Revolution, Provincetown contained 20 dwellings, 36 families, and 205 inhabitants. But this, too, turned out to be a temporary settlement. During the war, the British used Provincetown as a naval supply base for vessels such as the *Somerset*, which participated in the battle of Bunker Hill and went aground on November 3, 1778, off Peaked Hill Bar, located near Provincetown's "back shore." Some residents stayed in town long enough to capitalize on England's loss. As a high-ranking officer of the British navy reported, "From all I can learn, there is wicked work at the wreck, riotous doings. Truro and Provincetown men made a division of the clothing, etc. Truro took two-thirds and Provincetown one-third."[20] For the most part, however, residents again abandoned Provincetown for more protected surroundings inland.

Nonetheless, Provincetown was quick to rebound after the Revolutionary War. By 1790 Provincetown had a population of 454 people (211 women) living in ninety-five households. Its salt industry was on the rise, and nearly thirty fishing vessels were traveling to the Grand Banks, returning with a total of 11,000 quintals (1 quintal = 100 pounds) of cod.[21] When the American Congress issued the Embargo Act of 1807, which closed all U.S. ports to export shipping, Provincetown harbored twice as many vessels, a total of sixty-two, ranging in weight from 38 to 162 tons. In 1808 the town of Provincetown sent a letter to U.S. President Thomas Jefferson pleading for an end to the embargo, stating as its reason the deleterious effect the act was having on Provincetown residents, their "interests being almost entirely involved in navigation and the fisheries."[22]

The War of 1812 proved to be even more disastrous to Province-town's developing fishing industry when British warships, particularly the *Spencer* and the *Majestic*, took control of Provincetown Harbor and enforced a blockade. In 1813 residents called for a special town meeting to address "the present unhappy situation of the town by reason of the war; and to devise means for the enemy's demands in the future."[23] The British made life unpleasant in Provincetown, forcing fishermen to pilot British ships and, according to one resident, making "us do what we didn't wish—to carry water to them and provisions. However, I once carried them some frozen potatoes—there is some consolation in that."[24] Other forms of resistance were evident: Provincetown residents succeeded in smuggling fish to New York and in benefiting from an on-shore trade with British officers, who often paid in gold. Continuing their tradition of skirting the law, Provincetown's residents traded across enemy lines, their activities prompting the U.S. Treasury Depart-ment to denounce "the mass of the population [who] are interested in their [illegal contraband] concealment, and so far from giving assis-tance, threaten such opposition as renders the attempt . . . futile."[25]

The War of 1812 was the last international entanglement to hamper Provincetown's beginnings as a thriving seaport, for soon afterward both its population and its economy enjoyed unprecedented gains. From 1830 to 1890 Provincetown's population swelled from 1,710 to 4,642. Its salt and maritime industries complemented this trend as the town embarked on its own kind of industrial revolution. It was a time that Yankee residents in particular would remember with nostalgia and pride, since Provincetown soon fell into the hands of Portuguese immi-grants and never again regained its nineteenth-century economic prowess.

This era saw the rise not only of Yankee whaling captains and wharf industries but also of women's entrepreneurial ventures and Province-town's unceasing need to import laborers. Indeed, before Province-town's seafaring enterprises rose to the fore, its residents built a series of saltworks, the first in 1776. Producing salt was a shore-bound under-taking run by those who did not go to sea: women, girls, older men, and young boys. When there were not enough at home, Provincetown brought in laborers from elsewhere, in this case, young boys from Boston. The saltworks occupied a good part of Provincetown's land, with windmills stretched along the shore and salt vats covering expan-sive patches, even entire blocks. In 1837 Provincetown housed seventy-eight saltworks and exported almost fifty thousand bushels of salt. Unfortunately, by that time the price of salt had plummeted from eight dollars per bushel in the late eighteenth century to only one dollar. The industry lasted until just before the Civil War, after which it was more economical to purchase salt elsewhere.[26]

Isolated at the end of Cape Cod, Provincetown residents have tried a variety of ways to build capital or simply to make ends meet. Besides its salt industry, a makeshift fishing settlement emerged on the strip of sand called Long Point (1.4 miles by boat from downtown Provincetown). Beginning in 1818, the Long Point community grew steadily under the leadership of John Atwood Sr. and others. They built a lighthouse in 1826, and by the 1840s, it had attracted two hundred residents, all of whom relocated for the same reason: to be closer to the local fishing grounds. Using small boats and sweep seines (nets), fishermen took advantage of Long Point's remote location, building thirty-eight houses, a school, and a retail store. By 1867, possibly because the local supply of fish had diminished, Long Point's residents had returned to Provincetown proper, along with their houses, which they floated across the harbor on barges before placing most of them permanently in the West End.[27] In the late twentieth century, Provincetown revived this part of its courageous seafaring past by furnishing the outside of the remaining Long Point homes with decorative blue tiles depicting a boat on water.

The Long Point settlement coincided with Provincetown's transformation from a freewheeling oasis into a lucrative and organized seaport. From the early to the mid-nineteenth century, Provincetown developed economically alongside other New England seaports. Yankee merchants and whaling captains prospered, and Provincetown became known not only as one of the East Coast's most important whaling and fishing centers but also as one of Massachusetts's wealthiest towns. In 1854 it had the state's highest income per capita of all towns, a far cry from where it had stood just decades earlier (or, for that matter, from where it stood in 1989, well below the state average), hovering dangerously close to the bottom of the economic barrel. "'They have [amassed] silver to an amount which would surprise the inhabitants of our country towns, where every man, woman, and child do not actually see in the course of a year so much solid coins as one individual, not infrequently, possesses in Provincetown,'" remarked one writer in 1830.[28]

Provincetown captains rigged schooners and brigs for both whaling and salt-banking trips south to the Falkland Islands and the coast of Brazil, north to the Davis Strait, northeast to the Grand Banks, east to Georges Banks, and southeast to the Azores, the Cape Verdean Islands, and the coast of Africa.[29] Successful whaling ventures yielded hundreds of barrels of oil and thousands of pounds of whalebone (technically the baleen plates of the right whale), the oil needed for lamps and candles and the whalebone preceding flexible steel in, for example, umbrellas and corsets. The value of both products escalated from the early 1800s leading up to the Civil War, and seaports like Provincetown, by 1846 the fifth largest whaling port in the United States, flourished.[30]

Yankee whaling and fishing captains, wharf owners, and local merchants consolidated Provincetown's loosely structured whale grazing, cod fishing, and saltworks into dozens of lucrative "wharf industries," thus transforming Provincetown into something of an "industrial beehive," to use local historian George Bryant's term.[31] Although the official count varies, fishermen and entrepreneurs built approximately fifty-four wharves in Provincetown.

Provincetown's wharves—the fragments of which still elicit seafaring nostalgia—were critical to its success as a whaling and fishing seaport. The wharves made Provincetown Harbor into an accessible and desirable destination for countless maritime merchants. They allowed some of Provincetown's larger vessels to load and unload without running aground, and the ones containing marine railways made it easy for boats of all sizes to dock or dry-dock for repairs. Some of the longer wharves hosted row upon row of fish flakes—wooden platforms used to dry and cure fish—as did most front and back yards, the cumulative effect of which lent a notable stench to the entire town. In 1809 one visitor warned, "The flakes or frames on which the fish are dried are . . . intermixed with the houses . . . and the effluvia that escapes during the process is generally of the most unpleasant description."[32] Apparently the problem continued, as another traveler revealed nearly seventy years later: "Besides the sand, the most striking thing in all of Provincetown to a stranger is an all-prevailing odor of fish. It is not as you might innocently suspect, a simple odor, but a very remarkable combination of smell, in which, if you entirely give your whole nose to it, you may distinguish every imaginable offense which a fish can commit."[33]

The wharf industries channeled nearly all of Provincetown's business ventures onto their wooden platforms and walkways. On the wharves captains enjoyed one-stop shopping for essential supplies and equipment like nets, anchors, chain cables, and ice. Many of the wharves also housed sail lofts, storage facilities, ship chandeliers, blacksmith shops, and tryworks for extracting cod liver oil. Some sold groceries; others peddled vessels from dories to completely outfitted schooners. A number of wharves acted as financial centers, attending to local accounts, deeds, and loans and serving a vital function in a town and era with few banks but increasing numbers of people and monetary transactions. By 1854 Provincetown had its first commercial bank, the First National Bank, an offshoot of the Union Wharf Company. That same year the wharves serviced some seven hundred vessels: Grand Bankers, Georges Bankers, and cod and mackerel vessels.[34] In 1865 Provincetown sent 153 grand and salt-banking vessels to sea, and six years later harvested 1,348,590 pounds of fish.[35] It was a lucrative era not only for Yankee whaling and cod-fishing industries but also for Yankee residents' onshore ventures, for few people of other ethnic or racial backgrounds owned businesses in Provincetown. In 1865 Provincetown's population was 3,475, of which the majority were Yankees; 245 were of Portuguese descent; 185 were from Cape Breton in Canada; and 115 were Irish.[36]

Yankees built an economic empire in Provincetown during the nineteenth century and dominated the town's cultural, political, and religious resources. Yankee captains had been importing Portuguese sailors from the Azores and Scottish Gael seamen (also called "Herring Chokers") from Newfoundland; the latter immigrant community was able to blend in as white, while the former did not immediately affect Provincetown's status as a Yankee stronghold. During most of the nineteenth century, it was the Yankees who built the largest homes, owned and commanded the most lucrative vessels, ran the wharf industries, rented the most prestigious church pews, were the proprietors of nearly all the businesses, and held the most influential political offices.

Yet Provincetown's glory days as a lucrative seaport were brief, and Yankee townsfolk soon found their power, but not their prestige, slipping because they depended on two fickle industries with short-lived futures: whaling and salt fishing. Seafaring tensions during the Civil War damaged many of the salt-banking vessels, and immeasurably more daunting, the 1859 discovery of petroleum oil sent Provincetown's whaling industry into a steady, irreparable decline. In 1865, the Provincetown fleet had twenty-eight whaling vessels employing 498 men, 105 cod- and mackerel-fishing vessels carrying 1,260 men, twenty "coastwise-trade" vessels with 130 men, and 100 men engaged in shell-fishing. But by 1885, only 114 vessels remained, and by 1895 just forty-seven sailed from Provincetown Harbor. After the turn of the twentieth century, the Portuguese-dominated fresh-fish fishing fleet rebounded with the onset of large-scale refrigeration, and the total number of vessels climbed to sixty-three. But the last Provincetown whaling vessel, owned by Charles W. Morgan, completed its final voyage in 1921. Less than three decades after Cape Cod Oil Works and Nickerson's Whale and Menhaden Oil Works built refineries on Long Point in the late 1870s and near Hatch's Harbor in 1886, Provincetown's whaling and salt-banking industries slowed to a halt.[37]

While attempting to mobilize a replacement industry, Yankees fell hard to the pull of inland economic and educational opportunities and to demographic shifts within their own community. During the second half of the nineteenth century, the Civil War took the lives of numerous Yankee men and vessels and prompted scores of others to leave Cape Cod in search of work inland. At the same time, Yankees failed to reproduce at the same rate as their Portuguese neighbors did, and they intermarried with Portuguese residents, thereby changing the composition of both ethnicities. On February 18, 1874, the *Provincetown Advocate* revealed the extent to which Portuguese fishermen were displacing Yankees and setting up their own off-season ventures: "Among all of our fishermen, none are more hardy and adventuresome than the Portuguese, in fact they constitute the body of those who trawl for fish here in the winter."[38] In 1865, less than 10 percent of Provincetown's fishing captains were of Portuguese descent, but by 1885, they dominated the industry. Similarly, the percentage of residents of Portuguese descent increased from 5 percent in 1860 to nearly 45 percent forty years later. From 1870 to 1910, Yankees slid from forming a comfortable majority to representing roughly half of all residents in Provincetown.[39]

As their economic and social prestige waned, some Yankees simply left town for what they hoped would be greater opportunities elsewhere. For example, in the 1890s, Captain J. A. Matheson moved to Anacortes, Washington, to launch one of the first (salted) cod-fishing operations in the northern Pacific, and the former Captain Lewis Chapman relocated to Minnesota with several Yankee families. Other Yankees, however, stayed and challenged the incoming Portuguese captains by building their own fresh-fish fishing vessels. Captain Alex

The Cape Cod Cold Storage Company ca. 1910 was located at 125–129 Commercial Street. Postcard of the Pilgrim Monument and Provincetown Museum.

Kemp, for instance, Provincetown's last Grand Banks skipper, built the *Little Atlanta* for shore fishing.[40]

Even before the 1898 Portland Gale destroyed nearly half of Provincetown's wharves and wharf industries, a number of Yankees capitalized on the fresh-fish industry, which Portuguese immigrants had pioneered during the winter months of whaling's off-season. Yankees, who once owned large whaling and salt-banking vessels, invested their money instead in smaller boats so that they could transport a day's catch more rapidly. They also invested in Provincetown's newest on-shore technology, cold-storage facilities, to ice the incoming fish. In 1874 Yankees built the first of six fish factories, which used conveyer belts to transport crates of fish from the wharves into the freezers' upper stories. Inside, workers—both Yankee and Portuguese—prepared and packed the frozen cod, mackerel, herring, and an assortment of other saltwater delicacies that they then shipped to, most often, New York. The freezers contributed to both Portuguese and Yankee economic power by providing both jobs for all residents and facilities to package and transport new shipments of fresh fish.

The waning fishing industry notwithstanding, those Yankees who remained at Land's End set out to, first, solidify their claims to Provincetown and, second, create a replacement industry. In pursuit of this goal, they capitalized on the fortuitous *Mayflower* landing, which gave them access to two critical movements: a national one that was creating an American past by embracing historic moments and places, and a regional one that was creating and celebrating "Old New England." In 1874, the Reverend Elisa Nason of Boston highlighted Provincetown's regional significance: "The Pilgrims of 'The *Mayflower*' landed" there, he explained, and there "occurred the birth of Peregrine White, the first English child born in New England."[41] In contrast, John Wesley Hanson emphasized Provincetown's national importance. In his 1891 biography of William Henry Ryder, a *Mayflower* descendant, he insisted that "the American nation had its birth in Provincetown," which was where, too, the "germ of American republicanism," the *Mayflower* Compact, originated.[42]

Provincetown was not the only town in the United States at this time that was scrambling to replace its traditional—in this case, whaling—economy. In the late 1800s and early 1900s small towns from the Atlantic's northeastern seaboard to those farther inland witnessed the demise of their farming, quarrying, and lumbering industries as the Industrial Revolution spread throughout the nation and especially the Northeast. Some villages effectively disappeared, seldom heard from again, as their working classes migrated to burgeoning mill and factory towns and thriving urban areas. Others, like Saratoga Springs, New York, and Martha's Vineyard, Massachusetts, created new economies based on the expanding industry of tourism.

To entice middle- and upper-class tourists and to revive their increasingly quiet main streets, these northeastern villages created a mythic region called "New England" and a mythic time in the past called the "colonial." The term "colonial" was meant to capture a moment in American history that was not yet riddled by ethnic, racial, or class tensions. Indeed, New England residents created the colonial period in part to attract white tourists who were eager to flee what many felt were immigrant-ridden, congested urban areas and to return to preindustrial, supposedly conflict-free, rural enclaves. Aside from celebrating all that came with the building of the thirteen colonies, the colonial movement conveniently "forgot" or, more accurately, glossed over, the lethal troubles of the seventeenth century, including the clashes with Native Americans and the deaths from hunger, disease, and intra-group skirmishes. It was also a movement that carried implicit racial connotations, as it galvanized white Anglo-European Americans while simultaneously distancing itself from more recent immigrant groups.

Although many northeastern towns became "colonial" during the late 1800s, Provincetown waited until the early 1900s to launch its aggressive colonial campaigns. To be sure, up to the start of the twentieth century, tourists still thought of Cape Cod as a backward hinterland, even though some Cape Cod towns, like Provincetown, had been promoting themselves as resort areas for decades.[43] Nonetheless, by capitalizing on the concept of the colonial, Provincetown finally came into its own as a worthy tourist destination.

During the early twentieth century, Yankee women in Provincetown began promoting the imagined racial purity and economic tranquillity of a bygone colonial era by salvaging their heritage and prestige via exclusive ladies' societies. Although their Victorian sensibilities discouraged them from participating in electoral politics, they still ventured into the public arena as active "colonial enthusiasts."[44] Yankee women founded a number of clubs in Provincetown, including the Nautilus Club, organized in 1907, whose members vowed to "read, mark, learn, and inwardly digest"; and the Companions of the Forest of America, whose bylaws stated, "The object of this order is to unite for the purpose of promoting sociability, sincerity, and constancy. The Companions invite all acceptable white females of moral character, good habits, and sound mental and bodily health and respectable calling."[45] As these bylaws indicate, many, if not all, of these clubs excluded Provincetown's not-quite-white Portuguese, African American, and Cape Verdean women.

The most influential of these societies, the Research Club, fashioned Provincetown into a colonial outpost and elevated its Yankee histories and culture by organizing, publishing, and commemorating Provincetown's Anglo-European past. Buoyed no doubt by the completion of the Provincetown Pilgrim Monument in 1910, the club's original founders, Mrs. Mary Sparrow, Mrs. Grace Hall, Mrs. Anna Young, Mrs. Gertrude DeWager, Mrs. Elizabeth Atwood, and Miss Julia Knowles, extended invitations that same year to select women of *Mayflower* lineage, all of whom were "aristocrats of New England." To reinforce their familial connections, they referred to one another as "cousins," and in-

Photograph of the Research Club's float during an unidentified parade, ca. 1927. Courtesy of the Pilgrim Monument and Provincetown Museum.

deed, most apparently were descendants of only one *Mayflower* passenger, Stephen Hopkins.[46]

The Research Club helped turn Provincetown into a colonial village first by publishing a series of articles on Provincetown's Anglo-European history. The club met monthly in the off-season, and its officers insisted that all members contribute to the group's intellectual nourishment by researching and delivering papers. At each meeting, in addition to outside lecturers, at least one or two members presented papers which, almost exclusively, championed Yankee history and culture. Soon after Yankee women founded the club, cousin Julia Knowles married the editor of the *Provincetown Advocate*, Howard Hopkins, who arranged to have the club's papers published. "Colonial Music," a piece by Reba Bush Lawrence, is a typical example of the Research Club's bias:

> We who are descendants of the Massachusetts colonists may be pardoned for a certain pride in the history of music in America, for it was the settlers in New England who were responsible for the development along this line, which led directly to all that is good in the way of music in the United States today.[47]

Histories of Provincetown's once-thriving Yankee whaling and fishing industries proved popular, as did stories of its legendary lifesaving stations, its former schools, and its oldest cemetery.

Next, Research Club members erected several outdoor markers to remind residents and visitors of Provincetown's place as a national historic landmark. Because town officials had already named many of Provincetown's streets after prominent *Mayflower* Pilgrims, like Alden, Bradford, Standish, and Winslow, and other Yankees had just commemorated the landing of the *Mayflower* with the Pilgrim Monument, the Research Club chose other historic events. Their first tablet honored the four Pilgrims who died during their brief stay in Provincetown Harbor: Dorothy Bradford, James Chilton, Jasper Moore, and Edward Thompson. Following that, the "colonial enthusiasts" marked the location of the Pilgrim women's first wash day, the approximate landing spot of the *Mayflower* in the West End, the spring from which the Pilgrims supposedly drew their first buckets of fresh water, and the place where the Pilgrims "first encountered" Native Americans. Notably, many of these sites drew attention to women's lesser-known participation in the historic landing.

The Research Club's attempts to institutionalize Provincetown's Yankee legacy culminated in the Provincetown Historical Museum, which they founded, purchased, and ran from 1923 to 1956. Ideas for a museum germinated when Cousin Gertrude DeWager visited Nantucket in 1921, explored the island's popular whaling museum, and then urged her fellow club members to salvage Provincetown's historic artifacts. At first they housed its small collection, with the permission of the Yankee-run board of selectmen, in the town hall. But when the collection outgrew this space, they looked to the famous Benjamin Lancy Mansion in the center of town at 232 Commercial Street, which was for sale. After contacting the owner, a "real" cousin of DeWager's, and raising three thousand dollars from Yankee residents and relatives, they made the down payment on the mansion. In 1923, two years after DeWager's initial plea, Cape End's *Mayflower* ladies opened the Provincetown Historical Museum to the public.[48]

Like women's reform efforts elsewhere in the United States, the Research Club's activities took on a two-sided nature. On the one hand, they created and expanded public and political roles for women. The Research Club gave middle- and upper-class white women an oppor-

48 The Water Front, Provincetown, Cape Cod, Mass.   5103-29

The Pilgrim Monument ca. 1910 stands atop High Pole Hill and looks down
on all of Provincetown. Postcard courtesy of the Pilgrim Monument and
Provincetown Museum.

tunity to participate in local politics and to influence Provincetown's
collective memory of the past. On the other hand, such associations
often produced and reproduced class, ethnic, racial, and religious hierarchies. For instance, the past that the Research Club preserved and institutionalized played down the legacies of Provincetown's nonwhite
or less-white residents, including those of Native American and Portuguese descent. In addition, Research Club members were not concerned with Provincetown's social or labor problems or with forging relationships that crossed class and race boundaries. Indeed, some Research Club members also belonged to Provincetown's local Ku Klux
Klan chapter. Instead, they focused on maintaining a certain status quo
by institutionalizing their histories and positions as white middle- and
upper-class "aristocratic" women and by redrawing the boundaries
that separated residents who differed by class, race, and ethnicity. Their
aim was to re-create an Anglo-European past at Land's End, and the effect was to bolster Yankee authority while portraying Provincetown as
a desirable colonial outpost. The Research Club was active for several
decades, during which time Portuguese fishermen and their families
displaced Provincetown's Yankees.[49]

Yankee residents' most dramatic effort to articulate their rightful claims to Land's End, Cape Cod, and the nation as a whole resulted in the Pilgrim Monument, a towering 252-foot, all-granite, phallic shaft modeled after the Torre del Mangia in Siena, Italy. The same James Gifford who apologized at the opening ceremonies of the Old Colony Railroad because Provincetown had no "ancient monument" joined other prominent Yankee men of Provincetown and elsewhere to commemorate the landing of the *Mayflower* Pilgrims with just that, an ancient monument. James H. Hopkins, Joseph H. Dyer, and Artemus P. Hannum were among those who joined Gifford in 1892 to create the Cape Cod Pilgrim Memorial Association (CCPMA).[50] Like the Research Club and countless organizations outside Provincetown, the CCPMA was swept up in the Progressive Era's nationwide movement to create and commercialize an innovative, colonial past. Alongside their daughters, wives, and sisters in exclusive ladies' societies, the CCPMA erected a series of public history tablets to commemorate the *Mayflower*'s landing in Provincetown. They also eventually established a permanent collection of memorabilia associated with Cape Cod's Yankee history. But their primary concern was to secure financial backing for a magnificent monument that would perch atop High Pole Hill, overseeing all of Provincetown.

The CCPMA built the monument for the same reasons that Plymouth had built a monument more than fifty years earlier: to attract tourists by calling attention to Provincetown's historic, indeed legendary, significance. They also built it to correct historical records, which credited Plymouth rather than Provincetown for being the *Mayflower* Pilgrims' "first" landfall.[51] Those promoting the monument insisted that like the Statue of Liberty and the obelisk at Bunker Hill, Provincetown's Pilgrim Monument represented nothing less than the ideals of liberty and freedom on which Europeans laid claim to the United States. Apparently the U.S. Congress and the state of Massachusetts agreed, for each contributed 40 percent of the $90,000 needed to erect the monument. The remaining 20 percent was split evenly between contributions raised inside and outside the CCPMA.[52]

The CCPMA marketed the monument as a necessary reminder to a nation that seemed to be losing sight of its legendary beginnings, its status as an independent province, and its future as an aspiring democratic country. To solicit contributions, the CCPMA distributed booklets reiterating a number of patriotic pieces, including, for example, an article from *Harper's Weekly*:

We are gradually coming to realize in this country that we have a history, and one of the best assets of a nation is its past. The revered memory in which that past is held is a sign of the present growth of the
land. For a great and simple shaft to stand upon the spot which first
saw the Pilgrims, where the famous Compact itself was signed, is as
fitting and proper as a shaft to stand upon Bunker Hill.[53]

They also quoted the Reverend Edward Everett Hale of Boston's South
Congregational Church, who insisted that "the compact drawn up at
Provincetown [was] as important as the Declaration of Independence
and was its forerunner."[54] The CCPMA even went one step further by
contending that "the monument will be both a welcome and a warning
—a welcome to the persecuted, a warning that the laws of this land of
their refuge must be respected, that 'liberty' does not mean license, but
government of self from selfish propensities."[55] In a final plea for contributions it noted, "It is desired to make the erection of this memorial
at Provincetown a popular movement, and to give all law-abiding individuals an opportunity to show their appreciation and patriotism by
subscribing."[56]

The festivities surrounding the building and unveiling of the monument drew thousands to Land's End. The pomp and circumstance associated with the "Laying of the Cornerstone" ceremony in 1907, for instance, lured a multitude of onlookers as President Theodore Roosevelt
paraded through town and then up to a bare High Pole Hill. "Getting
Ready for Provincetown's Great Day," the *Boston Sunday Post* announced three weeks before the cornerstone ceremonies.[57] "Provincetown All Dressed Up for Its Noted Guests," the *Boston Journal* declared
the day before the event.[58] The dedication ceremonies attracted an equal
amount of fanfare. This time, in 1910, President William Howard Taft
made the pilgrimage to Land's End. The title of an article in the *Boston
Post* reveals the extent to which Provincetown basked in the glory of the
monument's grand opening: "Eyes of the Nation on Provincetown
Today: Mighty Warships Gather, Distinguished Guests Arrive, Whole
Town a Blaze of Color for Dedication of Great Monument."[59]

Some visitors raced out to be one of the first to climb all 116 steps
and sixty ramps to the top of the monument. Others may have learned
about it from travelogues or friends who brought home souvenir items
like postcards and pieces of cobalt blue china.[60] More adventuresome
tourists may have seen what looked like a needle in the Atlantic Ocean

—on a clear day the monument is visible from a distance of forty miles —and decided to make its home their destination. In his 1937 book, *Cape Cod Pilot*, Josef Berger (aka Jeremiah Digges) described the monument's unique history of immigration and labor. The Pilgrim Monument, he explained, is

> thoroughly American in its makeup. Although the Pilgrims had never been to Italy, the design is Italian, the plans were made by an army engineer of French and Swiss descent, it was built by the Irish and is taken care of by the Portuguese; and annually it is climbed by several thousand *Mayflower* descendants.[61]

From the dedication ceremony in 1910 until 1929, when the number of visitors dropped for the first time in two decades, the monument drew thousands of visitors to the tip of Cape Cod every summer.

The Research Club and the CCPMA were two of the last Yankee associations to organize in Provincetown in the name of their ancestors. By the mid- to late twentieth century, even though the Pilgrim Monument still loomed large, Yankee culture in Provincetown had diminished significantly. Their political institutions, including the board of trade and the board of selectmen, began accepting Portuguese members and leaders; their economic enterprises were few and far between; and their cultural influences seemed unremarkable to many residents and visitors. One Provincetown native whose mother was a Yankee and whose father was Portuguese admitted in 1997 that "the Portuguese part of the family was a lot more interesting. I always thought that my mother's side of the family was a little bland. The food was bland. . . . I think [Portuguese] culture is a little more excitable, a little more interesting, lively."[62] Aside from failing to secure economic and political gains, Yankees reproduced at a slower rate than did their Catholic Portuguese neighbors, who typically had large families. The membership list published annually in the Research Club's official "program" reflected this decline. The 1926/27 program listed eighty-seven active members and six "in memoriam," but by the 1955/56 season the number of cousins in memoriam, sixty-nine, was twenty-four more than the number of those listed as active members.[63]

Be that as it may, the colonial revival was an ingenious Yankee coup in a town that was well on its way to becoming known more as a Portuguese fishing village than as a colonial Yankee outpost. In an elaborate and timely series of ceremonies, the Pilgrim Monument re-created, at least momentarily, the authority and prestige that Cape Cod's Yankee residents had enjoyed for decades. Erecting the monument and having it dedicated by the U.S. president helped create a replacement industry, rescue a town that was failing economically, and mitigate the presence of what some Yankees considered "undesirable" "dark-skinned" immigrants.

Provincetown residents and promoters looked back to its early past —its "age of discovery," its Pilgrim heritage, its era of lawless disorder, and its economic heyday—to remake Land's End just as it was transitioning from a Yankee whaling seaport into a Portuguese fishing village. These historical projects emphasized the central contributions of Anglo-European Yankees while shrouding Provincetown's more recent history of immigration and ethnic conflict. In so doing, they represented Yankee efforts to intervene in the present and future through discussions of the past. After the "watering place" era, promoters latched on quickly to Provincetown's charm as a colonial village.

Yet those who carefully designed campaigns to refashion Provincetown were unable to predict the outcomes of their earliest calls to the persecuted and patriotic. Phrases such as "'liberty' does not mean license" suggest the anxiety boosters harbored as Provincetown became a resort town based on freedom. Yankees made Provincetown into a thriving seaport during the mid-1800s and had a replacement industry and a new monument in place by the early 1900s. Yet they still lost their hometown to other sets of pilgrims, both foreign and native born. Indeed, they could not foresee at this early stage how their newly created colonial outpost would soon blossom into a haven not only for Anglo-European "colonial enthusiasts" but also for foreign-born immigrants seeking economic and political advantages and for gay men and lesbians seeking freedom of expression.

Soon after Yankees promoted Provincetown's colonial past, Portuguese immigrants invoked similar narratives of liberation to claim their place as citizens of Land's End. And less than a decade following the monument's grand dedication ceremony, "maiden ladies" and "bachelors" began to seek out Provincetown because it was rumored to be an accepting enclave. Over time, gay men and lesbians would not only visit Provincetown en masse but would also call on Land's End to live up to its name as a haven for oppressed pilgrims. One late-twentieth-century guide to Provincetown began, for example, with this passage: "First things first: It's Provincetown, it's P-town, it's Paradise. And ever since the Pilgrims first landed here, this fishing village on the tip of Cape Cod, Massachusetts, has been providing the perfect oasis for people in need of an escape."[64] Eventually, the kinds of visitors who migrated to Provincetown because of its reputation as a refuge soon prompted townsfolk to reconsider their painstaking efforts to paint the monument as a beacon for the persecuted. In other words, many residents born in the shadows of the towering shaft on High Pole Hill would soon come to question the monument's message by welcoming some pilgrims while discouraging others.

2

"The Perfect Compromise"

Provincetown's Portuguese Pilgrims

Provincetown itself has of late, indeed, been seized by a new band of Pilgrims, the Portuguese, who succeeded the Yankees in the fisheries, and who now themselves are finding other lines of effort more attractive. One finds himself as much in a foreign land as is possible here in America, in Provincetown, in spite of the lofty monument which commemorates the first landing of our fathers. . . . There is something good to be said for the Portuguese which is not so marked in the natives of Cape Cod. [The Portuguese] are rather notably courteous and lively and have added a note of joyousness and vivacity which may be more superficial than the sturdy graces of the English character, but is, nevertheless, agreeable as met by the traveler.

—Wallace Nutting, *Massachusetts Beautiful*, 1923

WALLACE NUTTING'S POPULAR TRAVELOGUE, *Massachusetts Beautiful*, enhanced the colonial revival project.[1] Its portraits of New England life described the area in such detail that tourists could easily find villages by train, steamer, and, later, automobile, and they encouraged Americans to take pride in their homeland by promoting the historic and cultural landmarks of the Northeast. But Provincetown presented a unique conundrum. How could Nutting romanticize this quintessential colonial village—the landfall of the *Mayflower* Pilgrims— when it housed an increasingly influential population of Portuguese immigrants, the very kinds of people that xenophobic travelers from congested urban areas were trying to escape?

In the end, Nutting solved what many Anglo-European Americans regarded as the immigrant "problem" by tapping into tourists' desires not only for excursions to historically noteworthy sights but also for trips that promised "authentic" yet harmless experiences of ethnic life. These jaunts typically included some form of "alienated leisure" that allowed tourists to distance themselves—ethnically, racially, and socioeconomically—from those they toured. Alienated leisure gave white middle- and upper-class tourists an opportunity to reassert their cultural, racial, and class privileges and to reaffirm their faith in an American hierarchy of bodies, ethnicities, and labor.[2]

Drawing on tourists' turn-of-the-century desire to celebrate an American past and present, Anglo-European Yankees promoted Land's End in "sense-of-place" guidebooks. Although Nutting's *Massachusetts Beautiful* may have been New England's most popular early-twentieth-century travelogue, other books offered equally detailed descriptions of Provincetown and its emerging racial complexity. In her 1918 *Cape Cod: New and Old*, Agnes Edwards encouraged white middle- and upper-class tourists to commemorate the landing of the *Mayflower* with a visit to Provincetown, in her words, the "home of our forefathers" and also of recent Portuguese immigrants. In a tone meant to tempt rather than dissuade, she dared tourists to "descend from the [Pilgrim] monument . . . [to] see in a graphic exposition the amazing preponderance of this quiet, comely race," whose members present "every shade of color from almost black to creamy olive, and every grade of refinement in [their] foreign countenances." The Portuguese residents, she explained, are "smiling men and women [who] without any spectacular ovation [have] silently, persistently, inconspicuously achieved occupation of Provincetown." Portuguese immigrants "are the fishermen, the storekeepers . . . their daughters are waitresses in the hotels and teachers in the schools. . . . There are Portuguese women who cannot speak English; Portuguese men who marry the daughters of Cape Cod stock." They emigrated, Edwards continued, from "the Azores, and some from Portugal, and there is more or less a feud between them, and more or less resentment against them all by the natives." Lest this tension threaten middle- and upper-class sensibilities, Edwards quickly reassured her readers, "But they are thrifty and law-abiding people and here, as elsewhere on the Cape, their industry and picturesqueness contribute something not without value to the general life."[3] Edwards recommended Provincetown by reminding visitors of its place as a historic landmark, by patronizing and racializing Portuguese residents, and by promising an exciting but harmless brush with working-class ethnic

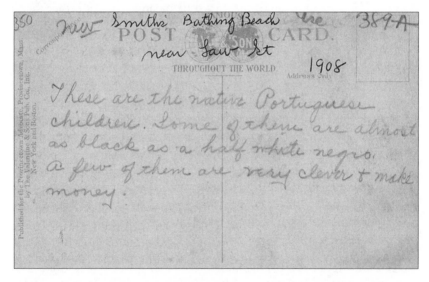

A 1908 postcard entitled "Children on the Beach" uses Portuguese residents—in this case, children—as tourist spectacles to promote Land's End. Postcard courtesy of the Pilgrim Monument and Provincetown Museum.

life. In short, she exposed the complex racial and ethnic dynamic whereby white people simultaneously appreciated and degraded those who are seen as not white.[4]

Many travelogue writers attracted visitors to Provincetown by portraying its Portuguese residents as exotic but tame foreigners. In 1932 Arthur Tarbell, author of the popular *Cape Cod Ahoy!*, noted that in Provincetown "every other passer-by on the streets is a dark-skinned member of another race . . . yet they are good citizens, law-abiding, industrious, and thrifty, these Portuguese."[5] Four years later, Katherine Dos Passos, wife of the half-Portuguese writer John Dos Passos, characterized Portuguese boys and girls as a "brood of swarthy black-eyed children" and the "Bravas" as "black Portuguese . . . [who are] a cross between savages of the Cape Verde Islands and exiled Portuguese criminals."[6] Nancy Paine Smith was one of many writers who repackaged working-class tasks as well as people into picturesque attractions. In the 1931 edition of *The Provincetown Guide Book*, Smith penned an essay entitled "How to Amuse Yourself in Provincetown" and nudged tourists to "visit the 'freezers' where twenty million pounds of fish are exported annually."[7] Journalists also prepared visitors arriving via the Boston boat to look out for "bronzed youngsters," "the Portuguese diving boys [who] line the end of the wharf, ready to plunge into the water for tossed coins."[8] Provincetown's wharves, fishing vessels, and fish factories permitted visitors a rare view of the strength and rigor associated with diminishing forms of working-class labor.

Most of the Portuguese immigrants who chose the United States arrived between 1880 and 1924.[9] Unlike earlier U.S. immigrants, who came mostly from northwestern Europe and west Africa, the immigrants arriving during this period came primarily southern Europe. According to immigration records, each year an average of twenty-six Portuguese people (twenty-four men and two women) arrived (legally) in the United States from 1820 to 1830. With the exception of 1833, which marked the beginning of the First Carlist War in Spain (1833–1839) and which saw a marked increase in male immigrants (636, most probably escaping military conscription), the numbers remained low throughout the first half of the nineteenth century. In 1850, Portuguese immigration rose sharply, with 546 newcomers (350 men and 196 women) and continued in the several hundreds until 1872 when, for the first time, more than 1,000 people (960 men and 351 women) entered. From 1850 to 1880, approximately 70 percent of all Portuguese immigrants landed in Boston, with fewer reaching New Bedford or New York. They made the journey in those early years on small vessels like brigs, schooners, and barks that each held approximately thirty-eight passengers.[10]

In the last decade of the nineteenth century, the number of Portuguese men and women gaining entrance to the United States increased precipitously as steamers with a passenger capacity of nearly 100 each had joined a fleet of larger vessels to transport American-bound Portuguese immigrants. In 1893, for example, 4,248 Portuguese immigrants (2,706 men and 1,552 women) made their way to the United States. The number of Portuguese immigrants continued to rise from 1872 to 1921, the latter year registering an all-time high of 18,856 (12,479 men and 5,377 women) legal immigrants.[11]

Most of these Portuguese immigrants settled in Massachusetts. New Bedford was often the initial stopping point, and from there Portuguese immigrants typically moved on to Fall River, Taunton, Provincetown, or Gloucester. Other states with high concentrations of Portuguese immigrants were California, Rhode Island, Connecticut, New Jersey, and Hawaii. Brazil and Canada also became New World homes for Portuguese immigrants.[12]

Most of the Portuguese immigrants to the United States, including those settling in Provincetown, came from the Azores.[13] Also called the Western Islands, the Azores consist of nine islands extending for more than 375 miles across the middle of the Atlantic Ocean, from northwest to southeast. One Provincetown writer described the islands as "armfuls of flowers in bowls of deep blue water . . . [which] except for the brief storms and a rainy season . . . know little of gray skies or cold."[14] Their latitudinal positions align the archipelago in almost a straight path from Washington, D.C., to Lisbon, Portugal. Flores is the island farthest west and is about 1,000 miles from continental Europe and 1,300 miles from Newfoundland. Santa Maria, the one farthest east, is 700 miles from the coast of Portugal and 750 miles off the coast of Africa. Unlike the inhabitants of continental Portugal, only 1 percent of whom engaged in the fishing industry on any level, a high proportion of Azoreans were fishermen and sailors. Although the Azoreans and the Portuguese from Lisbon arrived at the same time in Provincetown, the continental Portuguese immigrants tended to look down on the Azoreans as less educated and less skilled. According to the late Grace Goveia Collinson, a Provincetown native who taught Americanization classes for Portuguese immigrants during the 1930s and 1940s, 80 percent of Provincetown's Portuguese immigrants were from the Azores and 10 percent were from the mainland. The remaining 10 percent came from the Cape Verde Islands, Fuzeta, and other parts of the former Portuguese Empire, such as Brazil.[15]

Although they thrived initially, after Portugal's civil war in the early 1800s and its revolution at the turn of the twentieth century, the mainland neglected the Azores and their inhabitants. In the 1930s, Works Progress Administration writer Josef Berger (aka Jeremiah Digges) took note of Azoreans' distinct immigration experience by admitting that they were of "island origin; that is to say they came here not from the mother country in the first place, but from a possession far from the mother country, thus being twice removed."[16] When Azoreans arrived in the New World they identified first as "Western Islanders" in order to distinguish themselves from their Lisbon neighbors and only later as Portuguese immigrants and Portuguese Americans.

Both economic and political factors caused the Azoreans to leave their homeland for the United States. A comparatively lucrative means of making a living from the sea, educational opportunities, and the promise of freedom "pulled" these immigrants to Provincetown. But they also were "pushed" out of the Azores. A depressed economy and the lack of educational options prompted both men and women to leave for the New World. The men left in search of better jobs, and the women left simply to find any job. In the Azores, many women wanted to become schoolteachers, but with few schools and even fewer educational resources, this desire remained a dream rather than a reality for most. The other option was to get married, an escape that many women soon realized led to lateral rather than upward mobility.[17] Many first-generation Portuguese immigrants in Provincetown remained "poor," part of the working class, and only semiliterate for their entire lifetimes. But even during the Great Depression, the economic and educational conditions in Provincetown were better than those in the Azores, especially for women.[18]

In addition, during the middle to late nineteenth century, Portuguese men left for the New World to dodge forced military service, an obligation Azoreans especially resented as continental Portugal failed to ease their economic burdens. A spirit of adventure was also sometimes enough to spark the desire for seagoing voyages and unknown lands. Above all, Portuguese and Azorean immigrants believed that America and Provincetown, the "birthplaces of freedom," would offer them independence from the overbearing economic, social, and political constraints in postrevolutionary Portugal.[19]

Although many Portuguese seafarers came to the New World and to Provincetown during the precolonial and colonial eras, in the nineteenth century Yankee whaling captains recruited Portuguese sailors with increasing frequency. Indeed, as immigration scholar Maria Baganha points out, "Although rooted in the imbalances of the Portuguese socio-economic structure, Portuguese emigration to the United States was only initiated after direct inducement from the American economy."[20] In New England, the Azores were known as "the Western Islands whaling grounds," and Yankee captains used this area not only for whaling but also for replenishing supplies and acquiring sailors. Many Yankee captains left New England intentionally with a "skeleton crew," adding Azorean or Cape Verdean sailors during the early days of their voyages. Others left New England with what they thought was a full deck then realized once they were near the Western Islands that some of their men were unsuitable or likely to abandon ship. The port of Horta on the island of Fayal was the Azores' most popular and central port. From the mid- to late 1800s, when New England's onshore opportunities and falling whaling profits prompted many of its native-born men to forgo arduous fishing voyages, Portuguese crewmen and enslaved Native Americans often filled the void. In 1961 Samuel Morison described this exchange of men and labor: "American clipper ships were . . . manned by an international proletariat of the sea."[21]

In a town built on historic "firsts," the first Portuguese immigrant to make Provincetown his home has received a predictable amount of attention and storytelling. Most likely, Portuguese smugglers and traders visited Provincetown Harbor before the *Mayflower* landed, and definitely by the early 1700s, yet Manuel Caton, a lone rebellious seaman, has served for nearly a century as the heroic "first" Portuguese pilgrim to settle in Provincetown.[22]

Caton's tale is both romantic and celebratory. It depicts Portuguese men and, by extension women, as exotic, courageous, seafaring people who risked their lives to lay claim to Provincetown. It also adds to an image of the local Portuguese as the descendants of pirates, adventurers, and freedom lovers who contributed to the town's reputation for lawless disorder. In the early 1800s, Caton, as the story goes, was a young man from Lisbon who ran away from home for a life at sea. Although a gang of pirates captured his escape vessel and enslaved the entire crew, Caton managed to escape. Some say that the captain of the pirated ship forced Caton to deliver an important message or to pick up much-needed medical supplies in Provincetown and that once on shore he simply never returned. Others contend that Caton escaped in Boston and only later made his way to Land's End. Tales like these allowed Portuguese residents to take pride in their ancestors and to claim Provincetown as their hard-won home. Likewise, Caton's story also added to Yankee tendencies to promote Provincetown's Portuguese population as exotic and vivacious.

Herman Jennings, one of Provincetown's local historians, contended in 1890 that Provincetown's first Portuguese resident was Joseph Cross, a whaling captain born in Lisbon in 1813, who immigrated without fanfare to Provincetown at the age of thirteen.[23] Although the names and dates may vary, the pattern remains the same: the first Portuguese immigrants to settle in Provincetown were young, able-bodied seamen who arrived in the early 1800s, worked in the whaling industry, and discovered Land's End because of the close maritime ties between the Old World and the New.

Azoreans devised strategic and ambitious ways to reach Provincetown. Although hundreds of Azorean men, women, and children found Provincetown by formal immigration routes, just as many, if not more, entered Provincetown illegally. Regular shipping services between the Western Islands and Boston or Providence were relatively safe, and fishing, whaling, or smuggling ventures also allowed immigrants to reach New England.

After the initial wave of sailors, most of the Portuguese immigrants who chose Provincetown had learned about it from friends and relatives already there. Word-of-mouth more than relocation services or local newspapers informed Azorean immigrants of their options.[24] When Portuguese and Azorean immigrants arrived in Provincetown, they settled in the West End with kin and kith from the Western Islands. Central Street westward, including Montello, Conant, Pleasant, and Mechanic Streets, made up the Portuguese neighborhood. Its distinguishing feature, still recognizable despite the recent gentrification, is the more compact neighborhood whose houses are smaller and closer together than the larger homes of Yankees and artists in the East End.

Some Portuguese immigrants built homes in the East End, while a handful of Yankees settled in the West End, but for the most part the Portuguese and the Yankees took up residence on opposite sides of town.

In 1975, Grace Goveia Collinson recalled her family's decision: "My mother made the inevitable mistake of every immigrant. She sought her own people."[25] The mistake to which Collinson was referring was the language, race, and class barriers that all residents reinforced by choosing to cluster together. These barriers represent two intersecting dynamics: geographic exclusion and regulation put in place by East End Yankees who did not want Portuguese neighbors, and geographic choice and inclusion related to social mobility as recent arrivals networked professionally and personally with their neighbors. After 1873 and the arrival of the railroad and after numerous Portuguese and Azorean immigrants moved there, the West End became, in the minds of some residents, the "wrong" side of the tracks.

When Provincetown's Portuguese immigrants first arrived in the United States, they found a country anxious about gender, race, and citizenship. At the beginning of the twentieth century, Anglo-European men and women across the nation were celebrating American histories and ideals of freedom while simultaneously expressing concern about the United States' latest arrivals. In an 1896 sermon on the American nation, for example, Reverend C. E. Harris of the Centenary Church in Provincetown urged his Yankee parishioners to "get our good men into office" lest immigrants take their places.[26] By the early 1900s, social anthropologists, politicians, and Immigration Restriction League (IRL) officers began taking note not only of the immigrants' countries of origin —from the most desirable northwestern European countries to the less desirable southeastern European areas—but also of their racial and ethnic backgrounds. In their estimation, the whitest men were also the strongest and, hence, the best qualified to be American citizens and to defend American ideals and territories.[27]

Portuguese immigrants held a distinctive place in this emerging American-based ethnic and racial hierarchy. When Irish and Italian immigrants arrived in the United States in the early 1800s, they, too, were classified as not white.[28] But during the nineteenth century they came to be perceived as more racially similar to Anglo-Europeans, and in effect, they "became" white. Similarly, from the late 1800s into the early 1900s,

Portuguese immigrants often fit the historically changing and socially constructed—rather than biologically fixed—category of whiteness because they were European and Christian rather than African or Jewish. Nonetheless, they sometimes were regarded as black, or, more generally, as not entirely white because of their complexion and mixed—Portuguese-Azorean-Cape Verdean-African—heritage. In 1920, immigration officials in Providence demonstrated the significance of race by recording each newcomer's "complexion" as "white," "fair," "rosy," "natural," "olive," "dark," or "brown." Reinforcing long-standing divisions, Portuguese immigrants from the mainland typically fell into the "natural" category, while officials usually placed the "Western Islanders" on the "dark" end of the spectrum.[29]

When they reached Land's End, Portuguese immigrants encountered another set of racial distinctions. A number of "old stock" Yankees held influential political and economic positions and lived in the East End of town. Nestled into the West End was a close-knit enclave of less wealthy Azorean and Portuguese immigrants, and interspersed throughout town were groups of white artists. These geographic patterns corresponded to a class- and race-based hierarchy. White Anglo-European Americans positioned themselves at the apex, followed in descending order by white Nova Scotians and Irish Americans, light-skinned Portuguese mainlanders, dark-skinned Azorean immigrants, black Cape Verdeans, and, finally, black African Americans.

In order to distance themselves from their new neighbors, Yankees designated Portuguese immigrants as both racial others and religious and cultural "foreigners." For the most part, when Protestant Yankees distanced themselves from Catholic Portuguese immigrants by referring to them as dirty, ignorant, dark-skinned immigrants, they did so in subtle or verbal rather than overt or physical ways. Mimicking Portuguese accents, for instance, allowed Yankees to designate Portuguese residents as uncultured and undereducated while proclaiming themselves as the exact opposite. In 1910 a journalist for *New England Magazine* characterized Portuguese speech patterns as a kind of broken "drawl." He quoted Manuel, a Portuguese fisherman, as follows: "'Me,' said Manuel, 'me like ma'k'rel. Hima fine. Hameneg [ham and eggs] no good. Maka me seek. Me like catcher de ma'k'rel, eater de ma'k'rel. Hima so great! Ma'k'rel she-alla-right."[30] The same writer also quoted a Truro fisherman as saying, "Them dum Portegees ain't got no sense."[31]

Religious differences were equally serious, and some Provincetown Yankees formed Ku Klux Klan (KKK) chapters. In 1918 Agnes Edwards noted that although Yankees "resented" the invasion of Portuguese residents, they nonetheless accepted them as "thrifty" and "law-abiding." In 1942 Mary Heaton Vorse alluded to more hostile racial tensions in her anecdotal history of Provincetown, *Time and the Town*: "The latent animosity of a dying dominant race, for the more fertile race which [was] supplanting it, flared up bitterly" as the Provincetown Klan "burned a fiery cross on the grounds of the Catholic Church."[32] Unlike the strategies of the Pilgrim Monument team or the Research Club, the KKK responded to the displacement of Yankees with intimidation and violence.

Over time, Portuguese immigrants became Portuguese American citizens, a process that transformed their identities, alliances, and opportunities to be good Americans and even better capitalists.[33] Portuguese immigrants did not, however, "melt" into the New World; they did not leave behind their customs and rituals to become uncontested or "uprooted" Americans. Nor did they retain all their Old World traditions.[34] Rather, Portuguese immigrants became Portuguese American citizens by moving into segregated neighborhoods, taking Americanization classes, establishing entrepreneurial careers, and adhering to rituals from their homelands while acquiring and creating new ones in Provincetown.

In the late 1800s, Portuguese immigrants mobilized a steady reproduction of capital and goods. Joseph Manta became one of the first Portuguese entrepreneurs in Provincetown when he risked fitting a 150-ton schooner for year-round trawling for fresh, rather than salted, fish. Manta's vision required capital, innovation, and a crew of willing men. The returns on his initial and subsequent voyages far exceeded the costs. Soon his crew had enough capital to buy their own boats and to build their own houses in Provincetown. Indeed, while Portuguese immigrants in places like New Bedford and Taunton sank deeper into poverty at the hands of mill owners and factory foremen, Portuguese entrepreneurs in Provincetown and those in agricultural industries in California prospered.[35] From 1840 to 1920 Portuguese men in Provincetown took the place of most Yankees as both the owners and the captains of fishing vessels. The Yankee writer Edward A. Ross conceded as much in 1914 when he admitted, "All down Cape Cod these [Portuguese] fishermen have well nigh replaced the sea-faring Yankees. Provincetown, the spot where the Pilgrims first landed and which was settled by the *purest* English, seems to-day a South European town."[36]

The money that the Portuguese men earned from fishing soon filtered down through the West End neighborhood and into entrepreneurial ventures like barber shops, bakeries, grocery stores, and restaurants. As Mellen Hatch observed in 1939, the Portuguese "do about all the fishing and own many of the boats. They run stores, and garages, and taxis, and rooming houses, and gift shops, and oil trucks, and they do all of these things well."[37] Even though few residents of Portuguese heritage in Provincetown and elsewhere went into skilled professional careers, they still prospered at Land's End in fishing, unskilled trades, and service industries.[38] Some also made money in real estate, a precious commodity in a town only two streets wide.

Portuguese women and men entered Provincetown's service economy with seeming ease. In so doing, they speeded Provincetown's evolution into a resort serving both foreigners worthy of being toured and entrepreneurs benefiting from the new tourist trade. Some Portuguese men turned their fishing boats into excursion or sightseeing boats; others fished on some days and took tourists out on other days; and some turned the industry of chasing whales in order to kill them into the art of chasing whales so that tourists could view them. Similarly, a few men, including Joseph Nunes and Arthur Costa, turned their hobby of crisscrossing Provincetown's vast expanse of sand dunes into profitable dune-taxi businesses. At the same time, Portuguese women worked outside their homes packing fish in the "freezers," baiting hooks in the fishing sheds, cooking in the local restaurants, and working in retail stores like the New York Store (on the corner of Standish and Commercial Streets). Indeed, Provincetown's new service economy also gave scores of Portuguese women like Amelia Carlos an opportunity to become entrepreneurs, as the most popular woman-owned business was running a home as a boardinghouse. Portuguese women, men, and their families opened their homes and shops to a variety of artists and tourists, including those who identified in the 1910s as "bachelors" and "maiden ladies."[39] In so doing, they prospered while unwittingly participating in Provincetown's transition into a gay resort.

Portuguese immigrants' cultural traditions accompanied their entrepreneurial ventures. In their homes and in the local restaurants where they cooked, Portuguese women served such culinary specialties as baked haddock in a sauce of tomatoes and spices, mackerel fried or baked in milk, kale soup, and sea catfish served *vinha d'alhos* (marinated in vinegar, garlic, cloves, and peppers). Portuguese delicacies like linguica (a kind of sausage) and sweet rolls still are popular and are offered throughout town in restaurants and grocery stories.[40]

Through their names, Portuguese immigrants revealed both their willingness to become Portuguese Americans and their reluctance to let go entirely of Portuguese identities and traditions. Many Portuguese residents kept their Portuguese names and the popular practice of nick-naming, while others anglicized their names or were forced to do so when they entered the United States. For example, the Portuguese fishermen attending Arthur Duarte's Old World Feast celebration in the early 1900s included those with common Portuguese surnames like Silva, Costa, and Viera, as well as those with anglicized names like Chapman, Marshall, Allen, Snow, Paine, Cook, and Patrick. Because so many Portuguese Americans had the same surname, nicknames became a necessity. "Johnny Kitty," "Johnny Powerful," "Codfish," and "Sonny" referred specifically to individuals and "the rat family," "the regulars," and "the dirties"—the distinguishing characteristic implied —designated entire families.[41]

Federally funded "Americanization classes," which were popular from the late 1930s into the 1940s, helped Portuguese immigrants become American citizens. In a special town meeting on September 30, 1937, the principal instructor for the classes, Portuguese native Grace Goveia Collinson, reported that "interest in attendance has in fact been so keen that the members have postponed fishing trips in order to attend."[42] Goveia held roughly one hundred classes for the "Americanization Program" during that year, with attendance of nearly 80 percent. She helped sponsor events like "I Am an American Day," while the superintendent of school, Alton E. Ramey, stressed the importance of learning "the American Way of Life."[43]

Two annual festivals highlighted Provincetown's Portuguese culture: the Menino Jesus (Little Jesus) celebration, brought from the Old World, and the Blessing of the Fleet, re-created specially for the New World. For several decades, the best-known and most frequently practiced Portuguese tradition was that of the Menino Jesus, which Portuguese and Azorean residents observed during the Christmas holiday. Rather than hanging trimmings from an evergreen tree, Portuguese Americans celebrated Christmas by going to Mass, visiting one another's homes throughout the day and night, and decorating a multi-tiered altar in honor of the Menino Jesus. While many Portuguese Americans in Provincetown now observe Euro-American Christmas traditions, for decades the open-house festivities of the Menino Jesus prevailed. In 1938, Federal Writers Project interviewer Alice Kelly offered a glimpse of how Portuguese Americans were negotiating their new surroundings when she described Mrs. Joseph Captiva as the "perfect compromise": "She is bi-lingual. She can cook a 'galvanized' roast of pork, or bake a pot of Boston beans with equal competence. She is well dressed and well educated. She is even modern in her viewpoint." At the same time, Kelly continued, "she never misses Mass on a Holy Day, and if a friend dies, she goes to the house to offer help and comfort and to keep vigil with the dead, as her grandmother and great grandmother did before her in her homeland. And on Christmas Eve her house is open to all the old country people in honor of the 'Little Jesus.'"[44]

To reassert pride in their homeland as well as their place and authority at Land's End Portuguese immigrants also re-created traditions in the New World, like the Blessing of the Fleet. Portuguese townsfolk transported "The Blessing," as it came to be known, to Provincetown after Arthur B. Silva attended one in Gloucester in 1947.[45] The Blessing started out as a one-day religious celebration that began with an early morning Mass followed by a fishermen-led procession down to the wharves. Once friends and families were on the water, they joined a single-file fleet of boats that passed in front of a visiting bishop or local priest who ceremoniously blessed each craft. "Provincetown Gay for Annual Rites of Fleet Blessing" announced the *Provincetown Advocate* on June 19, 1950. During this particular year Father James E. Cassidy presided with this message: "I have come to ask almighty God to bless these fishermen, their families and the inhabitants of this town, and pray that he is with the fishermen in their every journey to bring them in safely."[46] After the formal blessing ceremony, the boats and their passengers spent the day picnicking and partying near Long Point. In a 1997 interview, Susan Leonard, a half-Yankee, half-Portuguese native born in 1950, fondly remembered the early years of the Blessing:

> The biggest thing [about the summer] would be the Blessing of the Fleet, that was something everyone always looked forward to. It was really big. As kids we would look forward to it and would think about

it for weeks and weeks and weeks, whether the weather would be good and who was going to have what to eat. My grandmother would spend days with all of her sisters making food to take on the boat. It was big . . . it was one of the few days of the year that they really even let women on boats. It was considered bad luck [then] for women to be on boats.[47]

One of the most visible and public Portuguese American customs, the Blessing has changed in form and meaning over time. During its first year, 1948, it was a religious festival meant to "bless" the fishing fleet and a cultural event that brought Portuguese families together to celebrate Portuguese cultures, traditions, and labor. But as Provincetown became more dependent on its tourist trade and as the fishing industry waned, fewer and fewer Portuguese fishermen were willing to finance the expensive celebration, and fewer families and guests turned out for the festivities. During the 1980s and 1990s there even were years when the Blessing almost ceased to exist.[48]

But a handful of Portuguese townspeople decided to revive the Blessing and added to it the First Annual Portuguese Festival, a community-wide, week-long tourist extravaganza. The *Provincetown Advocate* inspired them in 1996 when it ran a story about that summer's notably "quiet" Blessing ceremony attended by only four fishermen. It followed the story with an editorial imploring the townspeople to breathe life into future Blessings of the Fleet. What Provincetown needs, the editorial proclaimed, was a week-long celebration "of its fishing heritage, its roots to the sea, its colorful inhabitants over the years, from the Yankee whalers to the Portuguese fishermen to the gay and lesbian business owners of today." "The Blessing," it concluded, "should always be a part of the celebration of Provincetown's history of hard work, diversity and deep faith in religion and the sea."[49] The Blessing and the festival included a parade with Portuguese bands and traditional costumes, a block party with Portuguese dances like the chamarrita, an outdoor fair featuring Portuguese foods and crafts, an evening concert of Portuguese music, and a formal blessing ceremony.[50] While the Blessing had always reminded visitors and townsfolk of Provincetown's Portuguese culture and influence, the 1997 Portuguese Festival and Blessing of the Fleet Ceremony seemed almost urgent in its insistence that Provincetown was a Portuguese fishing village both alongside and before its recent incarnation as a gay resort. The evolution of an ethnic cul-

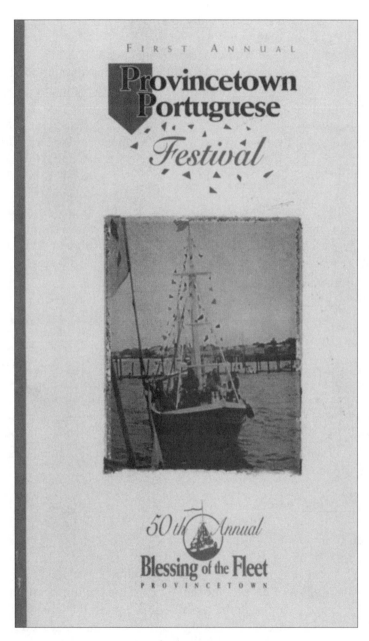

The cover of the brochure for Provincetown's first Portuguese Festival and the fiftieth anniversary of the Blessing of the Fleet, showing a traditionally "dressed" boat. Collection of the author.

tural ritual grounded in community to a consumer event geared largely to outsiders is not unique to Provincetown but has taken place in ethnic-villages-turned-resort-towns nationwide.

Portuguese celebrations and traditions were important to challenging Yankees' control of Provincetown and, later, to responding to gay and lesbian influences. When Provincetown's Portuguese community came together to launch the First Provincetown Portuguese Festival, the gay and lesbian business owners of the Provincetown Business Guild had just published their annual guidebook, which stated that Provincetown was "*Our* Town."[51] Some of the issues that residents were debating at this time pivoted on questions of masculinity, cultural pride, and ownership of space. Did Provincetown "belong" to one community more than another? In effect, the reincarnated Blessing was meant to remind townsfolk and tourists that at one time Portuguese fishermen were the masculine heroes of Land's End, long before the drag queens that populate its streets today.

Even though the Portuguese Festival made clear that Provincetown's ethnic population was becoming less intrinsic and more superficial to Land's End as townsfolk condensed Portuguese traditions, customs, and dances and sold them as a week-long ethnic affair, some parts of Portuguese culture still bind Provincetown to its ethnic past. The Portuguese Bakery, founded in the early 1900s, has a booming business in the center of town; Portuguese women bake traditional dishes and hold "flipper" (fried dough) parties; the small but steady Portuguese fishing fleet motors out to sea year-round; and St. Peter's Catholic Church (Provincetown's predominantly Portuguese Catholic Church) has a steady stream of devotees.

Part of becoming an American citizen entails negotiations over race, politics, and power. Although having large numbers or concentrated pockets of immigrants does not guarantee social or economic mobility, Portuguese immigrants gained socioeconomic leverage at Land's End in part because they mobilized a steady reproduction of goods and traditions as well as of people. Indeed, by the time the Immigration Restriction League convinced the U.S. Congress to pass the Johnson-Reed Act in 1924, Provincetown's Portuguese residents had wrestled a fair amount of control from what Mary Heaton Vorse referred to in 1942 as "the dying dominant race," the Yankees.[52] By 1896 Portuguese townspeople accounted for roughly half of the more than 3,500 residents.

Throughout the first three decades of the twentieth century, these numbers increased, and by 1931 Portuguese residents made up approximately 75 percent of the population.[53] Most townspeople and local historians agree that Portuguese residents gained control of Land's End because they reproduced at a greater rate than their Yankee neighbors did and because Portuguese men and Yankee women intermarried. One local Portuguese historian, the late Manuel "Cul" Goveia, argued a similar point in 1997: the Yankees "died off fast . . . [while] eventually the Portuguese influence and joy of living permeated the English so-called people. . . . Eventually it had to be, there [were] too damn many Portygees around."[54]

Strengthened by increases in people and capital, Portuguese residents eventually gained political power by appropriating many of Provincetown's trade societies and associations, soon outnumbering the Yankees in the chamber of commerce, the local council of the Knights of Columbus, and the Masons. Indeed, it was not long before a Portuguese American chaired Provincetown's board of trade and board of selectmen and, in perhaps the final coup, a Portuguese American became president of the Yankees' most treasured local institution, the Cape Cod Pilgrim Memorial Association, in 1997. Whereas Portuguese immigrants made little headway in electoral politics elsewhere in the United States, in Provincetown the opposite was true as Portuguese residents soon held a majority of all elected positions.[55]

Just as they succeeded in Provincetown's political and economic infrastructure, Portuguese residents gained cultural currency by actively resisting their assigned position as members of a different race. In particular, Portuguese immigrants countered Yankee portrayals of them as "dark-skinned" by promoting their own whiteness and Americanness. Some Portuguese immigrants stated plainly that they were white; others identified themselves as American, which often meant white. A few claimed the term "pilgrim," another periodically invoked marker of whiteness: "Look . . . we made the Cape. . . . You bet the [fishing industry] built it up. We're the Portuguese pilgrims. Us and the American fishermen . . . then the artists they come down . . . and then the writers . . . and the summer people. But we started it," insisted one Portuguese fisherman in 1938.[56] The same year another Portuguese fisherman, when challenged about his citizenship, asserted, "I am American. I belong to the Portuguese American Club."[57] Similarly, during World War II, Manuel Costa sent out Provincetown's town crier to deliver this message: "No-tice! Manuel Costa wants it known that he is as good an American citizen as anybody, having had his citizenship papers thirty years, and three boys to the front. But he will fly the Portuguese flag or any other flag he wants at half-mast when he wants bait, bait having nothing to do with patriotism!"[58]

Portuguese Americans also negotiated race and citizenship in Provincetown by painting their faces black and producing blackface minstrel shows from at least the early 1930s through the 1950s, the effect of which was to become white or at least whiter and, by extension, more American. Two Catholic associations with large Portuguese contingents, the Catholic Daughters of the Americas and the Knights of Columbus, presented New Deal Minstrels in 1934. These productions included typical blackface characters such as Sam, Topsy, Jocko, Rastus, Dinah, and Tambo and common blackface songs like "Waiting for Robert E. Lee" and "Darktown Strutters Ball." Similarly, the St. Peter's Holy Name Society presented the Holy Name Minstrels in 1959 under the direction of Frank S. Bent and Arthur Medeiros. "Mammie" and "Old Black Joe" were two of the featured tunes and the cast was made up of mostly, if not all, Portuguese Americans.[59]

Blackface minstrel shows perhaps more than any other event symbolized how Portuguese immigrants eased closer to a community of likeness, in this case a community of whiteness, by painting their faces black, ridiculing African Americans and aligning themselves with white Yankees. As historian David Roediger has argued, the simple act of smearing one's face black sent a symbolic message that those on stage were actually white and that being white mattered.[60] While distancing themselves from black African Americans, Portuguese blackface performers claimed a certain kinship with the white Yankees they sought to emulate. To be black in this country, Portuguese Americans learned, was to be linked to slavery and to lose the independence they crossed the Atlantic to secure. To smear one's face black also distanced Portuguese residents from Yankee assumptions that they were somehow inherently dirty. Indeed, some Yankees and other whites implied that Portuguese residents, because they were "immigrants" or "foreigners," were more polluted than the Yankees were. In 1938 Alice Kelly described the household of one Portuguese family, for example, as "immaculate," then noted that they "must have acquired cleanliness from Yankees."[61] Grace Goveia Collinson remembered in 1975 that Yankees often called her "a dirty black Portygee."[62] Thus, by putting on blackface for only a limited period of time then taking it off and reappearing as white, immaculate, and American, Portuguese Americans creatively forged a New World identity grounded in ideas about race and representation.

As Portuguese Americans became whiter in Provincetown and elsewhere, African Americans and black Cape Verdeans remained the targets of racial tension and prejudice. These darker immigrants and native-born residents provided a model of darkness by which whiter Portuguese and Yankee townsfolk could measure their own sense of whiteness. In the New World, Azoreans and mainlanders had learned to distinguish themselves from black African Americans as well as from their black neighbors in the Old World, Cape Verdeans. "The Portuguese of Provincetown . . . are not descendants of the Cape Verde islanders," Joseph Berger claimed in the 1930s. "They deplore the tendency of commentators and observers to confuse the two races, which, they point out, are wholly different, despite the fact that the Cape Verde Islands are under the Portuguese flag."[63]

From the late nineteenth into the twentieth century, Cape Verdeans learned the politics of race well enough to distance themselves from African Americans.[64] As the Cape Verdean writer Lucy Ramos explained in 1980, "Do you know the ridicule that a Black man faces when he says, 'I'm White, I'm Portuguese?'"[65] Some dark-skinned Cape Verdeans even refused to associate with African Americans because they believed they were white and African Americans were not. African American resident Douglas Roach, who grew up in Provincetown in the 1920s and 1930s, remembered that there was no color line to speak of until he was old enough to date. But at that juncture a number of Cape Verdean girls refused to go out with him because, they claimed, they were white and he was black. Roach also remembered an incident at a popular nightclub called The Ship (probably the Flagship, now Jackson's) in the 1930s. Anton Van Derek was at the piano, and when Roach walked in with three other African Americans, the owner told Van Derek to stop playing if the African Americans walked onto the dance floor.[66]

Although a small number of African Americans and Cape Verdeans have found that Provincetown provides them with the perfect resort town or hometown, racism lived on at Land's End throughout the twentieth century. Several townsfolk were appalled, for instance, when Douglas's kin, Edward S. Roach, and others penned letters to the

Provincetown Advocate in 1949 calling for an end to the blackface min-strel performances. On March 10, 1949, Edward Roach ignited the dis-cussion by commenting on the February 28 performance staged at the Provincetown High School by its students. After allowing that the fac-ulty "intended no harm," Roach continued: "Nonetheless, tremendous harm was committed. This stereotyped portrayal of the negro in the role of a knife-wielding, gaudy, boisterous, and clowning type is not only a vicious, incorrect interpretation of the Negro people, but a condemna-tion that only serves to feed the flames of racial hatred and misunder-standing." Roach admitted that Provincetown houses a few residents who hold undeniably racist and xenophobic views, yet he also made room for faith by invoking Provincetown's legendary past. "This town has always been noted for tolerance and fair-mindedness," he ex-plained. "Let us hope that this will continue."[67]

Roach's assertion drew a number of opposing responses, including letters to the editor and an editorial in the *Provincetown Advocate*. Ed Dahill defended the performances with a lengthy letter meant to ex-plain the benign historical trajectory that the jokes and songs followed. "We are quite willing to admit that comedy points up the 'follies and foibles' rather than the best points of the persons it presents. However," he went on, "we feel that this situation is inherently in the nature of comedy and that is has absolutely nothing to do with racial discrimina-tion."[68] Mildred Greensfelder sent in a remarkably similar point. The minstrel shows, according to Greensfelder, were "benevolent in effect, not malicious" because they "spread a geniality, a kindness in their ex-aggerated jokes, dialect, and mannerisms." "In closing," she wrote, "may, I, too, express a wish that tolerance and brotherhood may march on steadily to a glorious future in our wonderful town, Provincetown. But, please Lord, let us not forget how to laugh."[69] The *Provincetown Ad-vocate's* editorial decided to "go even further than" the previous letters. "We believe that the underlying philosophy of this movement, of which the attempt to raise the status of the Negro by banning the minstrel show is a part, is completely wrong." Indeed, they continued, "It is worse. It is a disservice to the Negro race."[70]

Roach responded to what he believed were "bigoted opinions ex-pressed in answer to [his] letter." In regard to the argument that the shows were neutral comedies, Roach retorted that "ridicule is the sub-tle destroyer of respect." He continued by taking issue with the previ-ous letters' assertions that humor knows no color, creed, or race. "Have any of these fair-minded citizens who refer to me as oversensitive ever been refused the right to eat in a restaurant? Or barred from a hotel?" he asked. "Have they ever suffered any of the many forms of outright discrimination perpetrated against the Negro people?"[71] If they had, he assured, they would better understand the way minstrel shows perpetuate racist ideologies and behaviors. Beatrix Faust agreed and thanked "our Negro citizens . . . [that] called this matter to our attention." Faust referred to the minstrel shows, even those "with no intent to hurt," as "a direct slap at thirteen million Americans, whose record of achievement of great difficulties and record of loyal service to the United States is second to none."[72] Townspeople didn't respond in the *Provincetown Advocate* to Roach and Faust. Although one month later, on March 5, 1949, the weekly ran the following front-page headline: "VFW Show Seen by Capacity Crowd: Minstrel Show and Band Concert Prove Top Attractions."[73]

Before most historians began considering race when they examined immigration patterns, James Baldwin was arguing that racial compromises were critical to immigrants' experiences when they entered the United States. Many immigrant communities, Baldwin maintained in 1984, soon forgot their ethnic differences when they joined the white underworld. "It bears terrifying witness to what happened to everyone who got here, and paid the price of the ticket," he argued. "The price was to become 'white.' No one was white before he/she came to America. It took generations, and a vast amount of coercion, before this became a white country."[74] Baldwin's analysis can also be applied to Provincetown: before they came to the United States, Portuguese and Azorean immigrants identified as Portuguese citizens, Azoreans, or Western Islanders; they would not necessarily have been identified as white; and they did not distinguish themselves from Cape Verdeans or Africans with the same determination. Thus by becoming white, Provincetown's Portuguese immigrants exemplified their belief in the United States' spoken and unspoken qualifications for full—meaning both social and legal—citizenship. They also demonstrated how, over time, this unique combination of people and events made Provincetown into the gay resort that it is today.

The distinctive history of the Portuguese community at Land's End, which was shaped by its particular immigration process, its encounters with race and class oppression, and its socioeconomic and political success, contributed much to the overall development of Provincetown. Yet like the Yankees, who imported Portuguese laborers only to watch them take control of Land's End, Portuguese immigrants also found that their economic endeavors had unanticipated outcomes. By the end of the twentieth century, for instance, with the First Annual Portuguese Festival, Portuguese townspeople were pressing more strongly for recognition precisely at the moment when their centrality was being challenged by the emergence and growth of new communities, this time formed by gay men and lesbians.

During the 1930s and before, racial, religious, and class contests — rather than debates about sexual or gender orientation—preoccupied Provincetown's Portuguese and Yankee residents. While townsfolk scrambled to escape or levy the mark of blackness, few, if any, seemed overly concerned with Provincetown's development into a haven for "unconventional" artists and gay and lesbian visitors.[75] Portuguese immigrants and their descendants were one of the four key communities that contributed to the making of twentieth-century Provincetown. Yankees preceded them, artists arrived next, and gays and lesbians were soon to follow.

3

"Paradise of Artists"

The popularity of [Provincetown] is what may be called an artist's paradise. The blending of sea and sand and the ever changing color of the foliage make it a picture of beauty on many canvases.

—Isaac Morton Small, *Just a Little about the Lower Cape*, 1926

THE STRATEGIES for marketing Provincetown shifted in 1899 when the renowned painter Charles Webster Hawthorne founded the Cape Cod School of Art (CCSA) at Land's End. In the mid-1800s the arts in New England had assumed new meaning as Americans began to shape and appreciate their regional histories and cultures in new ways. Artists, their studios, and their New England landscapes and seascapes had become prized tourist attractions, and by the time Hawthorne opened the CCSA, white middle- and upper-class travelers were already flocking to destinations where they could see an artist at work. Tourists were convinced that exposure to this kind of creativity could alter their lives in profoundly spiritual ways. They also believed that viewing native-born artists was a patriotic function, that being a good tourist was linked to being a good American.[1]

In the mid-1880s Provincetown's vast expanse of rolling sand hills reminded the Boston-based artist Marcus Waterman of the dunes he had painted in Algeria in 1879 and 1883. Provincetown captivated Waterman, who urged fellow Boston artists like Ross Moffett to "come on down to the end of the Cape, and see one of the most remarkable places in the country."[2] Even so, Provincetown regards 1899 as the official beginning of its art colony because that was the year Hawthorne arrived.[3] What made Hawthorne critical to Provincetown's fame was his decision not only to paint at Land's End but also to instruct there. The CCSA attracted hundreds of art students, dozens of well-known artists, and multitudes of tourists. On any summer day during this era, one was likely to stumble on the well-dressed Hawthorne teaching a large group of equally elegant women on a picturesque side street, in an overgrown garden, or along the waterfront. In 1900 the modernist Ambrose Webster joined Hawthorne and opened his Summer School of Painting. Soon after, George Elmer Browne started his West End School of Art; the Modern Art School on Lewis Wharf was established; and George Senseney offered etching classes.[4] By 1916 roughly six hundred artists and art students were spending the summer in Provincetown, and no fewer than six art schools were urging aspiring students to join them at Land's End. The *Boston Globe* encapsulated this artistic energy in a banner headline on August 27, 1916: "Biggest Art Colony in the World at Provincetown."[5] Artists sustained this momentum for decades: Ross Moffett and Heinrich Pfeiffer initiated the Provincetown Painting Classes in the 1920s; Henry Hensche continued the CCSA through the 1930s; and Hans Hofmann opened his Summer School of Art in 1935.

Unlike the necklace of galleries in the East End that make up a good part of Provincetown's art colony today, an array of art schools, associations, clubs, and studios formed the art colony in its earliest years. One year after the Provincetown Art Association opened its doors in 1914, the Provincetown Printers coalesced as a woodblock printing group. Visual artists founded the all-male Beachcombers Club and the all-female Sail Loft Club in the mid-1910s. And Hawthorne, Moffett, and others congregated at Days Lumberyard Studios at 24 Pearl Street, where the Fine Arts Work Center is currently located, as well as at the studio spaces at 4 Brewster Street. Later, during the Depression, the Works Projects Administration stepped in and kept the art colony afloat by funding a number of year-round artists including George Yater, Blanche Lazzell, and Vollian Rann.[6]

Besides the artists, Yankee businessmen also supported Provincetown's budding art colony. In 1914, prominent Yankees collaborated with artists to form the Provincetown Art Association and to fund its first traveling exhibition. William H. Young, president of Seaman's Savings Bank and a high-ranking officer of both the Provincetown Board of Trade and the Cape Cod Pilgrim Memorial Association, was also the first president of the art association, holding the post for twenty-two years. Moses N. Gifford, an officer on the board of trade and the CCPMA, was the art association's first dues-paying member. Other well-placed Yankees, including the president of the Provincetown Bank, a local judge, and the postmaster, all supported the art association during its formative years.[7] These men understood that hosting an increasingly famous artists' haven enhanced Provincetown's standing as a tourist destination. After all, how many "Old New England" "watering places" also had a famous art colony? And how many art colonies were able to market the working life of Portuguese townsfolk, the scenic beauty of a coastal peninsula, and the crumbling wharves of bygone Yankee whaling days all while claiming historic importance as the landfall of the *Mayflower* Pilgrims? In an increasingly competitive resort market, only Provincetown could offer all these features.

Indeed, no sooner had Hawthorne placed his wooden easel atop one of Provincetown's weather-soaked wharves than Yankee promoters added Cape End's new and exotic colony of artists to its reputation as a healthy "watering place," historic landmark, and Portuguese seaport. As early as 1900 writers such as Edmund J. Carpenter likened Provincetown to a "paradise of artists, filled as it is with quaint, picturesque nooks and corners."[8] The title of Nancy Paine Smith's 1927 work was telling in and of itself, *Book about the Artists: Who They Are, What They Do, Where They Live, How They Look*. In it Smith explained that "sightseers in our town ask first to have pointed out to them a Native. Next they say, 'Where is the art colony? We want to see an artist.'"[9] And in 1939 Mellen C. M. Hatch, author of *The Log of Provincetown and Truro*, spoke of the artists in an inviting way: "Provincetown was 'discovered' about the turn of the century by those strange people who like to put paint onto canvas." Hatch noted that "the artists live all over town, domiciled in everything from the shabbiest of shacks to what passes, at the Cape-tip, for mansions. . . . Perhaps more will find, in time, that the Cape-end, with wide dunes and the great sea, is a good place to search one's own soul."[10] Together, these plugs exerted a pull on travelers desiring ethereal encounters.

In addition to labeling Provincetown as a place that housed artists, Cape Cod and Boston journalists reported on the artists' unusual summer-time antics, most often characterized by the risqué costume balls that they produced every year. "Beach-Combers Ball at the Tip of the Cape, Gayest, Largest, Liveliest Ever," trumpeted one headline in 1923.[11] Some journalists were subtle: "Artists Are Queer Ducks."[12] Others tended to elaborate, like the one who wrote the following in 1924: "Beachcombers Ball Is Rich in Gayety and Color. . . . Provincetown's townspeople line the sidewalks on the way to the party place, and the artists and their company are furnishing the watchers with the thrills they are waiting for . . . the masquerading mummery includes the fairy folk of fiction."[13] Whether these writers used "gay," "fairy," and "queer" to indicate that the costume balls included homosexual and transgendered participants or themes is unclear but possible, for these terms took on multiple meanings at the time.[14] Regardless of how people translated the headlines, tourists seeking unconventional encounters capitalized on the possibilities permitted by this blend of costume and creativity.

Provincetown's new standing as both a serious art colony and a free-for-all artists' paradise illustrates how promoters capitalized on Provincetown's complexity as simultaneously safe and risky. It also hinted at the ways in which the art colony, like the Portuguese community, was more nuanced on the inside than it appeared from the outside. Indeed, while art colonies often carry the reputation of being liberal, gay-friendly enclaves, they can also contain conservative elements that reinforce rather than challenge conventional understandings of difference. What part did race, class, and sexuality play in the development of Provincetown as both an art colony and a lawless oasis? And how did the different sectors of the art colony contribute to Provincetown's evolution into a gay mecca?

Provincetown hosted two artistic communities: a visual one made up of painters and sculptors and a literary one containing novelists, journalists, poets, and playwrights. While these communities were interchangeable—painters worked on set designs, and poets took turns with brush and easel—distinctions based on discipline and method often separated the artists professionally and socially. The visual artists broke down further into "conservatives," sometimes called academicians, or traditionalists, who practiced realist or impressionistic art, and "moderns," or avant-garde cubists and abstract expressionists. Conservative artists such as Hawthorne, Browne, Richard Miller, Max Bohm, and Gifford Beal, plus the majority of the Beachcombers Club—which one art critic mused was similar to a French salon "'with a good bit of the all-American stag party thrown in'"—certainly held their own in Provincetown. Yet modern painters like Stuart Davis, Marsden Hartley, Ambrose Webster, Oliver Chaffee, and Marguerite and William Zorach were becoming increasingly prolific, especially following the success of the 1913 Armory Show in New York City. Modern and conservative artists divided the visual arts to such a degree that for just under a decade, from 1928 to 1936, they forced the Provincetown Art Association to hold two, rather than one, summer exhibitions, with the moderns holding theirs in July and the traditionalists presenting theirs in August. In the 1920s and 1930s Ross Moffett and Karl Knaths led the campaign against the art association's conservatism. After World War II, Hans Hofmann, Edward Hopper, and other abstract expressionists reopened the great divide between the two schools.[15]

Provincetown's early colony of visual artists also included splinter groups that worked and lived together. A good example is the Provincetown Printers, who pioneered the "white-line" woodblock print process in 1915. White-line color printing was a simplification of the laborious woodblock process. Instead of cutting up to ten blocks of wood per print, one for each color, according to traditional Japanese and German methods, the Provincetown Printers used a single block for the entire design. On one block they carved a "V" groove, which appeared in the final product as a white line separating each color. Influenced by avant-garde painters and cubist and abstract expressionist theories, the Printers chose bold colors, turned away from conventional floral motifs, and concentrated instead on café and seaside scenes that incorporated both realistic objects and abstract forms. The original Printers, a colorful and creative group of expatriates who came together first in Paris and then rented homes and studios near one another in Provincetown, included Ethel Mars, Maud Squire, Ada Gilmore, and Mildred McMillen. In Provincetown they teamed up with Bror J. O. Nordfeldt and Juliette Nichols, and within a year Blanche Lazzell, who later became one of the group's best-known modern artists, joined the collective.[16]

Provincetown's literary community was just as famous as its colony of visual artists and helped strengthen its standing as both a refuge of creativity and a historic landmark. The literary colony included novelists, journalists, anarchists, playwrights, and poets. Some were expatriate bohemians that frequented Gertrude Stein's salon in Paris, and others got their start in Greenwich Village. Mary Heaton Vorse, a novelist and labor organizer, was the first of this group to "discover" Provincetown, having arrived there with her husband, Bert Vorse, in 1907 for a summer retreat. Mary Vorse took it upon herself to tout to her Greenwich Village colleagues Land's End as a creative wonderland. The first wave of associates to join the Vorses at the tip of Cape Cod were the playwright Neith Boyce Hapgood and her husband, Hutchins Hapgood, a revolutionary journalist; the short-story writer Wilbur Daniel Steele and his wife, Margaret Steele, an artist; and the writer George "Jig" Cram Cook and his fiancée, Susan Glaspell, a novelist and a playwright.

The second wave landed in Provincetown between 1914 and 1916, when World War I forced hundreds of artists to leave Europe. During this time, John "Jack" Reed, a poet and reporter, came to town with his lover, Louise Bryant. Eugene O'Neill arrived in 1916, and the nucleus of the Provincetown Players took shape. A number of friends worked and socialized with this tight-knit group, including Terry Carlin (O'Neill's drinking companion), the set designer Robert Edmond Jones, and well-known modern visual artists like Marsden Hartley, Charles Demuth, and William and Marguerite Zorach. Although the socialite Mabel Dodge entertained most of the Provincetown Players at one time or another in her New York salon, in Provincetown she distanced herself geographically and psychologically by taking up residence near the back shore in the renovated Peaked Hill Bars Life-Saving Station.[17]

The story of the Provincetown Players' first two seasons is a well-known tale that typically begins in 1915 on the veranda of the Hapgoods' house with an impromptu performance of Neith Boyce's one-act play *Constancy*. A spoof on Mabel Dodge and Jack Reed's love affair, *Constancy* amused a room full of friends and colleagues, all of whom were already well aware of the romances taking place both on the stage and off. Robert Edmond Jones was on hand to arrange the set, and for the second play, *Suppressed Desires*, he juggled around various pieces of furniture before asking the audience to turn their chairs and face the living room. *Suppressed Desires* also was a romantic spoof, this time written by and featuring newlyweds Susan Glaspell and Jig Cook.

The 1915 season included two more plays that were staged on Lewis Wharf, the one-hundred-foot-long structure that Mary Heaton Vorse bought for $2,200 in 1915.[18] Lewis Wharf contained two small shacks and a larger two-story fish house, which was an art studio before its next incarnation as the first theater for the Provincetown Players (in 1920 and 1921 it housed one of Provincetown's first nightclubs, the Sixes and Sevens).[19] On July 14, 1916, the players staged three one-act plays on Lewis Wharf: *Winter's Night* by Neith Boyce, *Not Smart* by Wilbur Daniel Steele, and *Freedom* by Jack Reed. The second bill of the summer featured *The Game* by Louise Bryant, a reprise of *Not Smart*, and Eugene O'Neill's stunning drama of life and death at sea, *Bound East for Cardiff*. Earlier that summer O'Neill had arrived at Land's End in a despondent state, due in part to rejections by the New York–based Washington Square Players of two new plays, *Thirst* and *Bound East for Cardiff*. Coming to the rescue, the Provincetown Players produced both plays in 1916 and thus began O'Neill's hugely successful career.[20] Only four years later, he won the first of four Pulitzer Prizes for *Beyond the Horizon*, and two decades later he became the first and last American playwright to win a Nobel Prize.

The artistic and social cliques that constituted Provincetown's art colony helped make Land's End into a place where artists of varying abilities could thrive in their own social and methodological communities of likeness. Within these communities, artists with similar interests and methods delivered and received instruction and critique. They also found places that were ideal for exhibiting their work. The visual artists showcased their modern and traditional paintings every summer at the Provincetown Art Association, and the literary artists turned an old fish house into a perfectly suitable stage. Provincetown provided the props —the fishing sheds, dunes, seascapes, and townspeople—and with these plus the dozens of colleagues on hand and, critically, affordable accommodations, many artists thrived.

Provincetown's spectrum of originality and the sheer number of artists who lived there helped market Provincetown during the early 1900s and later as a creative outback for travelers "sated with the usual."[21] Beginning in the 1910s, bachelors and maiden ladies often headed to Land's End specifically because they had heard of its "openness" and "artistic nature."[22] Yet a closer examination of Provincetown's art colony offers two generalizations. First, some groups of artists like the Provincetown Players and the Provincetown Printers produced work and lived lives that challenged traditional gender, race, and class standards, whereas other groups, like the academicians, were far more conservative and exposed hierarchies without necessarily trying to dismantle them. Second, the politics that artists brought to their canvases and texts often correlated with their social and cultural values, thereby blurring the boundaries between "life" and "art."[23] For the most part, writers like Susan Glaspell and printmakers like Ethel Mars took risks in their plays and paintings as well as in their relationships, whereas

Charles W. Hawthorne, *Crew of the Philomena Manta*, oil, 1915. In Town of Provincetown Collection, courtesy of the Provincetown Art Commission.

artists affiliated with traditional disciplines and methodologies often lived traditional lives.

The conservative sector of the art colony, including Charles Hawthorne and many of his followers, ventured into previously neglected territory by painting complex and bold images of the everyday rigor that often shaped ethnic working-class life. Along with Winslow Homer, Hawthorne was one of the first American artists to illustrate some of the bleak and unforgiving circumstances facing fishing folk in seaport villages. Traditional artists often cast Portuguese residents as weather-beaten workers far removed from the comforts and niceties of white middle- and upper-class households. Hawthorne's famous *Crew of the Philomena Manta,* which now hangs in Provincetown's town hall, exemplifies his skill as a painter and his dedication to depicting Portuguese working-class tasks and temperaments. To be sure, many of Provincetown's Portuguese fishermen were showing signs of their oc-

cupations rather than their ages. But Hawthorne's sympathetic portraits of them suggest not only that they were hardworking and courageous but also that they were destined for lives of toil and drudgery.
Hawthorne's portraits of Portuguese women suggest similarly bleak
expressions and circumstances. Set often in the home rather than on the
wharves, portraits of Portuguese women like *The Fishwife* emphasize
women's roles as house-bound helpmates rather than entrepreneurial

Charles W. Hawthorne, *The Fishwife*, 1925. Provincetown Art Association and
Museum Collection.

Charles W. Hawthorne, *Selectmen of Provincetown*, ca. 1924. Friends of American Art Collection, 1924.952. Reproduction, Art Institute of Chicago.

adventurers. All in all, Hawthorne's paintings show the Portuguese townspeople's life in Provincetown as profoundly challenging and dismal.

In contrast, Hawthorne often, although not always, asked Yankee residents to pose as town leaders and dignified ladies rather than as weathered workers. In Hawthorne's *Selectmen of Provincetown,* for example, the three seated men, Herman Cook, Solomon Nickerson, and Caleb Rich, seem to have aged by using their minds instead of their muscles. Moreover, their authoritarian presence as the town's officials distinguishes them clearly from the town's laborers. They, too, are at work, just not on the wharves or in the streets of Provincetown but rather in the seemingly more lofty location of town hall. Besides portraying Yankee "fathers," Hawthorne painted Yankee women and girls in relaxed poses with flowers and ribbons in their hair and lush gardens or gentle seascapes at their feet. *Girl with a Yellow Scarf, On the Dunes,* and *Young Girl in a Garden* are portraits of ladies of leisure, belying the fact that many Yankee women ran their own businesses.

Hawthorne's eye for conditions mitigated by class and gender often became the lens through which others came to understand the place of Portuguese townsmen and women. One of Hawthorne's students, Houghton Cranford Smith, for example, remembers in his 1963 memoir, *The Provincetown I Remember*, the day he picked "a very small Portuguese man with a weather-beaten face who was one of the professional sailors" to pose for Hawthorne's class. Smith chose the sailor because he was "the most picturesque figure when he had his yellow oilers on." The "professional" fisherman in question agreed and immediately raced home to put on his "best Sunday suit." According to Smith, the fisherman "shaved, put on a boiled shirt and a too tight black suit and appeared at the studio all prettied up for us. Needless to say he looked like hell and we couldn't use him. . . . but we did later when he looked like the wonderful seafaring man he was."[24] In this way, artists perpetuated the notion that Portuguese fishermen were "picturesque" and "authentic" only when they appeared near the wharves and in proper fishing attire.

Smith also commented on women. Again, although his biases do not represent those of all artists in the traditional discipline, they do provide insight into the ways in which gender functioned in different

Charles W. Hawthorne, *On the Dunes* (detail), 1915. Telfair Museum of Art, Savannah, Georgia. Gift of Anna Belle (Mrs. Edward) Karow, 1915.

parts of Provincetown's art colony. Smith confessed that he and his male colleagues thought that the artist Nancy Ferguson "was pretty much of a joke." And he recalled "caricaturing the Suffragettes" when they arrived in Provincetown, "to the delight of the natives and the Portuguese."[25] Smith's views may have been extreme, but the conservative sector of Provincetown's art colony was constructed in blatantly patriarchal ways. Most of the instructors, for instance, were men, and nearly all their pupils were women. It is telling that Hawthorne became known as the "father of the art colony" and that the first Yankee to lead the art association, William H. Young, became known as the "father of the art association."[26] The popularity and exclusivity associated with the all-male Beachcombers Club, which still is active today, also helped give a distinctly patriarchal tone to Land's End.

The politics of race differed, too, across categories of artists, although here, as elsewhere, no hard or fast lines can be drawn. In 1916, for example, visual artists chose "A Night in Old Portugal" as the defining theme of its annual costume ball. "The highly fantastic and colorful frolic this year was presented . . . with 'charmalita' [sic] instruments by Azorean and St. Michael's natives." Although the night in question honored Portuguese residents and their traditions, it also symbolized the ways in which some artists regarded Portuguese people and their culture as exotic, festive, and "authentic."[27] In 1924 some artists paraded into town hall to one of the Beachcombers' costume balls as hooded members of the Ku Klux Klan.[28] While meant to amuse spectators and fellow costumed artists, the symbolic presence of the Klan suggested that its racist and xenophobic ideologies were comic, certainly not despicable, and bordered on the acceptable, at least among some artists in Provincetown.

Other artists distanced themselves symbolically from black and dark-skinned townspeople by participating in blackface minstrel shows. For instance, the minstrel show on August 24, 1916, directed by the modern sculptor Frederic Burt, included jokes and musical numbers performed by a variety of artists like George Elmer Browne, who sang "Camptown Races," and Charles Hawthorne, who sang "Old Folks at Home."[29] Paradoxically, while shaping Provincetown into a space of creativity, those artists affiliated with conservative methods sometimes reinforced the already unequal race, ethnic, and gender hierarchies.

Marguerite Zorach, *Two Women*, 1920. Courtesy
of the Julie Heller Gallery. Images like these
convey a sense of how modern artists imagined
and created Provincetown's homoerotic culture.

Avant-garde visual artists and the writers and poets with whom
they worked and socialized were not necessarily antiracists, nor did
they always view Portuguese residents as equals. But the Provincetown
Players introduced revolutionary ideologies of the 1910s that emphasized the New Woman and the New Radicalism—free love, infidelity,
extramarital procreation, interracial relationships, art as political, and
sex as politics—by acting out their latest ideas, emotions, and relationship dilemmas on stage at Lewis Wharf. Neith Boyce and Hutchins
Hapgood's *Enemies,* for instance, focuses on one couple's struggle over
marital infidelity. Jack Reed's *The Eternal Quadrangle* examines the pas-
sionate love triangle of Reed, Bryant, and O'Neill. Susan Glaspell's play

Trifles is a critique of the isolation and desperation of women in abusive relationships and of some men's inability to recognize even the most obvious symptoms of women's unhappiness. In his play *Not Smart*, Wilbur Daniel Steele criticizes hypocritical and sexist bohemian men who refused to take responsibility for luring young Portuguese women into the "not smart" circumstances that lead to extramarital pregnancies. O'Neill's play *Thirst*, also produced at Land's End in 1916, features the taboo themes of interracial sex and cannibalism.

The Provincetown Players and the modern artists who worked with them were part of a larger Progressive Era bohemian rebellion, which fueled Provincetown's transformation into an eccentric outpost. When expatriate bohemians returned to the United States at the onset of World War I, many of them made Greenwich Village their first stop and Provincetown their second. Because several well-known "Villagers" had popularized Provincetown at the onset of World War I, it was to Land's End and its rebellious reputation rather than to any other art colony that expatriate artists such as Charles Demuth, Marsden Hartley, Maud Squire, and Ethel Mars migrated. Demuth and others eventually spent time in art colonies like New Hope, Pennsylvania, and Hartley later joined Mabel Dodge Luhan at Taos, New Mexico. But except when they were in Greenwich Village, they came together as a group only in Provincetown, as many of them believed that other art colonies were, in Marsden Hartley's words, "futile" and "ineffectual."[30]

Bohemians were opposed to conventional gender standards, domestic arrangements, and bourgeois society in general. Bohemianism was, according to one British observer in the early 1900s, "understood to mean a gay disorderliness of life, cheerful bad manners, and no fixed hours or sexual standards."[31] As opposed to those bohemians who took pride in being impoverished and downtrodden, other bohemians, as the historian Allan Churchill and others point out, were white, educated travelers and artists of the middle and upper classes. The Provincetown Players fit into this subset of privileged bohemians, as did the visual artists who worked and socialized with them and who, unlike most of the Players, experimented with homosexuality in their work and in their lives. Sometimes referred to as "confirmed bachelors" and "maiden ladies," a number of these visual artists made their way to Provincetown. The men, particularly, distinguished themselves by emphasizing the kind of elegance and wit commonly associated with the

English gentry, perhaps best exemplified by Charles Demuth and Marsden Hartley.[32]

Demuth and Hartley moved to Provincetown because it was there that they found welcoming townspeople, inspiring seascapes, and like-minded intellectuals who appreciated their uncanny gender expressions and also respected both men as artists.[33] Demuth and Hartley met in 1912 in Montparnasse, Paris, at the Restaurant Thomas on the Boulevard Raspail, where Hartley and a group of expatriate artists dined regularly before the memorable day when Demuth "ambled" up to their table.

> It wasn't long before Charles made us particularly aware of him by a quaint incisive sort of wit with an ultra sophisticated, post eighteenth touch to it . . . carrying his cane elegantly . . . coming to our table as I have said, we all saying yes of course, and there was immediately much quaint banter afloat, interspersed with veiled *sous entendus* [hidden meanings], all of it fun, and I remember saying to Charles after the meal was over, I think you had better come and sit with us all the time, and so it was.[34]

Hartley's description points to Demuth's witty, English sensibility and also indicates the means by which expatriate artists identified and located one another, by frequenting known establishments, dressing appropriately, and becoming familiar with a certain coded speech in order to be able to interject or at least understand introductions laced with "veiled *sous entendus*."

After traveling in Europe from 1912 to 1914 and socializing in Paris with Gertrude Stein, among others, Charles Demuth went to Provincetown to join his fellow expatriate artists and the Villagers who already had summer homes there. One close friend of Demuth's, who also was in Provincetown in 1914, later linked Demuth to Cape Tip's equally famous bohemians by suggesting that Demuth gravitated toward "people of note," including Eugene O'Neill, Susan Glaspell, and Jack Reed.[35]

Once in Provincetown, artists like Demuth and other bohemians interacted with local residents by renting rooms from them, conversing with them in the streets, and patronizing their shops.[36] Demuth was not "out" regarding his sexual proclivities, yet they certainly were apparent from his elegant sensibility and appearance. Years later, Demuth's friend Susan Watts Street pointed to his unconventional yet tailored presentation:

> Demuth was extremely vain and dressed extremely well. I remember for instance, that he had a Donegal Tweed jacket and was perfectly handsome. And at Provincetown when everybody else was looking sloppy, Demuth would appear wearing a black shirt, white slacks, a plum-colored scarf tied around his waist, and black laced shoes, highly polished. . . . He had a high squeaky voice and a high giggle that sounded like the whinny of a horse.[37]

Demuth mobilized a homoerotically charged and elegant sensibility at Land's End. Indeed, by dressing as he pleased and refusing to abide by contemporary gender conventions, Demuth helped make Provincetown safe for and even accepting of affected bachelors. Moreover, not only did Demuth make his unconventional gender role public, he was proud of it and, according to one colleague, "very vain."[38] Rather than serving as a barrier, his effeminacy signaled to others that he had a different sexual and gender orientation and alerted men who might be interested in a homoerotic engagement that he was game.

Demuth's feminine appropriations caused others to feel a sense of anxiety as well as sympathy toward the unconventional artist. For instance, Demuth's colleagues decided to give him several nicknames: "Deem," short for Demuth and rather effeminate, and "Chuck," even more indicative of his "elegant" sensibility. Stuart Davis, one of Demuth's roommates in Provincetown, confessed that he and his friends coined the term "Chuck" because "he [Demuth] was too elegant to be called 'Chuck.'"[39] Rather than teasing or harassing Demuth, his Provincetown friends chose instead to express their approval or at least their understanding of his effeminacy by giving him an ultramasculine persona.

Two years after Demuth, the Villagers, and other artists had fashioned Provincetown into a summer retreat, the now famous but then struggling painter Marsden Hartley joined them and helped make Provincetown into a Dionysian wonderland. Hartley's visit to Provincetown was brief—he stayed only one summer—but memorable. In Provincetown Hartley found the camaraderie and comfort he had been seeking since he left Europe. His 1916 essay "That Great Provincetown Summer" put Provincetown on the map at that time and ever since as a free-wheeling outpost.[40]

Hartley went to Provincetown for the same reasons that other artists and writers did: World War I had made Europe unsafe, and Provincetown promised an agreeable alternative. Hartley had enjoyed Germany, especially Berlin, more than the United States because he believed homosexuality was more acceptable there, and when he returned from Europe, he found it difficult to make friends even among the Village bohemians. Although Gertrude Stein found Hartley interesting, her matriarchal counterpart in the United States, Mabel Dodge, could tolerate him only in small doses. In fact, Dodge asked him, for reasons unknown, to remove himself from her country home, Finney Farm, at Croton-on-Hudson, New York, just before he left for Provincetown.[41]

Locating spaces in which he felt at ease was difficult for Hartley, possibly because he inhabited alternative sexual and gender orientations. But Provincetown had a risqué atmosphere that satisfied and entertained him. He took advantage of the Provincetown Players' daily social fetes by spending time with O'Neill, Demuth, Glaspell, and Hutchins Hapgood and by engaging frequently in this crowd's raucous nightlife of drinking and skinny dipping.[42] Provincetown and its art colony also appealed to Hartley because it encouraged him to flaunt one of his gender-ambiguous outfits at its annual costume ball, which, like the elaborate costume balls in New York City, Paris, and Berlin, was a magnet for bachelors in search of homoerotic encounters. Indeed, on a daily basis, societal norms even in Provincetown frustrated Hartley, yet during the many costume balls he attended at Land's End and elsewhere, he dressed and appeared as a royal subject rather than an isolated deviant.[43]

Hartley and Demuth exhibited unconventional desires at a time when most people, including some bohemians and artists, believed that homosexuality was "inverted" if not "perverted."[44] But by appearing publicly and proudly as elegant bachelors, Hartley and Demuth challenged contemporary beliefs that condemned homosexuality. With the support of bohemians and natives, they made an elegant form of masculinity into an acceptable alternative, and they fashioned Provincetown into an outpost for outlandish characters, desires, and relationships.

■

William Evaul, *Mars and Squire*, white-line wood cut print, 1984. Courtesy of the artist.

Like Hartley and Demuth, Ethel Mars and Maud Hunt Squire were white, educated, middle- to upper-class artists. Squire was born in 1873 in Cincinnati, Ohio, three years before Ethel Mars, whose first home was in Springfield, Illinois. They met at the Cincinnati Art Academy in either 1894 or 1895 and from then on lived as "gay" maiden ladies and artists who regularly crisscrossed the Atlantic. Shortly after graduating from the academy, Mars moved to New York City and then traveled with Squire to Europe in 1902. After returning to the United States for a brief stay, they went back to Europe and settled in France in 1906. It was there that they met Gertrude Stein and became acquainted with Paris's intellectual and artistic expatriates at Stein's regular Saturday salon. It also was in Paris that Mars learned the traditional art of woodblock printing from Edna Boies Hopkins, who had studied in Japan. When World War I began, they drove for an ambulance squad before going back to the United States in 1915 and settling in Provincetown. After the war, in 1921, they returned to Europe and four years later discovered Vence, a small town near Nice in the Alpes-Maritimes that some artists in the early twentieth century compared with Provincetown because of its natural beauty and artsy atmosphere. Mars and Squire remained in

Vence in their villa, La Farigoule, painting and illustrating children's books until they died, Squire in 1954 and Mars five years later.[45]

Mars and Squire made it easy for onlookers to describe them and, by extension, Provincetown as eccentric. They had outlandish hair-styles and a unique artistic expression, and they contributed to Provincetown's reputation as an appropriate place to express themselves and their art. Squire's niece, Dorothy Squire, remembers her aunt as "stylish, as well as for her dressing as for her manners. . . . Her jewels had to be 'artistic' rather than 'real'; some of her bracelets were only brass, and a quartz shining on a ring made her as happy as if it were a diamond." Dorothy describes Ethel Mars as "a kind of gypsy: she wore long earrings, and had a half a dozen bracelets around each arm, ringing when she moved—To dress she never followed the fashion but only her own personal style."[46] A close acquaintance of Mars's offered a similar account of her attire: "She liked very strange things. Sometimes she liked very regular coats or suits, but she (would wear a) bright necklace, and a bright hat. . . . And she had skirts, of course. But the top, the blouse, was a very brilliant color . . . and she put a jacket on top of that, maybe tweed, but a little bit masculine."[47] Hutchins Hapgood also conveyed a sense of Mars's and Squire's flashy style in his autobiography, *A Victorian in the Modern World*: "'Maiden Ladies' does not fairly describe these two, who . . . led a life independent of man's conventions. Unconventional too was the appearance of Mars, at least, for her hair was dyed purple and her lips were orange; she resembled a Matisse portrait."[48] According to her heir, Ethel Mars "was well known every place she went, because she was quite an eccentric woman. She dressed in very bright colors and make-up, a lot of make-up. And anybody who knew her, also knew Maud Squire."[49]

Gertrude Stein's tale "Miss Furr and Miss Skeene" describes the couple's flamboyant participation in "gay" (upper-class, festive, and leisurely) life. Introduced by Stein as "The Tale of Two Young Ladies Who Were Gay Together and How One Left the Other Behind," the following is a brief excerpt from the lengthy, "singsong" piece:

> Georgine Skeene [Squire] was gay there and she was regular, regular in being gay, regular in not being gay, regular in being a gay one who was not being gay longer than was needed to be one being quite a gay one. They were both gay then there and both working there then. They were in a way both gay there where there some many cultivating

something. They were both regular in being gay there. Helen Furr [Mars] was gay there, she was gayer and gayer there and really she was just gay there, she was gayer and gayer there, that is to say she found ways of being gay there that she was using in being gay there. She was gay there, not gayer and gayer, just gay there, that is to say she was not gayer by using the things she found there that were gay things, she was gay there, always she was gay there.[50]

What designated a "gay thing" or a "regularly gay" person remains somewhat of a mystery. While the term "gay" sometimes indicated prostitution rather than homosexuality, neither Mars nor Squire engaged in paid sex work. It is more likely that before the 1920s the term "gay" referred to a part of upper-class society that enjoyed parties and leisure. What Stein's vignette makes clear is that independent women found places that encouraged the "cultivation" of their "voices" (artwork): "The voice Helen Furr was cultivating was quite a pleasant one. The voice Georgine Skeene was cultivating was, some said, a better one. . . . They were gay where there were many cultivating something." In addition to Paris and Vence, Mars and Squire regarded Provincetown as a place that encouraged them to "cultivate" their "voices" and to be "gay."

Mars and Squire formed a small professional and social circle with other same-sex couples and artists. Two women in particular, who worked with Mars and Squire in Europe and then joined them at Land's End, were the equally interesting "companions" Ada Gilmore and Mildred "Dolly" McMillen. Gilmore and McMillen also were white, educated, middle- to upper-class artists who had the means to go back and forth to Europe during the early 1900s. For a while their lives seemed to mirror those of Mars and Squire. Gilmore and McMillen met at the Art Institute in Chicago, where each studied from 1906 to 1912 and where Gilmore boarded at the McMillen household. In 1912 they moved from Chicago to Long Island and from there traveled to France, where both studied the art of woodblock printing with Ethel Mars. In 1913 Gilmore and McMillen joined Mars and Squire in Paris, and in 1915 Gilmore and McMillen accompanied Mars and Squire to Provincetown, where, unlike most artists, they lived at the tip of Cape Cod even during its loneliest winter months.

Gilmore and McMillen were "housemates," as one curator put it recently.[51] Whether or not their relationship had a sexual aspect is unclear

Ada Gilmore, *Gossip*, 1916. Collection of Napi Van Derek.

and, in part, irrelevant. Gilmore and McMillen were what another art curator termed "companions" who spent a number of years in Provincetown as a same-sex couple. In Provincetown they provided an example, as did Mars and Squire, of alternative domestic arrangements for women who chose to live with other women, no matter what the terms of their intimacy. Indeed, while confirmed bachelors made Provincetown into an accepting place by appearing in public in particularly campy or flamboyant clothes, maiden ladies did the same by striking out on their own, donning equally festive attire, and living independently of men, something few women at the time had the luxury of doing, owing to social and financial restraints. Indeed, maiden ladies like Mars and Squire and Gilmore and McMillen often were called "independent women" not because they lived alone but because they lived independently of men. Interestingly, Blanche Lazzell, who joined the original group of six not long after they arrived at Land's End, fit easily into their community of likeness. In reference to a physical ailment but perhaps also suggesting erotic attraction, Lazzell stated early in her career, "I am going to be an independent maiden lady. And I will show people I can be as happy as anyone."[52]

While Gilmore and McMillen's complex relationship continues to bewilder historians, it also suggests that sexuality in this crowd and during this era was not obvious. A few years after they arrived in Provincetown, Gilmore left McMillen to marry the woodblock artist Oliver Chaffee. Gilmore's move from a possibly homosexual relationship to a heterosexual one suggests that she might have been attracted to both men and women. Hartley and Demuth, too, engaged in heterosexual relationships, even though both were decidedly more interested in men. Similarly, descendants of Ethel Mars noted that throughout her life she took "many lovers."[53]

Many artists who engaged in some form of homoerotic coupling did not fit neatly into the Provincetown Printmakers, the Provincetown Players, or any other group of artists. For example, the artist Fred Marvin, Mary Heaton Vorse's half brother, lived in Provincetown for decades beginning in the 1910s. Marvin joined Mars and Squire in Vence and also studied with Hawthorne in Provincetown and Bermuda, for he was one of Hawthorne's more advanced students and, as such, was acquainted with Provincetown's traditional art colony as well as with its bohemian set. In Bermuda, as fellow artist Houghton Cranford Smith noted, "Marvin had with him an Italian boy who was a sort of valet or all man Friday." Cesco, the "Italian boy," prepared the artists' meals in Bermuda and then traveled with Marvin back to Provincetown where he continued "preparing all the meals for the boys."[54] After some time, Cesco opened his own restaurant and left the task of preparing the artists' meals to the artists themselves. Each week two different artists were made responsible for preparing their weekly meal together, thereby forming the Beachcombers Club, a private, homosocial yet primarily heterosexual social club.

Cesco and Marvin's story demonstrates how homoerotic relationships took shape in Provincetown. Cesco and Marvin lived together in what we might today call a "domestic partnership" for most of their adult lives and all of their time in Provincetown. Cesco remained with

CESCO'S ITALIAN RESTAURANT, PROVINCETOWN, MASS.

Cecso's Italian Restaurant at 209 Bradford Street was popular enough to warrant its own postcard. Postcard courtesy of the Pilgrim Monument and Provincetown Museum.

Marvin until the latter died in Provincetown in the mid-1940s. As Oliver Chaffee noted in a letter at the time, "I saw Cesco last Friday eve—after he phoned me—he looked tired out. I reckon he has earned everything he gets. I mean by that—he has [worked] day and night taking care of Fred who was helpless."[55] Occasionally, Marvin and Cesco traveled together to Europe, as was customary for artists and their companions.

While we have no evidence of either the private or the public sex lives of either Cesco or Marvin, Cesco's status as Marvin's "all man Friday," Marvin's associations with the unconventional Mars and Squire, and Marvin and Cesco's lifelong domestic arrangement indicate that they had an intimate and probably homoerotic relationship. Their arrangement also suggests that in Provincetown two men of similar or dissimilar classes and ethnicities could cohabitate in an ambiguous if not homosexual relationship during the early 1900s without becoming the targets of sustained ridicule or abuse. In other words, Cesco and Marvin demonstrate that before the 1930s homoerotic coupling was not only possible but even acceptable in Provincetown. It was, however, more acceptable for some than others and, as we shall see, more acceptable for visitors than for natives. The absence of public scandals that might point to evidence of homosexual relationships during this time in Provincetown indicates not that such relationships did not exist but that they coexisted with opposite-sex relationships.

Peter Hunt was a wash-ashore artist who helped normalize alternative gender sensibilities by forming a relationship with the local economy and with local residents. Like Mars and Squire, Hunt moved to Provincetown after serving as an ambulance driver in Europe during World War I, arriving in Land's End at least five years after Marsden Hartley's "Great Provincetown Summer" of 1916. According to one press release, "Mr. Hunt arrived in Provincetown with long blond hair, two Afghan dogs, a large black cape and a dwarf in attendance. He was known as 'Peter Lord Templeton Hunt'" or, as one native recently insisted, "a real queen."[56] Born in 1898 in New Jersey as Freddy Schnitzer, Peter Hunt cultivated a unique artistic method and peasant style of decorating furniture, had an outlandish appearance, lived with his mother, and became a permanent fixture of Provincetown's resident community.

Unlike bohemians such as Mars, Squire, Hartley, and Demuth, who stayed in Provincetown for one or more years but built permanent homes elsewhere, Hunt slipped from the respected category of visiting artist into the privileged group of resident artists. He did so by supporting the local economy and employing neighborhood children—his little "peasants," including artists Nancy Whorf and Carol Westcott—to help him in his studio, often called his "peasant village." Hunt integrated his life and work into Provincetown's community at large. In this way, he demonstrated how white middle-class unconventional men could be eccentric but also worthy of respect.

Eleanor Bloomfield and Ivy Ivans became part of the social and economic fabric at Land's End by opening a guesthouse in the East End in the late 1910s and subsequently publishing a home-improvement manual. Bloomfield and Ivans were wash-ashore "spinsters," one an artist and the other a "happy home maker," who created a world at Land's End that, for intimate and practical purposes, was independent of men. Bloomfield and Ivans were white maiden ladies from New York who came to Provincetown for the summer before becoming permanent residents in 1921. To date, no sources have described Bloomfield and Ivans as lesbians, and given the times, this is not surprising. Even though one longtime summer resident of Provincetown recently claimed that they were not lesbians, she also admitted that she had no way of knowing for sure.[57] Fortunately, Bloomfield and Ivans left behind an unusual though revealing scrap of evidence: a home improvement booklet entitled *A House That Is, or a Tale of the Ship's Bell.*

According to *A Tale of the Ship's Bell*, Bloomfield and Ivans were ambitious and creative women who first rented a house and took in boarders before buying property of their own in the far East End. Once they had some land, they bought a house on Commercial Street and moved it—a common practice in Provincetown—to 2 Allerton Street, where it stands today. In the booklet, Bloomfield and Ivans refer to themselves as "independent women" and "spinsters," common terms for maiden ladies that predate the more modern lesbian identity.

Bloomfield and Ivans shared an intimate and perhaps erotic relationship based in part on conventional domestic arrangements. They introduce themselves in *A Tale of the Ship's Bell* by alluding to their homoerotic relationship and describing their situation as follows:

> One of us being an artist and the other a happy home maker, what [could be] more natural than we should hunt up a house by the sea . . . being "independent women"—so-called dependent on our own resource making, we came to our own conclusions . . . namely, a Provincetown home of our own we must have.[58]

After the introduction, they describe how they found, moved, and began renovating their "sturdy Puritan house."

Rather than writing just about household repair, however, Bloomfield and Ivans made a point of revealing their same-sex domestic arrangement and their opinions of men. They admitted, for example, that they received "helpful hints" from an article in *Good Housekeeping* on "a man-made kitchen" but, they insisted, a "man-made kitchen with woman-made touches, makes a pretty good combination. Men, so it seems, do have their use, which of course is nothing short of stark heresy for two spinsters to voice."[59] Toward the end of the booklet they reiterate the irrelevance of men to their lives by discussing the manner in which "Neighbor Nutley" dropped in to offer advice. "Most men are mostly alike. They sort of seem to feel that we women folks must be 'given instruction.' Every once in a while, however, they do tell something worth while. That's why we keep on such chummy terms with Neighbor Nutley."[60]

Bloomfield and Ivans disclose the nature of their relationship in a subtle way by revealing their domestic identities as "spinsters." They also explain their "independent" lives and decisions, demonstrate their ability to perform seemingly "manly" tasks without men, and confront their readers' presumed prejudices. At the end of the booklet they concede, "Yes, we both know exactly what you are thinking, even if you are too polite to say so," that a pair of "old maids" think one thing then feel they must tell the world. "To which, let us reply, that we forgive you for calling us old maids—in fact we rather like it, even if spinster would have been more kindly."[61] While the circulation of this small booklet is unknown (a local resident discovered it in the attic of an old house), Bloomfield and Ivans's friends, acquaintances, and fellow residents probably found their publication both intriguing and instructive.

Although more liberal than many small towns in the United States, Provincetown still struggled with certain forms of homophobia, for not all artists or visitors fared as well as the independent women and bachelors discussed here. Antoinette Scudder refers to this homophobia in a poem she published in the early 1930s. Entitled "The Lesbians"—an identity that was new to Provincetown in the 1930s—the poem features two women who stayed at the Peony Cottage on Beach Point (in the row of identical "Days' Cottages" that line the waterfront in Truro, less than half a mile from Provincetown). With no small amount of contempt, Scudder introduces the first lesbian as follows:

> The stout and blowsy blond . . . always wore
> A sweater none too clean and knickerbockers
> That slipped and bagged above her coarse yarn stockings;
> Her hair of a nondescript shape, neither yellow nor brown
> And moist grey eyes that were always slanting and rolling,
> Yet gave an odd impression of movelessness.

Scudder's tone then changes when she describes the second woman:

> And the other one, the slim and wistful one—
> Eyes of a sea spirit—green and azure blending
> To a silvery remoteness. Lithe and small,
> She always made me think of a lonely bird,
> Straining its tenuous pinions of pearl and fawn,
> Unequal to a struggle.[62]

Scudder notes that "they were both artists." She also tells a story of resentment and anger toward the lesbian who did not conform to traditional gender practices but instead wore "knickerbockers" and "coarse yarn stockings" and had a "nondescript" haircut. Even their artwork marked "the slim and wistful one" as more benign than the other, "the stout one modeled queer / Symbolic things in clay, all feet and stomach / And the other painted landscapes with a soft / Vague sweep of color that puzzled and eluded."

Like other visitors, these lesbians may have wanted a private, secluded vacation, yet as Scudder indicates, "There was talk about them from the very first." Regardless of the "talk," "They would work apart —one of them in the house / And the other down the beach—but they would drop / Their tools and brushes a dozen times a day / To wander and seek each other and, on finding, / Would hug and fondle in a mawkish fashion."

Apparently, however, there was trouble in paradise. According to Scudder (the poem is written in a first-person narrative): "Sometimes, the fat one would go off on a prowl / And leave the other under lock and key." One day Scudder and a friend were walking past the cottage and heard "the captive whimpering in the house / Like a hurt animal" —a supposed cry for help, which led Scudder's friend to remark, "'There are some things I can't stand or understand.'" On a different night they heard "the grotesque couple" engaged in a squabble. Scudder and her friend intervened by dragging "the fragile one" to safety while "the fat one stayed there on the moonlit beach, / Awkward and helpless—with distorted tear-drops." Scudder tells how she removed herself after the traumatic event to the home of an older Yankee woman whom she described as "a grave and quiet / Person of fifty years [who] teaches Greek / in a girls' college." Scudder complained to the college professor that "some things / Are merely nasty," a comment that inspired her mentor to read aloud a passage by Sappho before asking, "'My friend, can any of us judge?'"[63]

Although Scudder writes in the preface to her collection that "the characters or incidents of the poems are entirely the work of her own imagination and have no reference to any living person or persons," she also states that she has "faithfully endeavored to reproduce the atmosphere of a certain locality." *East End, West End*, the title of Scudder's book, is an unmistakable reference to Provincetown, and the Peony Cottage, built in 1931, still stands today. In the end, Scudder's work is significant not because it re-creates an actual event but because it describes residents' responses to gender and sexual transgressors.

Scudder's poem reveals, first, differences in gender presentations and in residents' responses to masculine women. The "mythic mannish lesbian," to use Carroll Smith-Rosenberg's term, is cast as a predator, a woman who has assumed, visibly and defiantly, the characteristics of a man.[64] The mannish lesbian is "stout" and "fat." She designs "queer things in clay," sheds "distorted tear drops," and "prowls" like an animal while imprisoning the "wistful one"—her prey—under lock and key. The more feminine of the two is helpless and apparently in need of guidance to save her from a brutish lover and a destructive relationship. But the ending suggests how the writer came to a greater understanding of lesbian relationships, when the quintessential "good" lesbian—an older, wiser college professor—invokes the poetry of a classic lesbian text to question Scudder—herself a poet—about her homophobic assumptions. Did "the lesbians" renting the modest Peony Cottage come from a working-class rather than middle-class background? In other words, were they called "lesbians" instead of "maiden ladies" or "spinsters" because they lacked a gentrified sensibility or status? It is possible, given the place and time, that they were condemned for their sexual and gender orientations—again, the masculine woman more than the feminine one—as well as their class backgrounds.

Ultimately, the complexity of the art colony helped Provincetown develop into a busy resort town. For those people who appreciated more traditional artistic styles, boosters referred to Charles Hawthorne and his art classes that met daily on Provincetown's beaches, wharves, and side streets. If promoters wanted to depict Provincetown as especially "avant-garde," they pointed to Ross Moffett, the Provincetown Printers, and other nontraditional visual artists, like Ambrose Webster. Finally, when writers wanted to boast of Provincetown's status as an outrageous and "gay" (festive) or "queer" (unusual) outpost, they focused on the Provincetown Players, the tramp poet Harry Kemp, "confirmed bachelors" like Marsden Hartley and Charles Demuth, and "maiden ladies" such as Ethel Mars and Maud Hunt Squire. Indeed, because of, not despite, its diversity, Provincetown's art colony helped the townspeople fuel a replacement industry.

Portuguese and Yankee residents took advantage of their hometown's new popularity with painters and writers. Many residents capitalized on the artists as a new class of consumers by renting spare rooms in their houses and turning their old fish sheds into art studios or galleries. Others stocked their stores with art supplies, took artists out in their boats on fishing or sightseeing excursions, and invited them into their restaurants and shops. For example, John Francis, who had an Irish mother and a Portuguese father, helped artists find and furnish homes and apartments. Manuel "The Sea Fox" Zora took artists fishing and helped Scott Corbett write *The Sea Fox*, a novel about Portuguese rum-running and fishing in Provincetown. Like other Portuguese residents, Zora often posed for classes of artists and used these opportunities both to make money and to improve his English.

Even so, the artists' and townspeople's relationships were complicated and often depended on representations of "authenticity." The artists often rendered Portuguese residents as "picturesque" objects in their attempts to capture "authentic" forms of ethnic working-class life. They also tended to romanticize the Portuguese as somehow more real or exciting than the Anglo Americans. In 1935 Josef Berger noted that Portuguese immigrants have

> "lived" their stories, their song, their drama, rather than written or sung or set down for the stage these reflections of the life they lead. Their "escape" literature has been life itself. . . . Rescue, tragedies, exciting adventures at sea are all part of the day's news here, and as is usually the case with such a people, they are the subjects for art, rather than the artists. The racial cultural heritage, if such it might be called, which they have given the nation they have given vicariously through the pen and stage of others, of those writers who have come here and found in them a wealth of the stuff of which stories and plays are made.[65]

Most onlookers regarded Portuguese natives as exotic working-class objects, a view that glossed over their potential to become artists or to succeed in fields beyond the fisheries. But just as the artists fancied themselves experts in their portrayals of Portuguese working-class life, many Portuguese residents criticized the artists' work and asserted their own skills as artists. Although Houghton Cranford Smith referred condescendingly to the Portuguese residents as his "admirers," he also admitted that his work sometimes fell short of their standards. Once when Smith was working on a painting of a large schooner, a fisherman approached and requested a preview. Smith refused because it was unfinished but agreed to show the fisherman his work as soon as he completed it. "The day came to show what I thought was one of my best canvases," Smith recalled, "[but] when I set it up for him to look at it he said, 'Jesus Christ, can't you do no better than that?'"[66] The tramp poet Harry Kemp overheard a similar exchange roughly a decade later. In Kemp's version, the Portuguese fisherman declared, "That there ain't quite right; never seen a ma'k'rel [mackerel] like that before; don't look at all like that when I heap 'em up in the boat from the nets."[67]

Besides commenting freely and frequently on artists' work, a number of Portuguese residents became artists themselves. One Portuguese fisherman-turned-shoe-cobbler, "Joe Half-Dollar," displayed in the window of his cobbler's store "before" and "after" models of an old shark-bitten boot. When asked to explain his window display, he insisted simply that it was "his art."[68] Portuguese resident John "Johnny Kitty" Enos had the misfortune of breaking his leg, thereby ending his fishing career. After observing local artists to pass the time, Johnny Kitty decided that he, too, would take a chance with brush and easel. After several unsuccessful attempts at "original" watercolors, Enos concentrated on Cape Cod scenes, joined the art association, and sold the first canvas, *Cape Cod Bird*, that he entered in an art association exhibit. As one writer noted in the early 1900s, "It can truly be said that men like Johnny bridge[d] the unusually wide gap between the arts and fishing in the best Provincetown tradition."[69] Portuguese residents often began second careers as artists when they encountered bad or disabling luck in their initial economic endeavors. Examples of fishermen who became artists highlight the permeability of these categories and of Portuguese residents' abilities to maneuver within a limited band of options.

In addition to challenging claims of artistic authenticity and authority, Portuguese and Yankee townspeople took advantage of the liberal attitudes of certain sectors of the art colony and formed their own unconventional relationships. Gay and lesbian natives and wash-ashores assumed a unique identity in Provincetown, being referred to as "our queers," as opposed to "visiting queers." Our queers opened shops, ran guesthouses, and intermingled freely with neighbors and fellow towns-people. While the bohemians expanded the possibilities of how one might behave at Land's End, our queers made sure that after the bo-hemians departed, an alternative presence remained.

Our queers occupied a special position on the fringe of Province-town's year-round community. Although they did not always fit per-fectly in Provincetown's year-round residential community, they were without question a part of that community. They enjoyed the privileges that came with being natives and permanent residents of Land's End even as they engaged in unconventional sexual interludes. Our queers became one of the most diverse communities in Provincetown, for they included white upper-class Yankees, working-class Portuguese natives, residents of mixed Yankee and Portuguese heritage, and a variety of wash-ashores of neither Yankee nor Portuguese background. Many were artists, some famous but most not. Some repeat visitors slipped into the category of our queers, even though they never lived in Provincetown permanently. Tennessee Williams, for instance, did not remain in Provincetown, yet townspeople insisted on an affiliation with him because he visited Land's End repeatedly in the 1940s and, more important, because he became famous. Like the *Mayflower* Pilgrims' landfall, Williams's visits became a part of Provincetown's noteworthy and marketable past.

In general, our queers had as much, if not more, to lose than did the visiting artists because they were subject to the whims of small-town mentalities and limited economic resources. Moreover, they were not part of the exempted culture of visiting bohemians, meaning that they could not "misbehave" in the name of creativity and then simply skip town. Indeed, the town's residents often subjected our queers to stricter expectations. At the same time, however, our queers enjoyed certain protections and privileges as insiders rather than outsiders. Their fel-low townspeople accepted them on the condition that they demonstrate their respect for Provincetown, rather than disrespecting it, as residents believed that many visitors did, as a free-for-all, "anything goes," des-tination.

This fragile interplay prompted many native queers to "come out" in places other than Provincetown, their hometown. New York City was a local favorite because of its proximity, its reputation as a gay enclave, and its promise of anonymity. During the 1930s and 1940s, Christina Alden (pseudonym) spent intimate time with her female companions in places other than Provincetown. According to one of her relatives, Christina's Yankee family "cloistered her away" when they were in Provincetown because they feared she might draw attention to herself as a lesbian. In contrast, Ofelia Silva (pseudonym) was supported by her immediate family yet still felt the need to come out during the 1940s in New York City. While reminiscing about the post–World War II era, one Portuguese native hinted at the way residents kept quiet when it came to our queers:

> We always went to see Stella's late show [at the Atlantic House]. Stella kept asking him [Tennessee Williams] to write a couple of stanzas for her blues. I was right there at the table and Ofelia Silva was there, also a Provincetown girl, who loved Stella Brooks. That was a hell of a combination going on; [but] we can't talk about that.[70]

Even though most townspeople believed that they were protecting gays and lesbians who grew up or lived permanently in Provincetown, native queers did not feel, as many outsiders did, that coming out was safe in Provincetown. The tradition that our queers invented of coming out elsewhere continued throughout the twentieth century.[71] For Provincetown's natives then as now, coming out conjured up fears of verbal harassment, mockery, alienation, and intimidation but seldom of overt violence. Most of the gays and lesbians who faced physical harassment in Provincetown, however, were visitors rather than residents.

Our queers included Patricia Smith (pseudonym) and her companion Mary Costa (pseudonym). Smith, who was born in 1895 in New York, moved to Provincetown at an early age and by 1926 had bought property on Commercial Street where she owned and ran a local shop. Mary Costa was of Portuguese descent, was three years younger than Patricia, and worked in the shop as a "clerk." While Mary appeared somewhat "tomboyish" and townsfolk referred to them as a "couple," onlookers still regarded them as "normal" because they were hardworking and respected members of the community at large who played down their nonconforming relationship and gender presentations. "They were always together and they were in business together, [but] nobody paid any attention to them. They didn't bother anyone," Provincetown native Francis Alves recalled in 1997, "and we didn't object to it."[72]

Peter Hand was a wash-ashore that took advantage of Province-town's accepting climate and entrepreneurial opportunities. Hand was a self-identified gay—meaning homosexual—summer visitor who had no birthright to the group of our queers, since he was not a native, but who eventually slipped, like Peter Hunt, into that charmed category by setting up a business and a residence in Provincetown. While living in Quebec, Peter Hand and his partner first came to Provincetown for a vacation in 1932. Unlike many bachelors and artists who visited Province-town in the early twentieth century, though, Peter had no idea Provincetown was "artsy" or gay friendly. Like hundreds of other French Canadians, Hand and his partner, whom he called his "friend," simply chose to vacation on Cape Cod one summer. But after discovering Provincetown, Hand returned there with his partner each year until 1946, when he bought an old captain's house. It was this house, which Captain Ezra Cook built in 1840, that Hand made into one of Province-town's first openly and exclusively gay male guesthouses.

Hand's memories point to the familiarity and intimacy unconventional visitors forged with their host families in Provincetown. Indeed, Hand's story is emblematic of many bachelors who happened upon Provincetown, found rooms with Portuguese families, and enjoyed their stay enough to return repeatedly. When fishermen's wives rented rooms to him and other men, Hand recalled nostalgically, "We became one of the family. They cried when we came and they cried when we left. And we did too."[73]

Countless Portuguese residents welcomed alternative visitors into their homes and often formed familial relationships with them. Florence Corea Alexander, whose father immigrated from Fuzeta, Portugal, and whose mother was from St. Michael in the Azores, was born in Provincetown in 1919. She has been the proprietor of Corea's Beauty Shop on Conant Street for more than fifty years and still enjoys a steady clientele. In 1996 Florence spoke about her mother's tenants:

My mom used to rent the upstairs, the top floor that my daughter lives in now, and we had a couple of boys that moved in. . . . They were gay; they lived upstairs in Mom's house. And they would say to my mom and my dad, but of course my father, he was Portuguese, so he was kind of funny in funny ways like that, he didn't know what it meant. And so they would come down and they would say to my father, "You know, we're gay. But I'm going to have my mother come down and visit, so don't tell her that I'm gay." . . . Oh, they were nice boys. Very clean. They didn't bother us, and we didn't bother them. I mean, we got along fine with them. Even today I get along fine with them. I have a lot of friends who are gay that I really get along with. I mean, I don't mind it just like they don't mind us. We're all human, we all do whatever we want. Every family has one in the family that is that way.[74]

If the accommodations suited them, the maiden ladies and bachelors, who hailed mostly from the Northeast but also from Canada and Europe, often returned to the same boardinghouse for both short and long visits year after year.

But Peter Hand's recollections complicate the prevailing narrative that Portuguese residents welcomed gays and lesbians with open arms. Indeed, rather than unconditionally accepting all unconventional visitors, Hand suggested that the townspeople were more likely to accept those who fit in easily, those who were "clean" and "nice."

People were, let us say, mostly very tolerant. It was very live and let live . . . as long as you don't do anything disruptive. Of course we have incidents . . . you can't be 100 percent perfect. . . . [In Provincetown] it's your own life and you don't have anyone with a thumb on you pressing you down.[75]

Hand's story was typical in that he gained the acceptance and respect of most of the local residents because he assimilated easily, did not "do anything disruptive," was white, and had income to spare. He also belonged to the group of our queers because he eventually made a commitment to Provincetown by supporting the local economy.

While becoming a part of Provincetown's resident community, Hand introduced a fundamental change in Cape Tip's tourist structure by opening a guesthouse for men, thereby sending a message to outsiders that Land's End was gay friendly. Whether or not Hand's guesthouse, or others like it, welcomed all gay men or only those who were white, wealthy, and discreet, is unknown. Nonetheless, by opening a men's guesthouse, Hand carved out a comfortable and safe space in Provincetown for gay men. In so doing, he helped fashion Provincetown into a gay male resort, for gay visitors no longer needed to mingle, at least in terms of housing, with Provincetown's Portuguese or

Yankee residents. Over time, this trend toward exclusivity grew to include more gay-owned guesthouses, shops, and restaurants. It also escalated to the point that if gay visitors so chose, they could avoid Portuguese or Yankee natives of any sexual or gender orientation altogether.

Our queers and the bohemians and artists who joined them helped make Provincetown into a place where alternative relationships were possible. They did so by integrating socially and economically as they became seasonal visitors as well as year-round residents and merchants. They were also able to do so because most townsfolk were willing, for a variety of reasons, to overlook gender and sexual irregularities. Indeed, in contrast to the way residents took note of racial others in the early 1900s, most townsfolk looked the other way when gender and sexual dissidents began to settle in Provincetown. In the words of native Clement Silva: "We could tell [they were gay], but we never made anything of it. I mean it was no big thing, they were just people like I was a person, and we tried to treat them all just like that and there were not that many in those days either, there were very few." Many were seasonal visitors but some, he recalled, were "from in town—there were 'townies' that were gay, but it was just like we were friends and always had been friends and it would never change."[76] Our queers, the artists who joined, and the townsfolk who supported them collectively carried Land's End to unforeseen destinations.

While Provincetown had a reputation for centuries as an unusual and outrageous outpost, its new status as a famous art colony compounded and even exaggerated its standing as incorrigibly outlandish. Although Yankees might have preferred a more demure colonial outpost and a more conservative collection of artists, they could not deny the financial benefits of hosting a famous art colony. Portuguese residents realized these benefits too, as artists paid them rent with one hand and painted them as picturesque objects with the other. Still, Provincetown's spectrum of originality sparked debates about the place of modern art in a town that celebrated both a patriotic and unruly past. On the one hand, modern art took on "un-American" connotations and received a cool reception from critics in Provincetown and elsewhere. When avant-garde painters introduced alternative styles at the New York Armory Show, critics accused them of "insanity," "anarchy," and "immorality."[77] Closer to home, Abbie Cook Putnam, Yankee native, town librarian, and self-proclaimed art critic, commented on the Art Association's exhibits from 1915 to 1930. In her catalog she noted that the modern works were "no good," "rotten," and "rotten as usual."[78]

On the other hand, Provincetown's burst of creativity worked well with its reputation as a safe harbor and a birthplace of American freedom. In 1922 Nancy Paine Smith encouraged tourists seeking patriotic pilgrimages to visit Provincetown, where "the artists are hospitable to each other . . . [and] every school is welcome and examples of their work are on exhibition. In its democratic atmosphere, and in a town now cosmopolitan, but with roots deep in a Puritan past, here where the sea and the land meet, is being wrought, perhaps, a truly American art."[79] And even today art critics and artists alike praise Provincetown for nurturing a kind of ingenuity that is distinctly American. According to New England artist Ray Hues, for instance, because of their trailblazing woodblock method, the Provincetown Printers can be credited for creating "the only truly American art form."[80] Similarly, not long after the playwright Eugene O'Neill and the Provincetown Players forged a chilling yet refreshing alternative to Broadway's musicals, Land's End took on yet another patriotic badge, this time earning the title of "birthplace of American drama." The Provincetown Players forged an alternative version of theater in the United States and, consequently, helped shape Land's End into the most important art colony in the country as well as into a bustling summer resort. After enjoying two summer seasons on the abandoned Lewis Wharf, the Provincetown Players moved to MacDougal Street in Greenwich Village, where they staged daring plays under the direction of George Cram Cook. Yet the legend of the Provincetown Players remained at Land's End and drew hundreds of visitors each year. While the original group of Provincetown Players would never again coalesce at the tip of Cape Cod after their final 1916 summer season, Provincetown became known not only as the home of the famous Provincetown Players but also as the birthplace of American theater. From this point on, troupe after troupe of actors, directors, producers, and playwrights, including those of the Barnstormers Theater, the Provincetown Playhouse, and the Provincetown Theater Group, migrated to Land's End in hopes of re-creating at least some of the magic ignited by the original Provincetown Players.

Provincetown's fame as the birthplace of American freedom, art, and drama succeeded in transforming Land's End from an economically struggling seaport into an internationally famous art colony and vacation resort. The number of visitors, for instance, that climbed the Pilgrim Monument increased steadily throughout the 1910s and well into the 1920s. But the late 1920s and 1930s ushered in conditions which neither residents nor artists could have foreseen. The first surprise was the 1929 stock market crash, which took a slow but meaningful toll on townsfolk at Land's End. The second involved Provincetown's status as a resort town as residents began in the late 1930s to question the "kind" of visitors it was attracting. Intense scrutiny over the class backgrounds of Provincetown's guests surfaced first, and interrogations regarding the sexual and gender orientations of visitors soon followed.

PART II

SURVIVING PROVINCETOWN, 1929–1969

Today Provincetown is a haven for the most diverse gathering of people to be found in any small community in the United States. Here, mingling with the informality and camaraderie of one large family, are Portuguese who live by their skill and hardihood in making daily harvests of the sea, Yankee folk of historic lineage, artists, actors, musicians, writers, city vacationists, sailors, and even a truck farmer or dairyman or two.   —newspaper clipping, September 4, 1937

IN THE LATE AFTERNOON on Saturday, December 17, 1927, Provincetown's streets were deserted; its shops had been boarded up since Labor Day; tourists were sparse; and artists were few and far between. It was a quintessential "off-season" day like that described by one writer a few years later: when it's "dusk . . . and the light is almost gone, you could shoot a gun up Commercial Street and never touch a soul."[1] Other than the industrial hum of local fish factories and the distant motors of Provincetown's small fishing and rum-running fleet, Land's End was still.

At exactly 3:37 P.M. the four-stack U.S. Coast Guard cutter *CG-17*, a former World War I navy destroyer called the USS *Paulding*, interrupted Provincetown's off-season slumber as it steamed past Boatswain Emanuel Gracie and Long Point's Wood End Coast Guard Station.[2] Under the command of Captain John S. Baylis, the *Paulding* had departed earlier in the day from Boston. In some respects, the *Paulding* was in the right place at the right time: its mission was to patrol rum-running activity in local waters, and during Prohibition, Provincetown was known for covert ventures of this sort.

What Captain Baylis and his crew did not know was that the navy submarine USS *S-4* also was cruising in Provincetown Harbor and conducting a series of calibration tests just below the water's surface. It was carrying its entire complement of four officers and thirty-four enlisted men and at 3:37 P.M. was about to surface just off Long Point.

As Boatswain Gracie watched the *Paulding* round Long Point, he sensed an impending collision and readied a surfboat that might help in rescue efforts. But the only person who knew for sure that the *Paulding* would hit the *S-4* was the lookout on board the destroyer, who caught sight of the *S-4*'s periscopes and shears just off the larger vessel's bow. According to retired commander of the U.S. Navy Robert Sminkey, the lookout relayed his sighting; "the Officer-of-the-Deck ordered the engines 'All Back Full'; and the rudder put over hard to port . . . hoping to pass to port over the still submerged stern of the USS *S-4*."[3] But the *Paulding*, steaming ahead at nearly eighteen knots, delivered a death-blow to the *S-4* when it rammed into its hull just forward of the conning tower. The *S-4* heeled far to port and sank within five minutes, finally resting 102 feet below the surface.

The actual collision tells only half the story. The true horror for Provincetown took place during the ill-fated rescue efforts that lasted nearly seventy-two hours. Boatswain Gracie was the first at the scene. He immediately dropped a grapnel and began sweeping the bottom until four hours later, at about 8:00 P.M., it hooked the submerged vessel. Gracie's surfboat tossed in the increasingly stormy waters until the grapnel snapped at around 3:00 A.M. By the next day two U.S. Navy vessels, the *Bushnell* and the *Falcon,* finally reached Provincetown Harbor, but because of choppy waters, neither was able to commence rescue operations. Once again Gracie went out and located the *S-4* with a new line of grapnel.

By about 1:00 P.M. on Sunday, roughly twenty-two hours after the collision, Tom Eadie, a diver onboard the *Falcon,* followed Gracie's line down to the submerged vessel. After tapping Morse code with a hammer on the submarine's hull, he heard a response from the forward torpedo room. Six men were still alive. The *Falcon* then sent two more divers, Bill Carr and Fred Michaels, down to the *S-4* to attach an air hose in order to give the trapped men some oxygen. Although the navy officers had air hoses ready, the increasingly treacherous gale force winds, churning seas, and freezing temperatures made each attempt vital: should they attach the air hose so that it would bring oxygen to the surviving men or fill one of the ballast tanks in order to raise the submarine to the surface? Under commands from above, Carr dived first and filled one of the ballast tanks. All looked on, some with sadness, others with frustration and anger, as a stream of bubbles escaped to the surface, indicating that a rupture in the tank was preventing it from holding air.

Despite precarious conditions and severely limited visibility below the surface, Michaels made the third dive, this time planning to attach the air hose so that it would bring oxygen to the men. He found the submarine quickly, but the agitated waters bounced him off the vessel and he landed, unable to move, in layers of dense mud. Those above tugged at Michaels's lifeline and enabled him to free himself. But he immediately got entangled in the wreckage of the S-4. Eadie dived down to assist, called for a hacksaw, and set Michaels free. Moments later Eadie realized that the jagged wreckage had cut part of his own diving suit; he had hoped to attach the air hose but had to be hauled to the surface when his suit rapidly filled with water. In the meantime, an oscillator affixed to the hull of the S-4 allowed those onboard the *Falcon*, including family members of the trapped men, to communicate with survivors below. "Is there any hope?" "Please hurry!" the men pleaded. They also tapped and received messages of farewell late on Monday once they received word that foul weather was preventing further rescue efforts. At about 6:00 A.M. on Tuesday morning, the crewmen of the S-4 sent one last message: "We understand."

Provincetown's residents were horrified by what they felt were misguided rescue attempts. If the submarine had been raised before the impending storm that precluded salvage efforts, the six men might have survived. Provincetown's fishermen were eager to raise the S-4 immediately, as was at least one private wrecking company, which had raised many ships in Boston Harbor and had motored swiftly to Provincetown on the night of the collision. But navy officers forced these men to the sidelines and refused assistance from any and all civilians. Mary Heaton Vorse was in Provincetown on the afternoon the S-4 was struck. She recalled years later that "everywhere groups of people were saying to each other, in low tones, 'Why ain't they done nothing? We'd save these men with our own hands.'"[4]

The S-4 disaster was one of the first tragedies to bring Provincetown's new and varied groups of residents together as a community. No one turned her back, looked away, or pretended that the waters of the harbor were beyond reasons to grieve. It did not matter who was a Yankee, a Portuguese immigrant, an artist, or one of "our queers." In 1942 Vorse described the town's collective sense of remorse: "Provincetown never forgets the *S-4*. There is a special terror in the memory of those men waiting, tapping their patient messages, and dying. Everyone in Provincetown had a feeling that it was their individual task to save these men and no one could do anything."[5] Whether man-made or natural, catastrophes of this sort served in Provincetown, just as they have in other large and small communities, to bring otherwise alienated souls to common ground. Less than two years later, the United States and Provincetown had yet another tragedy with which to contend: the 1929 stock market crash and the ensuing Great Depression.

The Great Depression caused devastating economic hardships for more than a decade and contributed, at least momentarily, to the restructuring of working-class family and community roles in urban centers and small towns across the nation. Men, who were both the sole breadwinner and the head of their households, could not support their families despite the federal government's efforts to keep the gendered labor order intact by issuing pleas like "Don't Take a Job from a Man."[6] Consequently, wives and children began moving slowly into the workplace as low-paid wage earners and displacing their husbands' and fathers' authoritative positions. Many ethnic working-class communities that once depended on established, Old World neighborhood aid societies and marketplaces, turned instead to Uncle Sam, President Franklin Delano Roosevelt, the New Deal, and emerging, corporate-owned chain stores.[7]

When Provincetown's senior residents remember the Great Depression, they often begin by recounting that times then were "pretty rough."[8] Fishermen, many of whom were also husbands and fathers, were absent for months at a time. Their wives swallowed their pride and accepted household provisions that the Works Progress Administrators (WPA) handed out at the town hall. Independent grocers ran up an unprecedented $75,000 in credit accounts, for hard-to-find clothing and meat and milk. During the winter, children made due with sneakers or cardboard-lined shoes. Year-round employment opportunities were nearly nonexistent, especially after the mid-1930s when local fishpacking plants staged unsuccessful strikes. And the price of fish dropped to an abysmally low one cent per pound.[9]

Despite being isolated at the end of a sixty-six-mile-long peninsula, Provincetown failed to escape the ripple effects of the 1929 stock market debacle. How, then, did it weather these severe financial setbacks? Were class, race, and gender distinctions lessened or reinforced? And what long-term effects did the Great Depression have on Land's End?

World War II brought with it a series of demographic and economic trends that affected seaport towns, rural villages, and urban enclaves across the country. Those most relevant to Provincetown—still a fishing village in decline and a tourist town in the making—centered on questions of leisure or, more specifically, on increases in time, money, and mobility. The value of the vacation industry and the number of eligible tourists had risen steadily throughout the twentieth century, but they escalated even more rapidly after the war. By 1960 the average working American had one more day of leisure time per week than in the 1920s and more than twice the amount per week than in the 1890s. Improvements in transportation, higher incomes, earlier retirement dates, longer life expectancies, and advances in technology allowed working- and middle-class Americans of all races and ethnicities to choose from a growing number of racially segregated resort destinations. Renewed allegiances to the United States, similar to those of the early 1900s, likewise inspired tourists to seek out towns with historic, artistic, or scenic significance.[10]

Provincetown rolled out several welcome mats for its visitors. Thanks to the Federal Airport Act, it now had a small airfield. Although Mike Diogo preferred landing on Pilgrim Lake and founded his Amphibian Airways in 1946, John Van Arsdale used Cape End's new airstrip for his Provincetown–Boston Airline as early as 1949. He charged $6.95 for a one-way trip and often offered an $8.95 round-trip "shopper's special." Six years later the townspeople were relieved to see the Mid-Cape Highway, also called Route 6, finally extended from Orleans to Provincetown. These improvements came none too soon, as the once cherished passenger train, owing to a lack of business, had made its final, painfully slow trip from Provincetown to Boston in 1938.[11]

Tourists on a quest for the historic, artistic, and "gay" satisfied their desires at Land's End. The Pilgrim Monument was standing tall during the postwar era and performed its duty of luring those in search of historic sites. And World War II brought artists and leisured travelers to liberal enclaves in the United States instead of to those in Europe. Already known to be "artsy," Provincetown underwent a renaissance of sorts in the immediate postwar period. Similarly, Land's End, formerly a "dry town," had been "wet" since the repeal of Prohibition in 1933 and had opened a variety of nightclubs. Provincetown's reputation as one of the liveliest stations on the East Coast's entertainment circuit lured adventuresome visitors and gave Land's End a risqué charm.[12]

World War II was a pivotal moment for the country as a whole and for Provincetown as men and women began during this time to identify and behave collectively as gay men and lesbian women.[13] As historians Estelle Freedman and John D'Emilio argue, World War II "created substantially new erotic opportunities that promoted the articulation of a gay identity and the rapid growth of a gay subculture."[14] For men and women already engaged in sexually unconventional relationships and groups, the war created new options and communities. And for those isolated and living far from where bohemians and their ilk congregated, the war facilitated life-altering changes.

This is where Provincetown's postwar story begins, but how does it end? Historians, artists, and cultural critics have analyzed the politics of Senator Joseph McCarthy and have described repressive postwar policies and expectations regarding gender and sexual roles at length. Some, like Joanne Meyerowitz, have also compiled narratives of nonconformists in order to recuperate those who were Not June Cleaver, as she asserts well in the title of her book by the same name. Still, as Freedman and D'Emilio put forth, the "repressive policies of the federal government encouraged local police forces across the country to harass [gay men and lesbians] with impunity. . . . Throughout the 1950s and well into the 1960s, gay men and lesbians suffered from unpredictable, brutal crackdowns."[15] Sexual and gender nonconformists were arrested in unprecedented numbers during this time in places like New York, New Orleans, Miami, San Francisco, Baltimore, Dallas, and Washington, D.C. How did Provincetown respond to the postwar moral panic?

4

Weathering the Depression

First off 'course it seemed strange here. An' a long time ago th' Americans an' th' Portuguese they didn't get on so good. But after ahile they
get used. An' they find out we're good fishermen. . . . It's a good place
to live. Good money an' chances for th' young people. They say its bad
times now, but we ain' never seen bad times like in th' ol' country.
                                        —Joseph Captiva, WPA interview,
                                                        February 15, 1939

CAPTAIN CAPTIVA was not alone in believing that even during the
Depression, the economic situation in Provincetown was better than the
best times in Portugal or the Azores. In a recent oral history interview,
resident Margaret Roberts agreed, stating that the Depression "was not
at all depressing to us because we didn't know anything much different
from it."[1] Similarly, in his 1954 history of Provincetown's First National
Bank, Gaylon J. Harrison spoke for many when he noted, "No one
starved to death here. There were no apple sellers on the corners. No
one committed suicide."[2]

But these sentiments tell only half the story. In 1938 Florence Brown,
former director of the Provincetown Art Association and Museum, explained to Eleanor Roosevelt that most artists in Provincetown "have
no means of support whatever."[3] The dearth of economic opportunities
prompted many of the town's residents, especially young Yankees, to
move elsewhere. An editorial in the *Provincetown Advocate* in 1938 even
went so far as to argue that the small-town syndrome, in which young
adults leave town en masse to seek employment in the cities, was "acute
and serious in Provincetown."[4] And as late as 1939, Frank Flores, the
town's health agent and WPA recreation director, reminded Provincetown's residents that "the situation in Provincetown is bad, worse than

you know. The welfare funds are exhausted. Soldier's Aide and Mother's Aide are also gone."[5] What accounts for these different views of the Depression? Thinking about the Depression as taking place in two phases—one before the WPA stepped in and one after—provides a helpful starting point.

In contrast to the mid-1800s, when whaling flourished and Provincetown prospered, the years between the two world wars brought few riches. The number of tourists climbed from the early 1900s until 1929, but they stayed no more than a day, a week, or, at most, a season. For the remainder of the year, residents had to rely on a hardy fleet of fishermen and a handful of cold-storage freezers. Mary Heaton Vorse described the problem: "The depression came so early to the Cape and deepened so slowly" that at first many residents were not aware of its existence or its effects. Based on observations from the 1910s through the 1930s, Vorse explained, "There were almost no rich people in Provincetown and few in actual want except through disaster. Fishermen are poor. There is always plenty of pinching and the hidden starvation of not the right kind of food . . . but people have held their heads up and expected to do for themselves."[6] Residents survived the first half of the Depression by living on meager resources and relying on a well-tuned economic system called an "exchange," a "family," a "swapping," and, in some neighborhoods, an "over-the-back-fence" economy.[7]

During the 1920s and early 1930s men, women, and children all pitched in to supplement the fishing and tourist industries. When the number of both vacationers and jobs inland fell in 1929, many townsfolk and artists were left with little or no income. But each day Portuguese fishermen sold their hard-earned catch for cash until there were no more buyers, and then they kindly, and not without pride, gave the remainder away to residents of varying backgrounds. In addition to actually feeding townspeople during this era, the fishing industry also employed residents in its cold-storage freezers.

During the early years of the Depression, Provincetown's economy of exchange also benefited from fishermen who supplemented their incomes with profits from the risky business of rum-running. Indeed, while beachcombing along the back shore, residents sometimes caught a glimpse of the covert rum-running activity just off the coast, or they stumbled across an abandoned case of liquor. According to some, fishermen like Manny "Sea Fox" Zora spent years outrunning the "feds" and trading with large "syndicates" from Boston. On darker nights Provincetown's rumrunners motored quietly out to the back shore, evading coast guard vessels while watching for signals from their suppliers. After docking, residents delight in telling, rumrunners would pay a trusted servant on land to call in a (false) fire alarm at one end of town, thus summoning the attention of local authorities and what the Sea Fox called "zealous drys," while they unloaded their liquid treasures at the other end.[8] While townsfolk relate these stories with a fair amount of sensationalism and nostalgia, there is little question that home-brewed liquor acted as a timely economic lubricant.

Although Portuguese men savored the autonomy and the social cachet they gained as fishermen and rumrunners, they could not have sustained Provincetown's economy without the support of women and children. Indeed, even though most residents today credit Portuguese fishermen for keeping Provincetown afloat during the Depression, paying retrospective tribute to an industry shrinking in importance, Portuguese women and children were also at the heart of Provincetown's barter economy.

Women and young girls of Portuguese, Yankee, Irish, and Scottish descent engineered much of Provincetown's communal economy from their homes and backyards. While their male relatives and neighbors were at sea, the women and children were on shore mending nets in the fish sheds, inventing fishing aids, washing fishing gear, working in the service industry, and setting up shore-bound business ventures. When they finished their chores at home and work, they ventured out as gatherers. One fishermen's daughter, Florence Corea Alexander, who was then a teenager, admitted in 1996 that times were hard during the Depression but also that nobody went hungry. With nostalgia and pride, Florence remembered that Provincetown's natural resources fortified meager incomes. Fresh fish was plentiful. Women also gathered shellfish, particularly quahogs and soft-shelled clams, at low tide, and cranberries and blueberries in the "backcountry" (now the dunes of the Cape Cod National Seashore). Backyard gardens, she recalled, enjoyed relatively long seasons, while during the lean winter months the oil company and the grocer allowed residents to delay payment until the more lucrative summer months.[9]

Many Portuguese women were able to make Provincetown's subsistence economy work because they were first-generation immigrants who had once lived in extreme poverty and knew how to make ends meet on an insufficient income. Others, like Mary Ruth O'Donnell, were second-generation immigrants who had inherited similar survival skills and learned to cope with a seasonal economy. The O'Donnells' financial situation was typical. While her husband was out fishing, Ruth worked at home, and they managed fairly well, she declared, with hard work and frugality. Pride and nostalgia also laced Ruth's memories: "You know we did it," she recalled in 1997, "and there was no such thing as welfare—my husband worked. . . . I think it brought a lot of families closer together because the only activities we could afford, such as playing cards, we did together."[10]

Provincetown's barter economy also succeeded because townsfolk enlisted their children as part-time workers and scavengers. The late Manuel "Cul" Goveia, also known by his pen name "Joe Lazaro," noted that during the Depression, boys and girls learned to fish by hand, dive for coins, carry baggage for tourists, sell pond lilies and seashells, run errands for the elderly and wealthy, and pick coal from the beaches and railroad tracks. Many families, Cul added, went without staples like milk, sold precious heirlooms, and were fortunate enough to secure "pay as you go" plans at neighborhood stores. In addition to generous Yankee shopkeepers like Herman Robinson and Duncan Matheson, a number of wealthier residents supported needy townspeople regardless of their ethnicity, class, or religious background by donating to local charities and families and by extending credit lines.[11]

Taking in boarders was also a part of the community economy on which poorer families especially, but not exclusively, depended during the Depression. Although an anomaly in its location in the East End, the household of Portuguese native Clement Silva was in most ways typical. In the 1930s and 1940s, while his father was out fishing, Clem's mother took in boarders at their home at 557 Commercial Street. As Silva reminisced in 1997, "We used to have at any time two or three gay guys that my mother rented to who were very nice . . . in my home on the water. And we had gay girls . . . my mother used to feed them, rent the room and everything else for three dollars a night."[12] Portuguese households were desperate for cash; bachelors and maiden ladies needed a safe place to stay; and artists needed inexpensive housing. A white well-off bachelor who was not threatening sexually, paid his rent on time, had no loud or messy children, and exchanged recipes with his landlady was the kind of guest that many Portuguese families, especially those with husbands at sea, welcomed.[13] Both the adults and children became close friends with their tenants, and it was these lifelong social and financial bonds that held Provincetown together when a controversy called "the queer question" erupted in the 1950s.

Provincetown's barter economy compelled residents to reach out to neighbors and encouraged artists and others to emerge from the isolation of their studios and apartments. In this way it bridged the narrow gaps between distinct social and cultural groups in town. While the men provided fish and liquor, the women gave away homegrown vegetables and home-cooked meals to neighbors and artists of many races, sexual orientations, and ethnicities. They exchanged these items typically for coal, wood, milk, a piece of art, or a friendly smile. This is not to say that the townspeople and visitors came together during this time without problems, but rather that during the Depression, the residents of Provincetown created a community of likeness—based on being poor—out of a fluctuating set of economies and visitors.

Although they were efficient in the short run, the same family and community economies that brought residents together were not as successful during the second half of the Depression, in part because one of the critical links, the fishing industry, suffered major setbacks. Although the industry had been slow all along, in 1938, the same year that unemployment rates escalated all over the country, one fisherman let Alice Kelly in on the dismal situation: "The col' storages ain' workin' none to speak of," and the fishermen were not bringing in the usual quantities of fish. But he remained hopeful: "Like I say, I don't think it'll last. We don' often have such long spells when it shtays bad like this. So maybe any day now I bring . . . a nice mess o' fish."[14] The Twenty-first Amendment repealing Prohibition compounded fishermen's troubles by removing the need for rum-running. While Provincetown's more ambitious residents moved the exchange of liquor into newly licensed bars and taverns, the distribution of wealth and goods shrank. By 1936 even the local government resorted to borrowing money from private businesses and other town governments.[15] Rather than despairing, however, during the second half of the Depression, Provincetown's residents turned, for the first time, to a new pool of WPA jobs and, for the second time, to an expanding pool of tourists.

When Provincetown's fishing industry collapsed in the late 1930s, President Franklin D. Roosevelt came to the rescue with the Works Progress

Administration. WPA officials and Provincetown's board of selectmen arranged an array of local jobs including, but not limited to, road and environmental maintenance (beach cleanup and mosquito and gypsy moth control), book and toy repair, town hall records research and organization, positions as nurses and household aides (also known as mother's aides), school lunch and sewing services, and a special boys' town project. Educational projects included a nursery school, recreation program (including summer camps and plays), art instruction, and "Americanization classes." Writing projects, associated with the Federal Writers Prolect (FWP), sponsored interviews and published guidebooks. And the Federal Arts Project (FAP), the Treasury Section of Fine Arts, and the Federal Theater Project funded paintings, murals, and plays. At the town hall WPA workers distributed flour, butter, eggs, and clothing such as men's long underwear, which many women hemmed into bloomers for their own use.[16]

WPA jobs brought hope to Land's End. "Blue-collar" jobs gave working-class residents, most of whom were of Portuguese descent, opportunities to work and bring resources into households struggling under the weight of Depression-era shortages. The FWP hired writers George Willison, Carl Malmberg, Josef Berger, and Alice Kelly to describe working-class Portuguese life during the 1930s. In their interviews with Alice Kelly, semiliterate Portuguese men and women told their life stories in a semipublic venue, often for the first time. Many boasted of their newfound independence, laid claims to being more adept fishermen than the Yankees were, and declared in no uncertain terms that they did not like working onshore. They also elaborated on Portuguese and Portuguese American traditions, as well as on the differences between the "old country" and the new. FWP assignments inspired Josef Berger to research and write travel essays on Provincetown's environment, population, racial elements, transportation options, rooming house availability, industry, and economic development. The products of Berger's work, *Cape Cod Pilot*, and some of the chapters in *Massachusetts: A Guide to Its People and Places*, part of the FWP's American Guide Series, promoted Provincetown and Cape Cod in descriptive and inviting essays.[17]

The economic exigencies of the Great Depression plus the commissioned WPA work also allowed visual artists to experience the challenges of working for a wage. Philip Malicoat, Blanche Lazzell, and George Yater were among those selected for FAP work. The Treasury

Section of Fine Arts, a government-sponsored project interested not just in employing needy artists but also in producing a distinctive American art, hired elite Provincetown artists. The best-known Provincetown artist who worked for the Treasury Section was Ross Moffett, who painted murals for the Provincetown town hall as well as for post offices in Revere, Holyoke, and Somerville, Massachusetts.[18] The FAP helped situate visual artists for the first time as potential members of the working, rather than the leisure, class. According to some art historians, the Depression and the FAP responded to both the creative and the financial needs of American artists while bringing government officials and average residents to regard artists as everyday workers rather than as aloof bohemians. Especially beyond Land's End, many people were able, for the first time, to watch artists at work and to see their paintings in high schools and post offices rather than in museums or galleries. In this way, the FAP demystified what it meant to be an artist and to appreciate art and, in so doing, brought artists closer to the average public.[19]

In Provincetown, though, this hands-on, or at least eyes-on, approach to art was already happening, as artists had always worked on the streets and beaches and often used "ordinary" people as subjects. Even though the artists may have remained physically removed from the public elsewhere, their accessibility in Provincetown was one element that had made Land's End attractive to tourists and art lovers alike well before the onset of the Depression.

Although in some ways democratizing the arts, the WPA also elevated them above the occupations of the other townspeople in Provincetown. A comparison of WPA pay scales shows the recipients' paltry but crucial weekly earnings and reveals federally sponsored class and race inequities. Whereas blue-collar jobs paid workers $12 each week, the FAP paid Provincetown's artists approximately $17 each week, and the FWP paid Berger and Kelly, among others, $27 per week.[20] Theoretically, the WPA projects were meant to instill a sense of pride in their participants as American workers contributing to the economy. Yet by paying the townspeople unequally, depending on the kind of work performed—digging ditches versus painting murals—the WPA projects institutionalized an inequitable sense of market value for each person's labor and worth as an American. In so doing, the federal government re-created the occupational and ethnic boundaries that the community economy had begun to blur. In some cases, this resentment percolated above the surface. In 1936, for instance, one "observant citizen" asked, "How many of the artists or writers on the dole are capable of producing anything worthy of the name 'art'? How many are mere social parasites and always will be—looking for a handout here or a free meal there—WPA or no WPA?"[21]

The story of the WPA in Provincetown was even more complicated than this, for despite being widespread, WPA work was often received with both resistance and shame. While artists elsewhere may have been proud to accept WPA work, some artists in Provincetown shied away from federal assistance, no doubt due in part to comments made by "observant citizens." Vernon Smith, the FAP supervisor for Cape Cod, noted at the time that one artist "wished to avoid any publicity of the fact that he was on WPA [assistance]. I even think he would be against a WPA show in Provincetown in order not to have it known in the town that he was among those chosen."[22] Some artists apparently felt that government funding was reserved for those with little talent. Katherine Witherstine Gilman, a Provincetown native and daughter of the artist Donald Witherstine (a student of George Elmer Browne), recalled that her father considered WPA help to be a form of charity and turned down WPA assignments, even though his wife urged him to accept them. Fortunately, Donald Witherstine and his family had outside financial help and could afford to dismiss these assignments.[23] Commissioned work often proved the most deprecating; for example, FAP officials instructed some Jewish artists to paint elaborate Christian murals.[24]

Likewise, blue-collar workers registered their resentment of the menial onshore work by not taking their jobs seriously. In 1939, Selectman Jesse D. Rogers warned the Association of the Unemployed (containing approximately 275 men and women) that no WPA projects would be available for "loafers." Rogers admitted to knowing that WPA projects were a joke throughout the country:

> The story of WPA work in Provincetown has not been a pretty one. After watching the fooling around, loafing and card playing on the job last spring I was disgusted and would have shut down on the project much sooner had it not been that I knew some of the workers were really deserving.[25]

Rogers threatened to eliminate the projects if the workers did not work. "I don't mean to kill yourselves," he pleaded, "but work." Refusing to work may have had something to do with the way fishermen in particular looked down on shore-bound vocations. Captain Captiva spoke for many when he explained, "Anybody'll tell you they ain no men can fish better than the Portugueesh. We can always get jobs on th' boats. I wouldn't want to work on land. Mos' Portuguese feels th' same way. Rather be independent. I like to be boss. An' I wouldn' never be happy without I had a boat under me." Later in the interview he added, "I wouldn' be no good on land."[26]

At the same time, however, many artists and blue-collar workers appreciated the opportunity to work and took advantage of it to become better Americans. Shirley Pell Yater's husband, George Yater, was one of many artists who enjoyed working on WPA projects. Yater even saved enough money to buy a camera and a boat.[27] President Roosevelt and local WPA officials also became heroes in the eyes of some Portuguese residents. Federal work opportunities and educational assistance in the form of "Americanization classes" prompted many of these immigrants to seek U.S. citizenship because the WPA programs had given them hope, in a way that their homelands could not, for a better standard of living.

Finally, the story of the WPA in Provincetown is one of institutionalized gender distinctions. Boys Town, a government-sponsored project for Provincetown's young boys, illustrates just this point. This project, which WPA workers and town officials such as the chief of police organized, taught teenage boys how to construct and operate a mock town government. Boys Town held mock town hall meetings, wrote a constitution based on the *Mayflower* Compact, and even traveled to the White House in Washington, D.C., for a reception. Officially, Boys Town was "an organization by which all junior citizens of our community [undertook] to govern their affairs and contribute[d] to the general welfare of the Town." It was meant to give "youngsters an actual laboratory course in democratic government."[28]

The message that WPA projects like this one delivered, however, was clear: young girls were not capable, worthy, or interested in learning how to act as citizens or participate in government affairs. If there had been a "Girls Town" project, it might have taught girls how to sew, clean house, or care for the sick, young, and elderly, despite their previous experience as entrepreneurs and fishing industry workers. The gendered nature of the WPA blue-collar projects helped institutionalize men as workers and citizens, and women as caretakers. The WPA paid men in Provincetown to repair roads, construct buildings, clear fields, and dig ditches, and it paid women to sew, nurse, and act as mother's aides. WPA programs at Land's End and across the country encouraged government officials and local residents to keep the established gender order intact during a time of shifting roles and responsibilities.

Pride also played a role in the other arena of Provincetown's late-1930s economic survival strategy. Although WPA jobs were helpful, Provincetown's declining fishing and rum-running industries forced residents to concentrate more than ever on cultivating a strong trade in tourists. After all, WPA projects were important stopgap measures, but they provided work primarily during the winter season and would not continue indefinitely. Residents thus had to swallow their pride and maintain economic order by opening their doors even wider to strangers. By 1936, tourism in Provincetown had begun to pick up again after a five-year lull. A number of factors contributed to this upsurge, including a brief respite from the Depression from 1933 to 1937 and an increase in leisure time for middle- and upper-class vacationers.[29] Automobiles also became more popular and allowed visitors to reach Provincetown more easily. In August 1936, Chief of Police John C. Williams stated that the summer season brought "the biggest stream of auto traffic that [he] can remember. The entire [police] department worked all day and most of the night to handle" the crowds, especially on holidays and weekends.[30]

After leaving town for a number of years, Mary Heaton Vorse also noticed a distinct change when she returned in 1936. She found that in addition to the "crop [that] was fish," Provincetown now "had another crop—tourists—and so had all New England. New Englanders have slowly, almost imperceptibly, changed from earning their living from farming, manufacturing, and fishing to the business of pleasuring, which is now its second source of income."[31] Vorse insisted that Provincetown was even beginning to resemble Coney Island, at least during the summer, because it had become crowded and more commercialized. Provincetown's seasonal prosperity allowed most residents to work during the summer, even when they took WPA jobs or other forms of assistance in the off-season. Consequently, they grew to depend on Provincetown's new crop of tourists and tried even harder to attract them. They also turned their attention to an infrastructure that would work well with the burgeoning demands for service. Their strategies for marketing Provincetown and for providing easier access to Land's End succeeded, and it was this success that led residents to begin attempting to control and police the "class" of visitors vacationing at Land's End.

Travelogues promoting Provincetown as a quaint vacation spot drew many visitors. Just as in the early 1900s, during the Depression promoters transformed Provincetown's history, landscape, and residents into marketable commodities to lure consumers and alleviate financial stress. During the Depression, however, promoters added Provincetown's nascent but noteworthy nightlife to its list of attractions. In 1936 in *Down Cape Cod*, Katherine Dos Passos and Edith Shay encouraged visitors to enjoy Cape End's "magnificent dunes and beaches" as well as its "narrow, foreign-looking streets."[32] Paul Smith, founder of the Provincetown Book Store, highlighted Cape End's entertainment and dining venues in *A Modern Pilgrim's Guide to Provincetown*: "Call the nightclubs to find the gayest entertainment, planned and impromptu."[33]

During the Depression, as in earlier decades, promoters described Provincetown and its visitors as "gay" or "queer" in order to brand Land's End as unique and bring in even more tourists. The following example published in 1937 is typical: "Advance reports that tonight's [costume ball] would be unusually 'gay' and 'nude' were borne out as the evening wore on, and sensationally revealing costumes were observed."[34] Another in 1939 stated simply, "Provincetown Ball Gay and Satiric."[35] The exceptions were writers who held on to Cape End's colonial heritage, like Lawrence Dame, who stated that "Provincetown doffs the mummers antics as soon as [the tourists] leave and resumes again her true role, that of a wise, merry, tolerant New England lady who knows that she has charm and wants to share it with appreciative souls."[36]

Yet beginning in 1934 and especially from 1936 onward, most guidebooks and articles focused on Cape End's outlandish art colony, sensational events, and increasingly infamous nightlife. In turn, they attracted a stream of visitors, many of whom were gay men and lesbians

Notice the frolicking sailors and maiden ladies on Commercial Street, ca. 1918. Postcard courtesy of the Pilgrim Monument and Provincetown Museum.

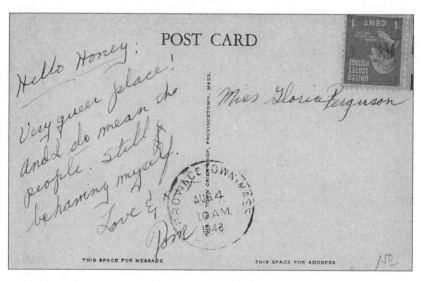

Postcards helped characterize Land's End as notably outlandish. "*Hello Honey*: Very queer place! And I *do* mean the people. Still behaving myself. Love and xxx Tom, 1948." Postcard courtesy of the Pilgrim Monument and Province-town Museum.

124

in search of accepting spaces. Indeed, because by the 1930s the terms "gay," "artsy," and "queer" were known as code words for places and people that tolerated gender and sexual deviants, Provincetown's reputation as such drew scores of sexually unconventional visitors. Land's End may have been particularly attractive during this time as places like New York City and San Francisco succumbed to the careful watch of oppressive purity crusades.

Entrepreneurs also lured tourists by selling and distributing postcards, which became popular in Provincetown and elsewhere at the start of the twentieth century. During the 1930s, tourist shops in Provincetown sold more than half a million postcards each year. One article, entitled "Summer Visitors Send Many Thousand Provincetown Postcards to All Parts," reported that images of the monument and the oldest house were the favorites and confirmed that selling postcards was proving to be one of the town's most lucrative businesses.[37] Most postcards re-created Provincetown's image as a colonial landmark and fishing village by featuring the Pilgrim Monument, town crier, narrow streets, and fishing wharves, but others captured rather queer images of Land's End, such as one that included two sailors and two maiden ladies intimately enjoying Commercial Street in the early 1900s. Another postmarked in the 1940s contained this handwritten message: "Hello Honey: Very queer place! And I do mean the people. Still behaving myself. Love & xxx Tom." Provincetown's postcard industry, in other words, reproduced Land's End as both traditional and eccentric.

Portuguese townspeople and entrepreneurs teamed up with Yankee residents to reignite Provincetown's vital tourist trade by bolstering the local service infrastructure. Whereas in the early 1900s Yankees nearly exclusively led the push to turn Provincetown into a famous watering place, in the 1930s Portuguese residents joined them and often took the lead. The board of trade, for example, headed in 1936 by its first Portuguese president, John R. Silva, endorsed a $25,000 advertising fund to promote Cape Cod as a tourist resort. Silva also wrote an open letter to the Provincetown business community asking it to congratulate the steamships that consistently brought boatloads of tourists to Land's End on a daily, albeit seasonal, basis. And in 1940 the board of trade began negotiating to extend the Mid-Cape Highway to Provincetown.[38] Portuguese fishermen also kept up or inaugurated sportfishing excursions. During this time, too, Joseph Nunes, scavenging for wood in the dunes, came up with the idea of letting some of the air out of au-

Postcard of George Washington Ready, the "original" town crier above (note the wooden sidewalk) ca. 1900 and photograph of the new town crier, Arthur Snader, below, ca. 1938. Postcard and photograph courtesy of the Pilgrim Monument and Provincetown Museum.

tomobile tires so that they would glide easily over sand. When Nunes returned from his scavenger hunt, he took to the street with a sign that read "Over the Dunes on Balloons with Joe Nunes," thereby establishing a dune-taxi business that for nearly half a century took customers out to the backshore.[39]

Making the trip to Land's End easier and providing entertainment once there was vital, but accommodations were equally important. In addition to maintaining the popular grand hotels, like the Pilgrim House, during the Depression townspeople offered a variety of enticing destinations. While only a handful of establishments catered to tourists in the early 1900s, by the late 1930s eleven hotels and inns, more than thirty restaurants, three nightclubs, and at least six summer cottages served vacationers in Provincetown. Single rooms also were available in both the West and East Ends of town for one to three dollars a night per person.[40] In 1936 Mary Heaton Vorse, accustomed to Provincetown's earlier and apparently quieter years, complained, "The whole town had become a rooming house. A stream of tourists choked the streets."[41]

Steering visitors toward these rooms and hotels and alerting them to restaurant specials became the job of Provincetown's "new" town crier. In 1935 the board of trade merged with the Town Crier Organization to revive the legendary town crier, the last one having traversed Commercial Street calling out the day's news in 1927. The new town crier, Amos Kubik, was a tourist attraction and a living relic. As Josef Berger noted at the time, the board of trade appointed Kubik and "provided him with a colorful [Pilgrim] costume (not worn, incidentally, by his predecessor) and a crier's bell. Up and down Commercial Street, therefore, still goes the town crier during the town's tourist season. The rest of the year, he doesn't bother."[42] The Pilgrim-clad town crier, who at one time was an integral part of Provincetown's year-round community before becoming a seasonal tourist attraction, is a perfect example of the way that Provincetown transformed its unique heritage into a marketable colonial attraction.

Despite these aggressive initiatives, Provincetown's residents exhibited a number of anxieties once they realized that trading a life at sea for a life coddling outsiders called into question the town's integrity. A sense of independence seemed especially important to recent Portuguese immigrants, who had left their homeland to seek certain American freedoms. But Provincetown's increasing dependence on outsiders alarmed others as well, like Mary Heaton Vorse, who asked, "How different is the mentality of a town which caters to tourists from one which holds itself, almost belligerently, aloof from 'off-islanders' while it makes its living from the sea?"[43]

While maintaining fishing boats, many fishermen and others looked also or instead to vacationers as income-generating sources. This meant that men who once earned their living from the sea and took pride in the independence promised by such a life now had to serve outsiders. Some fishermen, like Captain Frank Fratus and Captain Frank Gaspie, adjusted easily, changing their boats from ones that carried men to catch fish into ones that carried visitors to watch fish. Others were not so lucky or ambitious. Captain Captiva noted that he could "never be happy without I had a boat under me. . . . I don' know nothin' else, on'y fishin' an' the sea." Another fisherman, Manuel, stressed the importance of economic autonomy: "I wanted to be independent, see? Not say theesh 'yessir' an 'nossir' alla time."[44]

An even more telling symptom of local anxiety blistered once Provincetown's new open-door policy attracted numerous so-called undesirable guests. The late 1930s mark the beginning of Provincetown's formal efforts to control, police, and determine the type of summer visitor it would welcome. In August 1939 one writer lamented that "the fact was again proven—if it needs further proof—that it is not the number of people who come to town, but the kind, that contribute to or detract from our major business."[45] A few months earlier, a special town meeting attracted an unprecedented number of townspeople who turned out to vote on article 7, which would have changed police regulation section 19 to ban "shorts, halters, or immodest dress," except those worn by Boy Scouts, Girl Scouts, and athletic teams. But the article failed to get a two-thirds majority vote, in part because business owners, such as Paul Smith of the Provincetown Bookstore, argued that such stringent laws would discourage visitors from vacationing at Land's End. Seabury Taylor assured residents that the article would have a negative effect on local businesses, that it would "'hit Provincetown, and hit it hard.'"[46] Of the thousands of visitors who poured into Provincetown each summer, the ones perceived to be causing the most trouble were not, as one might guess, queers from New York City's anti-pansy backlash or middle-class gays and lesbians but, rather, working-class vacationers. In 1937 local officials attempted to run out of town

those visitors whom they labeled "gypsies," because according to officer Francis Marshall, they were "filthy and noisy" (unlike the "clean"
and "nice" gay visitors).[47] The group creating the most distress, however, were those of the "boat crowd variety."

During the late 1930s, visitors, residents, and artists alike urged
Provincetown to concentrate on attracting white middle- and upper-
class visitors. In 1937 artist Jack Beauchamp admitted that "Provincetown [now] lives in its summer business." Yet, he added, "inadequate
parking facilities and the presence of swarms of poorer tourists of the
boat crowd variety coupled with a dearth of first class tourist accommodations probably are the chief reasons why a better class of people
do not vacation here." The town, he warned, is declining in value and
is at a "crossroads" concerning its class of visitors and its character.[48]
Others urged residents to remove the large advertising banners span-
ning the width of Commercial Street and to clean up the streets or face
a "withdrawal" of people who spend money on seasonal rentals or second homes, renovate property, and pay substantial taxes.

Still, the most common plea was to stop catering to the "so-called
'boat crowds.'"[49] The "boat crowds" were, for the most part, white
tourists of all sexual orientations who made one-day, round-trip excursions by steamboat from Boston to Provincetown. Steamboats like the
SS *Dorothy Bradford* (named after the only *Mayflower* passenger to
drown in Provincetown Harbor) disgorged more than one thousand
guests, who flocked en masse to Provincetown's main and only commercial boulevard. These tourists had heard of Provincetown from
friends and publications and went there to see where the *Mayflower*
landed, to visit its famous art colony, and to experience its supposed
outrageousness.

In 1938 Bill Whyte tried to explain the boat crowd's perspective in
an article in the *Provincetown Advocate* entitled "What Do Boat Excur-
sionists Think about Their Visit to Provincetown?" He ended up instead
with the opinions of one of the crewmen onboard the popular SS *Steel
Pier* steamship. Whyte's main informant, "Honest John," was blunt. Because of all the publicity that Provincetown's risqué art colony received
in the Boston papers, the passengers, he explained, first "go ashore
looking for the artists and they don't find them. . . . They [also] expect
to see a lot of nude women walking around the streets. [But] they don't
see any, so naturally they are disappointed." According to Honest John,
the problem was not the paucity of artists or outlandish behavior. In-

Provincetown Wharf - Provincetown, Mass.

More than one thousand passengers descended from Boston boats onto Provincetown's Railroad Wharf (now MacMillan Pier, ca. 1910). Postcard courtesy of the Pilgrim Monument and Provincetown Museum.

deed, he asserted just the opposite: "You can't blame it on the *Steel Pier* if the artists go to bed with big heads from drinking and don't get up until 3 o'clock the next day." Ending his comments, Honest John tossed his steamboat company's hat into the ring of those responsible for making Provincetown into a successful, well-known resort: "The Cape Cod Steamship Company has really made Provincetown what it is today. If it wasn't for this boat, you would never hear of Provincetown."[50] Taken one step further, Honest John's claim also suggests that Provincetown owed its fame and the Cape Cod Steamship Company owed its fortune to the working-class day-trippers keeping both in business.

The Depression forced Provincetown's residents to compete once again for cultural and financial authority. The townspeople remember the first half of the Depression—before the WPA stepped in—with romance and nostalgia about the development of community during a time of crisis. But during the second half, when WPA jobs became available, the failure to resolve long-standing inequities divided the newfound community of likeness into groups defined by ethnicity, class, and gender. Indeed, although the WPA projects aimed to democratize the arts and labor, in Provincetown they ended up undermining democratization efforts by re-creating and institutionalizing hierarchies. Similarly, while meant to instill pride in artists and workers as income-earning Americans, the WPA jobs in Provincetown often created a sense of dependency and seemed to question the worth of those who accepted federally sponsored assistance. Residents responded to these paradoxes by asserting their independence and attempting to restrict access to Land's End.

Class difference was one of the first categories of exclusion to take hold in Provincetown. During this time, communities of likeness also formed around being white and becoming white, but overt and contested—rather than subtle and symbolic—displays of prejudice like that against the boat crowds were new. To be sure, some gay men and lesbians, like those featured in Scudder's collection, received a cool reception at Land's End, but during the 1930s the predominant forms of exclusion in Provincetown recognized class and race but were still blind to differences in gender and sexual orientation. Residents feared becoming another Coney Island, a resort area that once catered to the white upper and middle classes but by the 1950s had become popular with black and working-class New Yorkers. Not long after the townspeople tried to police working-class vacationers, however, local sentiments changed, as World War II set loose a national coming-out process and as gay men and lesbians descended on Provincetown en masse.

5

"Provincetown Tells the Gayflower Set: *Scram*"

Hear ye, hear ye, lads and ladies—Provincetown is gay with artist folks, summer theaters, bright shops and quaint tea rooms. . . . Truly Provincetown is a "must" on any Patriotic American Pilgrimage.
—*Historic Provincetown Calls You*, ca. 1940

"BUDDY-BUDDY-SHIPMATE! (This is a navy term of endearment which I have just picked up)," was the salutation that Tennessee Williams used in 1944 in one of many letters to his longtime friend Donald Windham. "I have just returned from a most extraordinary all night party on Captain Jack's Wharf, as a matter [of fact] the third consecutive of a series, but this the most extraordinary of all." Tennessee's night in Provincetown was exceptional, due, in his choice words, to a "rat-race" he entered with two gay men who owned a salon in town. Williams described them as a "couple of willowy rather pretty Jewish-looking intellectual belles [effeminate men]." Williams and the salon proprietors were competing for the charms of a local sailor. Tennessee bragged after the fact:

> One of the belles was unbuttoning the sailor's pants and the other mine. . . . Then all at once things start to happen! The sailor extends his arm, I extend mine. In one dervish whirl both belles are thrown clear of the charmed circle which from then on consisted solely and frenziedly of Tennessee and the Navy![1]

Painting a decidedly festive portrait, Williams's letters tell the story of a flourishing gay world in Provincetown during the early and mid-

Sailors inundated Provincetown during both world wars. Postcard courtesy of the Pilgrim Monument and Provincetown Museum.

1940s. They also describe the ambivalence with which this lavish lifestyle was received by straight and gay visitors and townspeople. For instance, although at times thrilled with his options for sexual partners —he dated a ballet dancer, a musician, a dancing instructor, and a language professor and was duped by "a piece of trade, a Yale freshman . . . [who] got away"—Williams also expressed frustration, noting on several occasions that "the town is swarming with belles but trade [masculine men] is scarce as hen's teeth, or rather that which is not too dangerous is." Williams compared Provincetown's "storm of belles" to "a plague of green flies, the sort that torment you on a summer beach, [they are] like Fritz [Bultman's] eternal case of poison ivy, or a woolen under-wear on a fierce sunburn." In a disturbing aside, Williams added, "The Portuguese natives have been beating them [the belles] up on the streets at night lately and I am not at all sure which side I am on . . . my own or the oppositions."[2]

After residents questioned the value of working-class visitors of the "boat crowd" variety, did they next target certain gay men and lesbians, perhaps those of the working classes who were not affiliated with Williams's select group of artists or sailors? Immediately after World War II ended, purity campaigns spread throughout the seaports, naval bases, and urban areas that had attracted and fostered gay life during the war. A collective sense of fear and paranoia cast homosexuals as "undesirable" and dangerous citizens, and postwar efforts to purge gay men and lesbians from jobs, neighborhoods, and nightclubs swept across the nation. According to the historian Nan Boyd, in places like

New York City, San Francisco, and Washington, D.C., a "tripod" of agencies—liquor control boards, police squads, and court systems—succeeded in closing dozens of gay bars and arresting countless homosexuals.[3] Would Provincetown, the reputed birthplace of democracy, fall victim to a similar fate?

During World War II, the conditions in Land's End were much like those during World War I. As Williams explained, the U.S. Navy stationed a good part of its North Atlantic Fleet in Provincetown Harbor, which meant that hundreds of sailors were strolling the streets and innumerable visitors were going to Land's End to meet or, perhaps, to have sex with them. Williams also alluded to the second similarity during this time, the many artists seeking refuge at Land's End. "The whole lunatic fringe of Manhattan is already here, Valeska [Gert], Joe Hazan, Robert Duncan, Lee Krasner and [Jackson] Pollock, the Bultmans and myself. Such a collection could not be found outside of Bellevue or the old English Bedlam," Williams joked in June 1944.[4]

In Provincetown during the 1940s and 1950s the arts underwent something of a renaissance when an eclectic mix of painters, writers, actors, and entertainers took up residence there. Some of the better-known painters were Henry Hensche, who succeeded Charles Hawthorne in 1935 at the Cape Cod School of Art; Hans Hofmann, who linked Provincetown to New York City by founding schools in both places; Reeves Euler, Robert Motherwell, Vollian Burr Rann, Ada Raynor, and Myron Stout, all of whom worked at Day's Lumberyard Studios; Yvonne Anderson, who helped found the Sun Gallery for younger artists in 1953; and, among others, Edward Hopper, Kranz Kline, Philip Malicoat, Tony Vevers, and Mark Rothko. Forum 49, a lecture and exhibit series on the future and meaning of the arts in Provincetown, and the establishment of the Chrysler Art Museum (where the Heritage Museum was and the Provincetown Library will be) further ensured the importance of Land's End as an art enclave during the cold war. *Time* magazine apparently agreed when in 1958 it named Provincetown the "undisputed summer art capital" of the country.[5]

Provincetown's reputation as a theater outpost, the revival of the Provincetown Playhouse, and the mere presence of Tennessee Williams nurtured Provincetown's artistic culture. Williams, who is rumored to have written part of *The Glass Menagerie* while in Provincetown (at the Atlantic House, according to the late Reginald Cabral, who owned the

"A-House"), drew several aspiring actors, like Marlon Brando and Montgomery Clift, each of whom hoped to secure lead roles in Williams's plays.[6] In 1961, Catherine Huntington, Virginia Thoms, and Ed Thommen organized the Provincetown Theater Playhouse and re-created the artistic environment of the original Provincetown Players by staging some of their early productions. Dozens of less famous but no less important actors, playwrights, set designers, and dancers, like gay wash-ashores Murray Wax and John Carbone, joined Huntington and Provincetown's newest theatrical troupe.[7]

A thriving entertainment culture complemented Provincetown's more formal arts programs. During World War I when Provincetown was still "dry," its reputation as an art colony, Portuguese seaport, colonial village, and salubrious resort was what attracted most of its guests. But by World War II, Land's End had been "wet" for more than a decade and had opened a variety of nightclubs, which, for "modern pilgrims," were even more appealing than its miles of scenic beaches and groups of artists. Provincetown's reputation as one of the liveliest stations on the East Coast's entertainment circuit contributed to its fame, helped along by such nightclub entertainers as Eartha Kitt, Ella Fitzgerald, Stella Brooks, and Billie Holiday playing at Cabral's Carriage Room in the Atlantic House and at Staniford Sorrentino's Crown and Anchor Hotel. Valeska Gert, whom Cabral described as "a wonderful woman . . . totally tanned, her hair cut exactly like a man . . . she was as free as the day is long," also was a hit at the Atlantic House.[8] Comedians like Dom Deloise and Lily Tomlin reportedly made their debuts in Provincetown at the end of this era. Some local historians and artists have argued that Provincetown was now hosting a more talented mix of artists and entertainers than it ever had before or since. According to local artist and art historian Tony Vevers, in the postwar era, artists succeeded in re-creating Hartley's "Great Provincetown Summer of 1916."[9]

Accompanying Provincetown's flourishing "gay" (festive) art world was an equally popular gay (homosexual) world. Provincetown's welcoming Portuguese households, lively art colony, alluring nightclubs, isolated location, and scenic surroundings appealed to thousands of newly liberated and economically flush gay men and lesbians.[10] Publications ranging from the *Provincetown Advocate*, which described the annual artists' costume balls as undeniably "gay," to magazines such as

Man's Conquest portrayed Provincetown as a harbor of sexual and gender possibilities.[11]

Some gay men and lesbians learned of Provincetown's reputation as they walked the streets of Greenwich Village. Others, like Alice Foley, heard about "P-town's" "artistic" climate from "friends of Dorothy." Calling one another "friends of Dorothy," a reference to the *Wizard of Oz*, or "Mary" and using terms like "artistic" to mean gay friendly, were passwords that gay men and lesbians used during this time. Because Provincetown was already known as "artsy" and because onlookers assumed that those people who moved to or simply visited P-town were queer, many closeted gay vacationers often told their parents and straight friends that they were going to less controversial places on Cape Cod like Harwich or Sandwich. In 1997 Foley explained how this worked:

> In 1952 I came down [to Provincetown] more often with friends but we always would tell our parents that we were going to Falmouth, because Falmouth was more acceptable. Provincetown was then pretty much known for being peculiar, a little queer. Falmouth had a boardwalk, like something out of "Happy Days," so it apparently was more appropriate and [it] made more sense for young people to go to Falmouth.[12]

Lenore Ross, Jack Richtman, Pat Shultz, Beverly Spencer, Murray Wax, John Carbone, and Roslyn Garfield were just a few of the gay men and women who had heard of Provincetown through friends, visited there in the postwar era, and remained as wash-ashores.

As did most resort areas at this time, Provincetown enticed tourists with a range of restaurants and clubs. In contrast to establishments in less risqué vacation destinations like Martha's Vineyard or Hyannisport and more like some of New York City's cabaret clubs, Provincetown's nightclubs featured gender transgressive entertainment and catered to tourists of dissimilar ethnic, gender, and sexual backgrounds. The clubs spearheading this entertainment culture included the Weathering Heights Club, the Atlantic House, the Pilgrim House, the Moors Restaurant, and the Townhouse. By the 1950s Provincetown's visiting and native gay men and lesbians had created a gay world at Land's End by inventing an elaborate social ritual organized in and around these establishments. The seasonal and daily—weather permitting—ritual, or "routine," as some residents recently recalled, served to establish Provincetown's gay tourist community in the postwar era, and it continues more than half a century later in the form of the "tea dance" and "after-tea tea" to structure gay leisure time at Land's End. Tourists partaking in the postwar routine found festivities altogether different from what most seaside resorts or hometowns offered.

New Beach, now known as Herring Cove, kicked off the merriment at noon. After a few hours of sun, surf, and, for some, sex, the crowd of mostly white gay men, plus a smattering of straights, "bull-dikes," femmes, and gay men and lesbians of color, began parading at approximately four o'clock from the beach down the road to the Moors Bar and Restaurant (the Moors was located at the west end of Bradford Street; it was sold in 2002 and torn down; now a complex of condominiums stands in its place). A local Portuguese couple, Maline and Naomi Costa (the latter of whom was reputed to have bisexual affairs), owned the Moors. The restaurant offered "authentic" Portuguese kale soup, linguica, lobster rolls, and chowder; employed visiting and native gay men and lesbians; and hosted an elaborate cocktail hour featuring the festive pianist Roger Kent. Kent orchestrated at least one hour of audience participation comedy skits and Broadway show sing-alongs, favorite pastimes of some white gay men who found empowering the fantasy aspects and the homosexual undertones of the theater. At least twice a week, as gay wash-ashore Jack Richtman remembered in 1997, fellow members of the staff or patrons hoisted Kent to the top of his piano where he put on a wide-brimmed straw hat, picked up a long cigarette holder, and sang "torch songs in soprano."[13]

At five o'clock, the revelers made their way down a sandy path (now Shank Painter Road) to the Weathering Heights Club (on the hill across the parking lot from the Grand Union, now a retail store). The infamously "husky" Phil Baoine, a Boston-based "teamster" who was, according to native Napi Van Derek, "as queer as a three dollar bill" or, in today's gay vernacular, "a big queen," owned the Weathering Heights and was also its headline feature.[14] A number of cross-dressing men and women waited on tables and performed as Baoine's "Weathering Knights" while Alice King, whom some have described as a short, stout, Italian "butch," managed the club and at times acted as the emcee. Baoine staged revues like "Christmas in July," delivered female impressions, told jokes after descending into the crowd from the ceiling on something like a trapeze or a large swing, and invited audience members on stage to participate in his skits. As Richtman remembered, "We all crawled up there [to Weathering Heights] . . . it was a place away from everything in a place that was away from everything. So that made it more cozy and wonderful." And Phil Baoine's act, he recalled nostalgically, smacked of "the girl in the velvet swing all covered with tulle again."[15]

A leisurely change of clothes and then dinner typically followed the happy-hour festivities. Some chose Lenore Ross and Pat Shultz's Plain And Fancy Restaurant, which selectively steered gay men and lesbians downstairs while herding straights and families upstairs. Others patronized the Bonnie Doone Restaurant (located where Muscle Beach is today) or the lively Flagship Bar and Restaurant in the East End (now Jackson's). For many gay and lesbian vacationers, however, the night was still young. Nighttime entertainment in the form of black, white, and mixed-race comedians, singers, and female impressionists could be found at the Town House Restaurant and Lounge (now Steve's Alibi); the Madeira Room in the basement of the Pilgrim House (now Vixens); the Carriage Room (now the Macho Room) upstairs at the Atlantic House; and the Crown and Anchor Hotel complex, which had formerly been called the New Central House, the Sea Horse Inn, and the Red Lion. A few smaller bars including the Pilgrim Club, near the Old Colony Tap, and the Ace of Spades, a lesbian hangout that eventually became the Pied Piper, also appealed in the postwar era to a mixed crowd of gays and straights.

For many gay men, though certainly not all, the daily ritual included opportunities for anonymous or semianonymous public sex. Besides capitalizing on Provincetown's acres of sand dunes during the day, after midnight many men looked for sex near the Pilgrim Monument or at a constantly changing but designated area of the bay beach now known as the "dick dock." Others chose to meet friends at one of Provincetown's after-hours cafés like the Hump Inn or Mary Spaghetti's place. The routine even extended into the late morning hours as men and women enjoyed breakfast at the Cottage restaurant, which a local family, the Feltons, had run before their gay son, "Dickie," assumed control. Just before noon the tourists headed back to New Beach to watch, among other things, the Weathering Knights, who carried Baoine over the dunes on a "litter" before ceremoniously tossing him into the surf: "He'd be covered in tulle all flowing and everything," Richtman recalled, "like something out of 'Pricilla, Queen of the

Desert'. . . and of course everyone would scream."[16] In this way, the clubs and their inhabitants acted like moving theaters of celebration, performing layer upon layer of rituals within rituals: the ritual of the secular pilgrimage to Provincetown, the ritual of club hopping, the ritual of Baoine tossed into the surf, and the ritual of Kent conducting sing-alongs, to name but a few.

Rather than catering exclusively to white gay men and lesbian tourists, as many entertainers in Provincetown do today, the postwar gender impressionists (now known as female impersonators), comediennes, singers, and ventriloquists performed for a diverse audience of both guests and residents. In other words, they created the conditions in which likely and unlikely bedfellows came together. Provincetown's gay and straight residents and visitors of mixed racial, ethnic, and class backgrounds fondly remember impressionists such as Arthur Blake, Craig Russell, Whalen Flowers (and his ventriloquist dummy, Madam), Phil Baoine, and Lynne Carter.[17]

Mary "Lil" Russe recalled in 1997 that her husband, John, a Portuguese fishermen, found time to visit Phil Baoine and even sat on his lap during one of the shows.[18] A Provincetown native, Anthony Joseph, remembered in 1998 that his mother, who warned him to stay away from effeminate, kerchief-wearing men, was nonetheless fond of Baoine.[19] And Florence Alexander, whose parents rarely went out for entertainment, admitted in 1996 that they went with their two gay tenants, who worked at the Weathering Heights, to a show there and had the time of their lives. Alexander's memories capture some of the magic:

> We used to have a Weathering Heights years ago on Shank Painter Road. . . . And Phil Baoine owned the Weathering Heights. Oh, he was a good husky man. And he would sit in the middle of the room on a swing, and he would swing and tell jokes and wear great big hats. Well, the waiters, they were gay, they lived upstairs in mom's house. . . . I took my mother and my father up to Weathering Heights. The two boys made a reservation. It was their anniversary. And Phil Baoine kept telling jokes. They were on a good side and they were a little on the raw side and, oh my father and my mother, they laughed that whole night long. Said that was the best time they ever had up there. So I'm glad we took them up. Because they never did go out much.[20]

The artists' costume balls and female impressionists inspired some straight Portuguese and Irish natives to stage their own "gay" events, in this case a wedding. Photograph courtesy of Ruth O'Donnell.

Provincetown native Marguerite "Beata" Cook played two roles: first, she offered to take fellow townsfolk to the clubs. "'Hey, you know that wasn't quite so bad, we should do this more often,'" they often confessed to her afterward. Second, in the clubs she often represented the "natives" to intrigued visitors: "Nobody [in the clubs] could believe someone was born and brought up here," Cook noted. At times she considered doing some kind of "native dance" when she noticed tourists pointing at her while whispering, "She's a native, you know."[21] Like its Portuguese-owned boardinghouses, Provincetown's clubs encouraged interactions between gay and straight visitors and townspeople.

While much of postwar America was struggling with McCarthyism and gender roles spelled out by mainstream media programs like *Leave It to Beaver*, in Provincetown's cabaret clubs a different set of hierarchies prevailed. Instead of incessant censure, gay men and lesbians enjoyed themselves unselfconsciously, at least for a short time, in a contained space.[22]

The carnival-like shows featured gender transgressors who performed impressions of masculinity and femininity with such vigor, grace, and style that townspeople and vacationers of all sexual orientations and backgrounds paid to see them at a time when gender irregularities were under attack. In part because it was illegal at the time, the impressionists did not cross-dress, as many drag queens do today, but instead focused on giving the impression rather than the appearance of a woman. Although Arthur Blake did not wear women's clothes, he had the ability, Murray Wax reminisced in 1997, "to make you think of Marlene Dietrich with a smile . . . or Marilyn Monroe with a gesture."[23] Typically, female impressionists negotiated the illegality of opposite-sex costuming by donning a simple "piece of tulle" such as a hat or scarf, which was enough to transform the performer, however momentarily, into the gender of his or her making. The cabaret spaces and performances sanctioned these gender transgressions while providing a specific site where diverse members of Provincetown's visiting and resident communities came together. By delivering impressions of masculinity and femininity, female impressionists re-created the artistic tradition of gender bending that earlier queers in Provincetown, such as Marsden Hartley, had inaugurated.

Transgressions in Provincetown's nightclubs assumed several forms. The Atlantic House, in particular, challenged racial boundaries by inviting entertainers of color who performed there for gendered and racially mixed audiences. Gay men and occasionally lesbians transgressed constructed gender boundaries by performing what it meant to be a man or a woman at the time, thereby calling into question the stability of gender ideals. Spectators crossed the boundaries between queer visitors and native residents by attending and participating in the impressionists' alternative gender performances.

Strategically, gender impressionists in Provincetown based their performances on humor in order to reconcile their appearances in a potentially homophobic environment and a clearly homophobic era. Humor was one way in which the impersonators could mitigate or explicate in a comical way the anxieties around gender and sexual transgressions, which delighted some and threatened others. "Camp humor" as anthropologist Esther Newton explains, "ultimately grows out of the incongruities and absurdities of the patriarchal nuclear family . . . camp humor is a system of laughing at one's incongruous position instead of crying. . . . [T]he humor does not cover up, it transforms."[24] Gay men and lesbians who were part of Provincetown's entertainment culture used camp humor to build community by making space at Land's End for semipublic forums that appreciated rather than condemned transgressive gender behavior.

Even though impressionists used these sites to connect with diverse audiences and to showcase alternative gender expressions, at the same time their performances confirmed the very gender boundaries that they intended to question. By masquerading ideals of femininity— "proving" that even in male garb men can be as or more feminine than women—impressionists were questioning the absurdity of strict gender categories. They also, however, reestablished gender ideals by reminding Provincetown's gay and straight guests that effeminacy ultimately belonged to women ("real" or otherwise) and not men.[25]

Despite the popularity of Provincetown's nightclubs and gender impressionists, Land's End still had its share of residents and tourists who took offense at these gay-affirming places and performers. For the most part, up until 1949, they either kept their frustrations to themselves, or they harassed gay men at night when most of the town was sleeping soundly. But in 1949 a confluence of local and national factors, including an increasingly noticeable gay community and an increasingly reactive and conservative political culture, tipped Provincetown's moral guard beyond its previous threshold of tolerance.

Outside journalists and tourists were the first to turn Provincetown's rampant gender bending into headline news. In 1949, for instance, *Mademoiselle* magazine claimed that Provincetown was "so full of phonies in July and August that it . . . had to pass an ordinance forbidding men to masquerade in women's clothes."[26] Outside interpretations like this one, which questioned the very existence of manhood in Provincetown, prompted the *Provincetown Advocate* to defend its native men: "A person unfamiliar with the town might gather from this that impersonation is a widely practiced habit here while most of us will contend that the bipeds who can honestly be called men make no pretense at being anything else."[27] At Land's End, masculinity, once measured by the kind of labor one performed, could now be proved more simply with gender-appropriate clothing and behavior.

Paul C. Ryan of the *Worcester* (Massachusetts) *Telegram* provided another example of postwar panic.[28] Ryan's 1949 piece "Provincetown 'Boys: a Problem" illuminated for western Massachusetts and the surrounding areas the gender sensibilities, ineffectual policing tactics, and welcoming attitudes that one might find at Land's End. Ryan first congratulated eastern Massachusetts for having a successful summer season and then stated that Provincetown claimed to offer "quaintness, old dwellings, the sand dunes and sea," which attract "legitimate artist[s] and art student[s]." Yet it is also, he maintained, "with this backdrop that P-Towners have found an increasing number of 'tourists' who flock into the town in early Summer and attempt to give the place a little 'atmosphere.' These 'boys' as the townies call them, are somewhat of a problem." The boardinghouses, which make up a significant portion of the business community, cannot agree on whether or not to house gay men, and "local enforcement officials cannot cope with the situation until some of the 'boys' get into trouble. Then they are heaved out of town. But for every two that go, two more appear." Ryan concluded by lampooning (and revealing) parts of the well-worn gay routine: "It is only after dark that the freak parade starts. The 'boys' flutter along Commercial Street to their various evening entertainment spots or snake along in their brightly colored convertibles to beach parties. Zebra-striped seat covers were in vogue this year for the open cars." After this brief description, he added, "Labor Day weekend was the season's climax. Out at New Beach the 'boys' held their annual 'convention' or mass beach party and more than 300 showed up for the affair. Everyone entertained."[29] Far from portraying Provincetown's gay vacationers as self-loathing inverts—as many writers, sexologists, and psychiatrists were apt to do at the time—Ryan's column instead revealed the resilient and fun-loving nature of Provincetown's postwar gay community.

The "boys problem" soon escalated into a battle between Portuguese and Yankee elected officials, police officers, conservative residents, and clergymen intending to rid Provincetown of its "boys" and Portuguese and Yankee residents and business owners (some of whom were gay) hoping to profit from Provincetown's popularity with a largely solvent subculture. Although some business owners despised most gay men and lesbians, and some elected officials and clergymen were sympathetic to them, for the most part, relationships of authority and dissent fell along these lines.

To bridge this rift and regain some semblance of social control, Police Chief William N. Rogers criticized those chamber of commerce business owners who employed "boys" and who "provide[d] them with quarters and [were] not loath to provide them with congregating places."[30] In December 1950 Rogers asked the chamber to support a stricter set of town bylaws so that law enforcement officials could more effectively prosecute the "exhibitionists" who, he argued, behaved in Provincetown as they would not dare to do in their own hometowns. Chamber president and Portuguese native Joseph E. Macara echoed Rogers's plea and explained how complicated the terms of local morality and normality had become:

> Each season . . . the number of "The Boys" continues to increase . . . and the abnormal actions of many become more public and brazen with the result that more and more normal people turn away from the town in disgust. . . . The problem will be difficult to handle, but it must be met and solved before the summer trade of the town is seriously damaged and before some climax in abnormality occurs.[31]

Two months later, in February 1951, the *Provincetown Advocate* responded to the chamber's concerns by rousing Cape Tip's hibernating residents and comparing their hometown to a guardian beast battling the evils of gender immorality. In an article entitled "The 'Queer' Question," it warned: "Sometime, and the sooner the better, Provincetown will have to take between its paws a somewhat baffling and knotty problem. The problem isn't pretty, pleasant or wholesome. But it is definitely with us." The "Queer Question" elaborated on "the problem" by deferring to an anonymous (and, in retrospect, highly suspicious) letter from "a patron of long standing who [was] a physician in Deep River, Connecticut." Apparently the Connecticut physician had informed Ralph C. Carpenter, a Yankee native, owner of Delft Haven Cottages, and a member of the board of selectmen, that he and his wife, "with regret," must cancel their trip to Land's End. The town and Carpenter's West End resort complex were "perfect vacation spot[s]," the physician conceded. But "the swarming numbers of 'queer boys' . . . [who] flood all over our favorite eating spots . . . cavort around Long Nook Beach, [and] almost fill the walks in Provincetown" had persuaded them to vacation elsewhere.[32]

By the following year, the board of selectmen had agreed on a set of regulations meant to rid Land's End not of all gay men or lesbians but of the more flamboyant and visible gender transgressors. "Selectmen Clamp Down on Gay Spots with New Regulations to Curb Evils," the *Provincetown Advocate* declared in June 1952. "Determined to raise the standards of Cape End places . . . [and to] eliminate objectionable features which have been on the increase in recent years," the selectmen hand-delivered the regulations to each licensed liquor establishment. The new provisions insisted that "no licensee shall employ or allow to perform on the licensed premises any so-called female impersonators, nor employ, cater to, or encourage the licensed premises to become the habitual gathering place for homo-sexuals of either sex."[33] Other rules attempted to ferret out obscene or suggestive language and dancing in ill-lit spaces, and some prohibited the presence of intoxicated persons and female bartenders. Throughout the 1950s, the selectmen and Provincetown's new chief of police, Francis "Cheney" Marshall, rewrote the regulations to better reflect statewide liquor license measures. In addition to the restrictions already mentioned, the revisions demanded that licensed establishments post a police officer on the premises and required all nonresidents wishing to work to register with the police department.[34]

Outside journalists, no doubt influenced by the ripple effects of McCarthyism, were quick to congratulate Provincetown on its homophobic regulations. Indeed, the "ten commandments," as residents referred to them, made Land's End the topic of endless discussion. In June 1952 the *Boston Traveler* applauded Provincetown for giving its "undesirables" a "swift . . . kick in the pants" and challenged other Cape towns to do the same to avoid the "unsavory mess" and economic "damage that was done to Provincetown." "It was Provincetown's own fault," the editorial proclaimed, for allowing "female impersonators" to drive "away the solid middle-class vacationists who didn't want themselves or their children exposed to embarrassing sidewalk scenes." "Now," it stated joyfully, "The selectmen have picked up the soap and gave [*sic*] the town a bath." The ten new regulations approved in June 1952, the article concluded, bar female impersonators from performing and "prohibit the 'habitual gathering' of homosexuals in any *restaurant, bar or club.*"[35] As the *Boston Traveler* disclosed, many journalists and "solid middle-class vacationists" demonized homosexuals as "undesirable" dirty guests who—no matter what their race, income, or parental status —were barred from the "solid middle class" because according to some vacationers, their gender and sexual transgressions soiled resort towns and their establishments.

The *Provincetown Advocate*'s decision to reprint the *Boston Traveler* article, entitled "Provincetown Cleans House," convinced some residents that the "ten commandments" would save Land's End, yet it persuaded others to register their outrage. On June 19, 1952, S. Osborn Ball commented on the absurdity of the selectmen's regulations and pointed out the influence of McCarthyism. Referring to "the recent ordinance issues from the local White House re: homosexuals," Ball argued that the regulations appeared to be unconstitutional and impossible to prove. He then reminded the readers of the unjust rationale fueling this hatred by offering comparable suggestions for "the local McCarthys to chew upon." He mused, "How about a little Blue-Eyed Boy ordinance? All it will say is that no club can hire, nor encourage to congregate, any lads with blue eyes, nor any lads even suspected of having blue eyes." The police caught one such blue-eyed boy exceeding the speed limit just last year, he teased, so we "can't afford to turn blue-eyed boys loose on the town, folks." Other "snappy little ordinance[s]," Ball suggested, might include one denying all women access to bars because "dames mix them up," even though "every one of them lead[s] the community in respectability."[36] Two weeks later, L. A. Martin used the regulations to question Provincetown's reputation as a birthplace of democracy: "If that [the ten commandments] is an example of the cleaning up you are advertising, it is no wonder the Pilgrims left for Plymouth."[37]

Business owners also resisted the regulations by refusing to police gender and sexual morality in their establishments. Beata Cook remembered in 1997 that one of her relatives, Friday Cook, who owned a popular local bar called Cookies Tap, was aghast at the selectmen's audacity even to propose the "ten commandments." The general attitude of most natives, she recalled, was that the regulations were "ridiculous" and "crazy."[38] This probably was especially true for local entrepreneurs who fit into one of the following categories: those who behaved or identified as gender or sexual nonconformists, those who had close friends or relatives who were gender or sexual nonconformists, and those whose clientele was made up primarily of tourists and natives who were gender or sexual nonconformists.

Confronted with this widespread resistance, local officials changed their tactics slightly—from decreeing to cajoling—when they appealed next to God-fearing "decent" residents. In August 1952, in a formal letter entitled "An Appeal to All Decent People in the Town of Provincetown," selectmen Frank Barnett, William White, and Ralph Carpenter made an impassioned, Christian-based, homophobic plea:

> We can no longer say "it can't happen here." It has and we are at this moment overrun with a throng of men described by Archbishop Cushing as "the lowest form of animal life." Unbelievable as it may seem, they have their friends, defenders, and supporters among our own people.

Portuguese women house them; "night club operators cater to them." We need everyone's help, they pleaded, to eliminate the "nests where the homosexuals congregate" to succeed in "this crusade."[39]

To be sure, many residents, local clergymen in particular, stood behind and probably helped draft the selectmen's "appeal," but a critical mass of natives, wash-ashores, and entrepreneurs disregarded it and instead issued their own ideas about decency and democracy. Before business owners could articulate these ideas, however, the selectmen made one last attempt to exert their power by using their capacity as the local licensing board to shut down at least one of the "nests where homosexuals congregate." One of the first establishments under attack was the Ace of Spades, which the selectmen closed temporarily in 1952. Eight years later, the selectmen targeted Phil Baoine and his Weathering Heights Club. In 1960 the board of selectmen refused to renew Baoine's seasonal victualler's license, which he had held for more than a decade, because, they contended, the application was one month late. Although Baoine's application had been late before and other applications also were tardy, the board saw fit to put only Baoine out of business.[40]

The heated debate over the Weathering Heights, its owner, and its patrons illustrates two important points: first, the degree to which the purity crusade swept over Provincetown and, second, the ways in which residents stood apart rather than together in the face of local moral panic. At two hearings, one late in May and the climactic one on July 18, 1960, more than three hundred townspeople and visitors came together to debate the Weathering Heights, Phil Baoine, and Provincetown's claims to morality. On one side stood the local officials led by Police Chief Marshall; clergymen such as the Reverend James Mott of the Universalist Church, Reverend Leo Duarte, and Reverend Thomas Mayhew, both of St. Peter's Church; prominent Yankee businessmen like John Van Arsdale and Ralph Carpenter; plus dozens of local Portuguese residents "vigorously opposed" to granting Baoine a new license. They agreed that nothing less than Provincetown's reputation and tourist industry, were at stake. They argued that places like the Weathering Heights polluted an otherwise pure Provincetown, that its clientele was undesirable, and that Baoine and his establishment were antithetical to the moral guard of Land's End.

Irving T. McDonald insisted that the club had a "certain reputation" for a type of "patron" to which it catered. "If we get rid of [these] undesirables," he urged, "we'll get the type of people that will more than compensate for the [economic] losses . . . it's time we cleaned up this town with a new and desirable class of people." I am not, he pleaded, "a Puritan or a prude," but Provincetown must not "see [its] birthplace for a mess of porridge."[41] Captain Joseph Roderick added that the sooner this club vanished, the better, and Custodio Silva claimed that he went to the Weathering Heights once, but "it turned my stomach in ten minutes." Finally, Father Duarte invoked God to argue that Provincetown's moral good was at stake in this decision and that if the board of selectmen did not deny this license, he would take it upon himself to summon his own moral militia. "I am opposing it because laws have not been complied with . . . because we don't know who the club members are . . . and for moral reasons—not that we haven't any [clubs] that may be worse. This would be a good step forward in eliminating these dregs of humanity."[42] In the end, nearly sixty townsfolk opposed granting Baoine a new license.

The other side, which included Yankee and Portuguese business owners, stood up for Baoine as a good citizen and cried foul at the selectmen's unjust treatment. Baoine's attorney, James Langan of Boston, countered the local patriarchs by arguing that "it was un-Christian-like to point the finger" at Baoine.[43] Baoine, Langan argued, had not violated a single regulation and had run his club properly. Thirty-three townspeople, including, but not limited to, Naomi Costa of the Moors, June Getzler of the Town House Lounge, Peter Hand, Mrs. Paul Smith of the Provincetown Bookstore, Mrs. Norman Cook of Adams Pharmacy, Sonny Tasha, and John Papetsas, turned out to approve granting

Baoine the license. Catherine Cummings spoke for many when she admitted that the Weathering Heights Club was perhaps the "least offensive and more orderly of [all] the places in town."[44] The ruins of the Weathering Heights building that stood abandoned on Shank Painter Road for half a century reminded onlookers that the postwar moral militia defeated Baoine, his admirers, his manager, and his Weathering Knights.

The selectmen made Weathering Heights a scapegoat in their efforts to impose order on Provincetown's increasingly unwieldy summer season and to punish the institutions that had encouraged Provincetown's gay routine. Baoine was an easy target. Most nightclub owners were either straight, like Maline Costa of the Moors, or one of "our queers," like Reggie Cabral of the A-House. Most owners, in other words, enjoyed a certain amount of native privilege and protection, especially in regard to the selectmen's policing tactics. To be sure, law enforcement officials raided Reggie's A-House nearly every decade from the 1950s through the 1990s and, on several occasions, suspended his liquor license. In 1977 the selectmen even tried to revoke his license altogether because of reports of public sex and sex discrimination (refusing to let women enter).[45] But Baoine had arrived in Provincetown with two strikes already against him: he was neither straight nor one of our queers. In what became his third and final strike, Baoine snubbed the local economy and bought all his supplies in Boston, thus refusing to assimilate economically.[46] Such blatant disregard of small-town politics sealed his fate.

One week after the Weathering Heights Club closed, a group of summer business owners petitioned the board of selectmen to cease its "arbitrary and discriminating nature of the delay and denial of business licenses" because they pretended to know "what is good for Provincetown." In their formal petition, which the *Provincetown Advocate* reprinted on July 28, 1960, they explained that their concern lay not necessarily with standards of morality but with the "effect that possible closings and future denials will have on the prospects of Provincetown as a resort town." "Provincetown," the petition continued, "is no longer a comfortable place to vacation and is quickly becoming also uninteresting and even annoying . . . as it becomes less comfortable and less interesting and less entertaining, our 'summer people' also become less." If the summer people—meaning gays and lesbians—depart, they explained, the only guests who will remain are the frugal "transient tourists," those residents once called the "boat people." The business owners agreed "to deliver justice to an individual who is persistently offensive is democratic; [but to] select a business or attack a group and cause economic suicide are other questions." If the board persisted on its path of arbitrary policing, businesses would suffer irreparable damage, the townspeople would lose jobs, vacationers would go elsewhere, and "a great deal of [the] color and quality that bring the summer source of income into this town" would be lost. Only "Coney-Island seekers and beatnik viewers" would make time for Provincetown, they assured.[47]

In no uncertain terms, these business owners pressured local officials into looking the other way when it came to Provincetown's gay visitors, and in so doing, they disabled the local purity campaign. The owner of the Provincetown Bookstore, Paul Smith, spoke for many entrepreneurs when he argued in 1960 that first, his business nearly always reflected the general economic climate in Provincetown and, second, this year, because of the selectmen's arbitrary policing, business was down 22 percent from last year. Total sales had not been this low since 1955, he observed, and sales for the week ending July 16 were down more than 33 percent and were the worst since 1954.[48]

Indeed, although some scholars today contend that beginning in the 1990s, corporate America realized that the profits to be made from gay and lesbian consumers outweighed the consequences of marketing to them, Provincetown's socioeconomic history suggests that this trend began in some places at least four decades earlier.[49] According to the economist Thorstein Veblen, "The basis on which good repute in any highly organized industrial community ultimately rests is pecuniary strength, and the means of showing pecuniary strength, and so of gaining or retaining a good name are leisure and a conspicuous consumption of goods."[50]

But even when the local business community was fighting on behalf of gay and lesbian rights to Provincetown, it was met with resistance. Individuals and groups of townspeople supported the selectmen, clergy, and police for designating boundaries of decency and morality at Land's End. Thomas Hennessey, a former Provincetown schoolteacher, congratulated the selectmen on their recent efforts to "improve the moral atmosphere of the Town and . . . requested [that they] continue their 'moral clean-up program.'" He claimed that he left Provincetown because of the "miserable moral climate" that the town was forcing on young children as it accepted money in its right hand while attempting to sustain "principles" in its left. "We have cleaned our streets, we have whitewashed our homes, we have scoured our town administration," Hennessey bragged. "Is it not too optimistic that each of us now will sterilize our minds by a return to those moral maxims so vital to a stable society?"[51] Jessica Lema of the Committee for the Preservation of Provincetown spoke out against, among other things, granting Phil Baoine a new license, and the Knights of Columbus made a point of commending the police force for its summer policing tactics.[52] Some residents, such as beach taxi driver Mathew Costa, even called for an increase in policing, especially in the area of the dunes between Wood End Lighthouse and New Beach (Herring Cove) where gay men, according to Costa, exposed themselves in "unnatural" ways and engaged in "disgusting scene[s]."[53] Gay men, they all agreed, corrupted native and visiting children as well as entire families.

In addition to institutionalized policing, gay men and, to a lesser extent, lesbians were subject to various forms of informal policing. Undoubtedly, ambivalent and hostile feelings toward the gay men and lesbians who frequented Provincetown appeared not only in court rooms and selectmen's meetings but also on Provincetown's streets. As Mathew Costa and other natives complained when gay men capitalized on Provincetown's sandy dunes to fulfill their sexual desires, local teenage boys and policemen attempted to curtail overtly gay appearances and actions on and near Commercial Street.

In the postwar era, native teenage boys continued the adolescent rite of passage, which their fathers and uncles had invented in the 1930s, of harassing flamboyant men and men who propositioned them. In August 1949 the *Provincetown Advocate* reported on a "gang crime wave" made up of local boys who harassed, robbed, and assaulted male tourists. Some residents also admitted recently that when they were teenagers in the 1950s and 1960s, they hurled bricks at the windshields of gay men's cars.[54]

Local and state police officers also harassed gay men for congregating on Commercial Street. Jack Richtman, who first visited Provincetown in 1952 and moved there decades later, found that after the war, Fire Island was nearly completely "gay," and there "you could just be anything you wanted . . . [but] Provincetown was not open to that and very scary at times and you could be arrested in the streets."[55] Similarly, Murray Wax remembered in 1997 that the postwar era in Provincetown "was not a time of real open-ness." On one occasion, the police approached him and some fellow gay men and lesbians, who had congregated spontaneously near town hall for a brief conversation, and demanded that they "move along." "This is not Nazi Germany," he complained to his boss, the well-known and influential Provincetown Theater director Catherine Huntington, "and I demand a formal apology."[56] Huntington secured that apology and in so doing helped set in motion processes of redress, or systems of protection, for gay men and lesbians who had been harassed. Indeed, almost as soon as gay men and lesbians stopped cowering and instead demanded the right to feel safe in Provincetown, influential townspeople went out of their way to protect them.

Like the local reactions to the "ten commandments" and the selectmen's "appeal," Provincetown's residents were quick to voice their disagreement over Provincetown's postwar police state. A series of letters to the editor and editorials in the *Provincetown Advocate* in 1953, for example, decried the "overpolicing" and "Gestapo" atmosphere of Provincetown's summer season. "A patron of one place reports that during a twenty-minute stay in one Cape End club three pairs of armed cops made their rounds of the place," one editorial reported. "He got up and left. Wouldn't you? In another place, after six visits by the police, 24 people decided it wasn't the spot for them, and departed." Another "plea to the police" stated: "To the Guardians in Blue: Do you realize that if this unnecessary nonsense continues and the town becomes a memory of the past that every one of the townspeople you are supposed to be protecting you will be hurting?"[57]

During the postwar era, white gay men and lesbians, backed by Portuguese and Yankee residents of all sexual orientations, queered Land's End. They did so by creating a thriving gay world there that celebrated rather than demonized gender and sexual alternatives during a time when gay celebrations were prosecutable offenses. In this way they took risks and put job and housing security aside to challenge the behavioral constraints that saturated much of postwar America.

Provincetown's postwar politics resembled and differed from those elsewhere. When the climate beyond Provincetown turned increasingly hostile toward gays and lesbians in the postwar era—when they became known as "un-Americans" elsewhere—in Provincetown they fought back as consumers of safe spaces and as what Liz Cohen calls "purchasers as citizens." The purchaser as citizen was "a consumer satisfying personal material wants [who] actually served the national interests, since economic recovery after a decade and a half of depression and war depended on a dynamic mass consumption economy."[58] Without question, gay men and lesbians were not recognized by mainstream markets or politics in the United States during this era as purchasers or citizens, but in Provincetown they were. In Provincetown they queered spaces that were primarily straight. And when some townspeople responded to a greater queer presence by attempting to control flamboyant "boys" through a well-staged purity campaign, other townspeople, recognizing their dependence on a mass gay market, thwarted their more conservative neighbors' efforts. In the end, financial success outweighed questions of morality.

While tracing this economically liberating moment in time, at least two factors stand out as problematic. First, racism continued to linger at Land's End as residents produced blackface minstrel shows well into the 1950s despite letters to the *Provincetown Advocate* that explained how these performances perpetuated racist ideologies. Indeed, Edward Roach published his letters in 1949, the same year Paul C. Ryan exposed Provincetown's "boys problem." The concurrent articulation of both race and gender concerns at Provincetown during the postwar era begs the question of why residents and visitors challenged gender and sexual constraints while letting racism continue without a similarly prolonged and vigorous debate. Eleven years after Roach published his objections, two African American tourists complained that they had been kicked out of a guesthouse because they were black. And at about the same time, Barbara "Mae Bush" Stevens organized a picket at a local eatery that refused to serve black patrons.[59] Second, and related to the first, are the unforeseen socioeconomic effects of this particular queering process, which ushered in displacements that led to, among other things, the re-creation of a racialized, foreign-born working class and the reproduction of a gender imbalance.

PART III

GENTRIFYING PROVINCETOWN, 1970–2000

> Here, at land's end, in the superb setting of this landscape, our gems are rich possibilities of human love, human pleasures, the splendid diversity and sameness of our longings. It is a place worthy of pilgrimage, where the elements arrange, as they conjoin, small tableaux of miracle and reversal. —Mark Doty, *Heaven's Coast: A Memoir*, 1996

DIANE CORBO began her "love affair" with Provincetown in 1970. From her desk as the director of Provincetown's Council on Aging, she recalled in 1997: "In the seventies it was definitely hippies, a lot of flower children, a lot of sleeping right downtown and camping. . . . The predominant people were artists and 'beatniks' of the sixties and hippies from the seventies, the remains of the beatniks, more into hippies then."[1] According to Corbo, these groups were in constant "crossover with gay people and they had great places to go here for gay people." Some of those places were the Atlantic House, the Crown and Anchor, and the Town House, establishments that were patronized primarily by men. But women carved out spaces for themselves as well, like the Ace of Spaces, owned first by a local father-daughter team, John and Frances Atkins, before lesbian wash-ashore Pam Genevrino and her partner, Linda Gerard, took over. Corbo remembers meeting, in the Ace of Spades, the "first wave" of lesbians, many of whom, like those elsewhere in the country, adopted butch or femme personas. Roslyn Garfield, Pat Shultz, Lenore Ross, Beverly Spencer, Alice Foley, Sandra Rich, Betty Villari, "Mae Bush" Stevens, Anne Kane, Phyllis Schlosberg, and Terri Vorelli, all of whom found Provincetown in or shortly after the postwar era, formed the nucleus of this first wave. Lesbians like Diane Corbo, arriving in the 1970s and 1980s, used the language of the women's liberation movement and thus became the "second wave."

Corbo moved to Provincetown for two reasons. First, she depended on Land's End as an escape from the pressures of working with terminally ill patients in the oncology and intensive care units at Yale University Hospital in New Haven, Connecticut. Second, she found comfort in Provincetown's acceptance of nonconforming people. Corbo's first connection with Provincetown bordered on the spiritual. "It was really very refreshing and renewing to me," she explained, "and being able to walk the beach any time of the day or night and find solitude and peacefulness really helped me in my work. I'd go back rejuvenated and I'd be able to continue." Regarding the second reason, Corbo put it this way: "My romance was with this Portuguese fishing village and those people are so wonderful and warm and they embrace—they get along from past to present with the beatniks, the hippies, and the gay people." After going to Provincetown on weekends, holidays, and summers for more than a decade, Corbo and her partner, Valerie Carrano, an epidemiologist doing research at Yale, finally decided in 1983 to buy a home of their own at Land's End.

In order to survive Provincetown's mercurial seasonal economy, Corbo and Carrano did what generations of maiden ladies and Portuguese women had done before them. They started a number of moneymaking enterprises and reconfigured their home at 462 Commercial Street into a house for boarders. Before becoming financially independent at Land's End, however, Corbo relied on assistance from her mother and uncle, both of whom became partners with Corbo in buying the house that soon became the Ravenwood Guesthouse. During the 1983 season, Corbo ran the guesthouse while Carrano continued to work in New Haven. Together, Corbo reminisced, they "took whatever jobs they could to pay the bills."

By 1984 Corbo and Carrano had devised a financial plan that would allow both of them to live year-round at Land's End. The plan included running the guesthouse as well as a restaurant and a pub. The latter, known as the Pub Down Under, featured the then-new Foster's ale and was located at 179 Commercial Street (now the Szechuan Chinese Restaurant). The more successful of the two was their restaurant, Snug Harbor, which was located at 157 Commercial Street (currently the Martin House). In order to buy and run Snug Harbor, Corbo and Carrano brought in as partners a gay male couple, Ted Alexander and John Mercer, with whom they had worked before, during summer seasons at Vorelli's restaurant. Together, they had plenty of experience: Alexander and Mercer had been fine-dining waiters in New Orleans; Corbo's father and grandfather owned successful restaurants in Connecticut; Carrano came from a "three-generation restaurant family"; and Corbo and Carrano had had a restaurant called the Eleven Forty Cafe on Chapel Street in New Haven. In its first years, Snug Harbor was a smashing success. Corbo remembers the long waiting lines even when they accepted reservations. Although they catered to local patrons from Provincetown, Truro, and Wellfleet, the bulk of their clientele were gay men who arrived in droves from the establishment next door, the Boatslip Motor Inn.

The foursome that owned Snug Harbor demonstrate how gay men and lesbians often worked together in Provincetown. To be sure, gay men and lesbians also worked and played in sex-segregated groups. Corbo and others have referred to this as the "quiet rift between gay men and lesbians at Land's End." In the 1970s and early 1980s, Corbo noted, "the gay guys and older queens didn't want to be bothered with the dykes and lesbians," and vice versa. But under certain conditions, the rift vanished. Indeed, native, wash-ashore, and seasonal "townies" of all sexual and gender orientations labored side by side in most restaurants, clubs, and retail establishments. They also socialized together after work or on their few days off, by visiting friends tending bar, holding private after-hours parties, or spending the day in some remote part of Long Point. Gay men were more than happy to patronize establishments owned by lesbians, such as the Plain And Fancy Restaurant, Snug Harbor, Town House Lounge, and Post Office Café (the last two owned by Phyllis Schlosberg and Betty Newman), and lesbians often joined the gay "routine" that featured female impressionists and sing-alongs and, later, drag queens and tea dances. Also, in times of crisis, gay men and lesbians created new kinds of partnerships. Corbo described how this took place.

"We had a good business," she explained sadly, "and then AIDS hit. And it hit hard." According to Corbo, the onset of AIDS put fear into at least two kinds of tourists: straight visitors, who were "afraid they were going to catch the 'unknown virus' from the toilets and from the forks coming out of the kitchens," and gay male vacationers, who "stopped coming to Provincetown for a while because they were afraid they would relax with their health precautions and they didn't want to be promiscuous." For Corbo and hundreds of other Provincetown residents of all sexual, ethnic, and class backgrounds, the AIDS crisis meant not only that businesses would suffer but, worse, that friends, partners, and family members would die. "It didn't take long for it to hit really close to home," admitted Corbo, "and that was my partner, Teddy, and he was gone in three months." Although Snug Harbor began losing money, keeping the restaurant open was particularly important to John Mercer because his health insurance was attached to the business. When Mercer died of AIDS two years later in 1991, Corbo and Carrano sold Snug Harbor to Glen Martin, who had been working for them as a waiter.

Resting easily did not figure into Corbo's survival strategy for her dream to live at Land's End. While running Snug Harbor and tending to Ravenwood, which were busiest during the summer, Corbo landed one of the few year-round jobs working for the local government. Using her expertise in medicine, Corbo worked for three years for the town of Provincetown as a town nurse. Provincetown already had one town nurse, Alice Foley, whose job had become consumed by AIDS work. Corbo joined Foley and managed Provincetown's remaining health needs, from newborn home care visits to blood pressure clinics for the elderly. It was here that Corbo established herself in public health as a trusted nurse for Provincetown's senior native and wash-ashore populations. When the municipal job to direct the Council on Aging opened up in 1990, several of Corbo's elderly Portuguese clients encouraged her to apply. Corbo was the director of the Council on Aging until 2001, at which time Carrano, who had been working in the public health office, took over.

Another, but by no means the last, hand that Corbo played in Provincetown pertained to her involvement in the now well-known organization called the Women Innkeepers of Provincetown. When Corbo established Ravenwood, it was a somewhat lonely time for her and other women guesthouse owners. She was new to the industry, baked muffins at 5:00 A.M. for breakfast, washed sheets well into the afternoon and evening, and did what she referred to as the round-the-clock "Provincetown dance" of nonstop work during the summer season. She knew a few other women who owned rental properties or guesthouses, and her hope was to seek them out for the purpose of friendship and community. She also hoped they might help her figure out where to buy soap and other supplies; she wanted to network with other women business owners; and, not least, she wanted new women friends. The first women guesthouse owners of whom Corbo was aware were Marge Betzold, who since 1975 had been running the Gull Walk Inn, and Gabriel Brooke, who in 1979 had started construction on the condemned building now known as Gabriel's.

Corbo's memories of Brooke are charming and telling. With a warm smile on her face, Corbo recalled, "I thought to myself, this must be a nutcase woman that would buy this house with a tree growing right in the middle, a tree so big that you and I could not see each other. And the whole house was like on a tilt." A few days after Brooke's purchase Corbo walked by and noticed a sign that said in effect: "Live here, work here." Brooke had organized a women's commune of sorts in order to renovate the building and open Provincetown's first "full service" guesthouse exclusively for women. "She was a trend setter, she really was," Corbo observed, even though she remembers being deeply "intimidated" by Brooke. According to Corbo's version of the beginning of the Women Innkeepers, she invited a small group of "women property owners" to her house for coffee but buckled under her fear of Brooke and neglected to invite her. Although Brooke happened to be away that month, she heard about the gathering and simply assumed that she had been invited. Brooke held the second meeting at Gabriel's, and from then on, the Women Innkeepers flourished.

Corbo's narrative of business and personal relationships at Land's End fits into three larger histories. The first concerns the AIDS crisis; the second reflects the steady increase of women entrepreneurs nationwide; and the third pertains to trends in gentrification, consumption, and citizenship. By 1985, just one year after Corbo and her partners opened Snug Harbor, twelve thousand men in the United States were dead or dying, and thousands more were infected with the HIV virus. This was the same year that Rock Hudson announced to the world that he had AIDS, and because of his popularity, AIDS finally entered public American culture.[2]

At Land's End, businesses suffered throughout the 1980s as both visitors and residents tried to understand what GRID, AIDS, and HIV status meant; how people contracted the disease; and how they might avoid becoming infected. Some people believed the HIV virus was spread through bodily contact of any kind, whereas others linked it specifically to bodily fluids of any kind. Alice Foley teamed up with Preston Babbit, the cochair of the Provincetown AIDS Support Group, and others, including the owners of the *Provincetown Advocate*, who allowed them to publish a weekly column on AIDS, to educate the townspeople and help those dying of the disease.[3]

Provincetown's system of nurturing people with AIDS was so well organized and so well respected that it drew men from all over the country whose last wish was to die at Land's End. Mark Doty's memoir, *Heaven's Coast*, is a tribute to the man he cherished, the devastation of AIDS, and places of refuge like Provincetown. Doty, who moved to Provincetown in 1990 with his longtime and HIV-positive partner, Wally Roberts, wrote, after Roberts died, about Provincetown's "brilliant days brimming over with warm October light that seem never to end." Provincetown "was like a balm," for Doty and Roberts, who took in "the huge pewtery gleam of the tideflats," and the "angelic waiter" who "welcomed us, a sort of everyday angel whose task it seemed to bless our meal, our visit, our days in a place that offered a sense of respite." It was also, he noted, like "home." Doty revealed one of Provincetown's loosely kept secrets: "One real advantage to living in Provincetown, for people with AIDS, is that the epidemic has hit here so hard, for so many years, that people have figured out appropriate systems to help those in need . . . elsewhere, understanding all of this can be a full-time job."[4] Doty wove the poetic through, around, and despite the practicalities of living with AIDS in Provincetown.

Well before AIDS changed the lives of men and women in Provincetown, working- and middle-class lesbians began establishing their own businesses at Land's End. Some lesbian entrepreneurs arrived during the postwar era, but an unprecedented number moved to Provincetown beginning in the late 1970s. But like the AIDS crisis, this was a national rather than a local phenomenon. Indeed, the last three decades of the twentieth century witnessed the beginning of local economic restructuring when both regional and federal agencies doled out loans and incentives for small-business ventures.

Women, no doubt motivated by the surge in women's liberation activism in the 1970s, got in line first.[5] From 1975 to 1985, the number of women establishing businesses increased by 56 percent and the number of men doing so rose by 26 percent.[6] Women-owned businesses grew at a rate of 57.6 percent between 1982 and 1987 and 87.8 percent between 1987 and 1992. By 1996 there were more than 7.7 million women-owned

firms, and by 1997 women were starting 70 percent of all new businesses.[7] As one study put it, the "growth of women entrepreneurship
was part of a more general expansion of innovation and business creation, resulting in new kinds of people becoming business leaders and
contributing to the gradual restructuring of local economies."[8] In step
with this broader shift, lesbians in Provincetown succeeded as entrepreneurs, consumers, and citizens.

Finally, the third national trend that left a lasting impact on
Provincetown during the last quarter of the twentieth century was
widespread gentrification. Like other coastal towns and gay enclaves,
Provincetown had pro-growth policies in the 1980s that led to real estate and tax inflation as well as to residential displacement.[9] Gay men
and lesbians finally claimed ownership of Provincetown and demanded that it live up to its reputation as a birthplace of freedom. At
this point Provincetown moved fully into a "consumerized republic," a
term Lizabeth Cohen uses to describe conditions "where self-interested
citizens increasingly view government policies like other market transactions, judging them by how well served they feel personally."[10] What
effects did this new "consumerized republic," this "Gay World," as one
visitor called it, have on Provincetown and its local populations?

6

"Sexism in Paradise"

The Portuguese people ran the town, they were the selectmen, and the fire chief, they were the insurance company, they were . . . [the] fabric of the town. . . . The Portuguese people totally welcomed the gay people to town; they also saw it as a way to make money.

—Gabriel Brooke, interview with author, 1998

THE WOMEN OF PROVINCETOWN have been critical to the success of the town's unpredictable seaport economy. From the early 1800s through the Great Depression, women introduced a number of cottage industries, including Provincetown's shoreline of seventy-eight salt-works. From the mid- to the late nineteenth century they oversaw tables of fish flakes and sustained Provincetown's only "real" factory, a shirt factory. And in the early twentieth century they worked in Province-town's cold-storage freezers and baited hooks in the fish sheds while the fishermen were at sea. Women also stood out as the backbone of Provincetown's barter economy by sustaining a swapping system of goods and necessities.

Before World War II, Provincetown women had no official political movement or language to conceptualize gender-specific financial gains —that would come with the lesbian-feminist movement of the 1970s— but they forged ahead nonetheless.[1] Some women, like Mrs. M. A. O'Neill and Mary Bryant, proprietors of the Octagon Inn and the Bryant House, respectively, opened their homes to boarders and tenants and in this way took financial responsibility for their families. At 368 Commercial Street, Mrs. Angus Matheson rented rooms in her home and cooked three meals a day for her tenants for $6 a week. Miss Annie Mac-Donald, whose house sat just in back of 300 Commercial, charged two more dollars than her neighbor did but also did her guests' laundry.

Charlotte Matta owned a pastry shop; Mary A. Bennet ran a grocery store; and Laura T. Small made a living as an insurance agent. Harriet Adams was even more creative. During the Depression she rented her home in town and lived rent free in one of the dune shacks on the back shore.[2] These women obtained and maintained power in a male-dominated, capitalist economy by striking out on their own. They also paved the way for generations of female entrepreneurs to follow. Indeed, although recent statistics tell a story of unprecedented gains for women entrepreneurs during the 1980s and 1990s, they leave out the working-class and immigrant women like those in Provincetown who began charting their own economic paths a full century earlier.

But Provincetown's turn into a gay resort shifted the local economy's gender balance in an unexpected direction. Even as some residents' anxieties were rising because of the perceived emasculating effects of the decline in fishing and increase in public gender transgressions, male economic authority thrived at Land's End as men displaced women as much as if not more than any other category of business owners. Provincetown's postwar transformation into a gay male mecca evolved at the expense of female entrepreneurs and working-class residents, many of whom were of Portuguese descent. Even though Provincetown had had a long-standing tradition of women-owned and women-managed enterprises, once gay men inundated Land's End and set up their own establishments, resident women lost ground. The accommodation business, for decades controlled equally by men and women, exemplified this trend. Whereas in 1966 women owned 110 accommodation businesses (classified by size and amenities as "camps and cabins," "inns," and "lodges") and men owned 106, thirty years later, men owned 83 accommodation establishments and women owned 27.[3] This shift reflects both the movement of gay men into Provincetown and the movement of native and resident men from the waning fishing industry into the increasingly lucrative service sector.

Indeed, the same capitalist service industry that allowed women to make financial headway before World War II encouraged scores of gay men to do the same, especially after the war. During this time, gay men helped hold Provincetown's homophobic backlash at bay while they secured economic, political, and cultural power. In addition to establishing the gay "routine," gay men mobilized a series of displacements that fell along intersecting lines of race, ethnicity, class, and gender. In other words, while gay men made Provincetown a more comfortable place for nonnormative visitors in general, they also made Land's End into a resort serving white gay men in particular. Local watering holes and tourist's favorites such as the Moors, the Weathering Heights, the Atlantic House, the Town House, and the Pilgrim House catered to and featured gay white men. Although African American women like Stella Brooks and Billie Holiday also entertained, and lesbian Portuguese natives like Ofelia Silva enjoyed the gay ritual, the majority of participants in Provincetown's postwar gay world were white and male. In the 1970s, the gay ritual changed slightly when disco "tea" dances held at gay male resort complexes, like the Boatslip and the Crown and Anchor, replaced the older generation's Broadway sing-alongs, but the gender and race imbalances remained intact.

Although white gay men did not necessarily displace lesbians, they certainly acquired more of Provincetown as their own. Gay men arrived in Provincetown with greater financial resources than lesbians had and gained access to Provincetown's capitalist service economy more rapidly.[4] Besides cornering the market on nightclubs and bars, with few exceptions gay men owned nearly all gay-owned businesses, including, but not limited to, bed and breakfast establishments, retail shops, and hotels. For instance, in 1966 gay men owned approximately six accommodation businesses and lesbians owned one. This gap only widened as time went on. By 1973 gay men owned fifteen accommodation businesses, and lesbians only four, and in 1990 gay men owned forty-four while lesbians owned eight.[5] Gay men also had considerably larger stakes in Provincetown's growing real estate market. They hastened Provincetown's turn into a gay mecca by withdrawing from the chamber of commerce because it did not intentionally advertise Provincetown as a gay place to gay tourists, and they immediately founded, in 1978, one of the United States' first gay business guilds, the Provincetown Business Guild (PBG). At the suggestion of PBG officers and members, who wanted more control over local licensing decisions, gay men also gained access to Provincetown's local government before gay women did. In 1979 PBG members helped Marvin Coble, an openly gay man, win a seat on the board of selectmen.[6]

Against this male-centered backdrop stood a number of lesbians of varying racial and class backgrounds who gained economic and political influence at Land's End before, during, and after the postwar influx of gay males. Lesbians moved into Provincetown as entrepreneurial leaders, cultural movers and shakers, and political actors. In short, lesbians managed to offset Provincetown's new postwar gender imbalance.

Most of these women were working- and middle-class entrepreneurs. As one editorial put it in 1966, they were "new Pilgrims seeking the 'new world' of broad-minded liberalism and entrepreneuring democracy."[7] Lenore Ross, who first visited Provincetown in 1954, came from New York City and had spent most of her vacations at Cherry Grove on Fire Island. She eventually started vacationing in Provincetown instead because as she noted recently, "Fire Island was just a playground and Provincetown was more substantial. . . . It really had more [than Cherry Grove] and I liked the freedom of being gay for the first time in my life. And in a town, not in a party town, in an actual real place."[8] Pat Shultz also arrived in Provincetown in 1954. "For the first time in my life I saw gay people openly accepted on the streets," she stated in 1997.[9] In 1959 Ross opened Provincetown's first openly gay-owned restaurant, the Plain And Fancy, and soon hired Shultz. After several profitable seasons, they bought a number of older homes each fall, renovated them during the winter, and then rented them out in the spring and summer. The fruits of these early endeavors matured into a thriving real estate business, Pat Shultz and Associates.

Other women joined Ross and Shultz and settled in Provincetown during this time. Roslyn Garfield arrived as a schoolteacher, a respected and likely occupation for women at the time. But at Land's End she branched out into male-dominated fields, embarking first on a career in real estate before becoming a prominent attorney as well as the town moderator. Barbara "Mae Bush" Stevens, who is part Native American and part Cape Verdean, also was a teacher but came to Provincetown and opened a Middle Eastern restaurant before landing a job as a U.S. postal worker. Alice Foley opened her own restaurant, Alice's, before becoming the town nurse during the AIDS crisis.[10]

Local residents contributed to the gay women's presence in Provincetown by welcoming them, taking them in as boarders and tenants, and supporting their businesses. Wash-ashore Beverly Spencer first visited Provincetown in 1947 at the age of twenty-four. She had been in the marines, and a fellow servicewoman, a native of Provincetown, brought Beverly home with her. Spencer explained how her friend's family gave her a place to stay and helped her get her first job at the Moors Restaurant. "I was well connected when I came into the community" because of this family, she recalled in 1997. "I never, never felt anything, any stigma or anything . . . the people they liked, they liked. It didn't matter about your lifestyle."[11]

Lenore Ross also spoke of the hospitality and assistance that she and Shultz received from local Portuguese families: "There were nice old ladies and families, town people that were very, very nice to us, I mean very helpful." Ross told a story about shingling a roof during one of their first years in Provincetown. She and Shultz were applying the tar paper in the wrong direction when their next-door neighbor, Portuguese resident Jesse Meads, a builder in town, called to them and pointed out their mistake. As Ross recalls, "so he helped us, not physically, but he instructed us on how to do it . . . and we worked in the winter, and it was cold, and his wife would come over with cracked corn and raisin wine to keep us warm."[12] Many of Provincetown's postwar lesbian wash-ashores cultivated industrious, thrifty, and self-sufficient reputations, which stood in contrast to gay men's notorious "routine." This is not to say that all gay men were festive party-goers or that Land's End lacked its share of rowdy "bull daggers," but that the townspeople took note of the larger numbers of gay men more often than they did of the smaller groups of generally discreet lesbians.

Like their prewar counterparts, the women who moved to Land's End during the 1950s and 1960s tended to assimilate. For the most part, they subsumed, though they did not hide, their identities as sexual or gender nonconformists. Quietly and discreetly, they eased into Provincetown's year-round community. Indeed, Ross, Schultz, Garfield, and Foley made barely a ripple when they arrived in Provincetown because independent women were not new to Land's End and because most of them sought, above all, to blend in rather than stand out. Stevens was an exception not only because she was part Native American and part Cape Verdean but also because she was a self-identified hell-raiser. "They don't ask questions, I mean they just accept it [being gay]," Shultz explained in 1997, "and that's really what makes it so wonderful."[13]

In contrast to the lesbians arriving at Land's End in the 1940s, 1950s, and 1960s, who mixed easily with gay men and straight townspeople and were integrationists in both theory and practice, many of the lesbians arriving in the 1970s and 1980s used the language of lesbian feminism to introduce a separatist agenda and to denounce Provincetown's mostly male atmosphere. How can such a "'gay' place," one woman asked in 1977 in the *Provincetown Magazine*, have so few "*womon's*" spaces?[14] Provincetown, she noted, had one woman's bar but no women's center or women's guesthouses. Another lesbian argued in the same issue that Provincetown epitomized "sexism in paradise" because most business owners who hired women gave them the lowest-paying and most menial positions. Provincetown, she declared, was a place for gay men that did not welcome gay women. "I am not 'gay.' I am a Lesbian," a third woman asserted. "Gay is male-identified. My experience as a Lesbian has nothing in common with that of the homosexual male but oppression for the 'crime' of same-sex sexual preference."[15]

The ways in which lesbians viewed and utilized Provincetown, however, were even more complicated than this binary suggests. Many lesbian wash-ashores, even those who arrived during the 1970s and 1980s as lesbian separatists, eventually decided that terms like "lesbian" and "gay" did not fully describe who they were. "I will not categorize or define myself as anything," wash-ashore Joy McNulty declared adamantly in a 1997 interview.[16] The same year Corbo agreed, "My lesbianism then and my lesbianism now is really for me a secondary [identity]—it is not the main focus of my being. It is very private to me and I am who I am first and that is part of who I am."[17] Denise Chamberlin, a self-identified "coffee freak" and entrepreneur who opened a gourmet coffee shop in Provincetown in 1995, arrived a full decade after the lesbian-feminist movement yet still felt boxed in by terms such as "lesbian" and "queer." Chamberlain recognized that the lesbian-feminist movement had produced a number of "smart" and "strong" role models, but as she noted in 1999,

> I feel like with some people if you tell them what you are then that's what you are. I like to just have a clear box and be able to be what I want to be. . . . I've definitely been gay for a long time but I never limited myself to that, I didn't ever want to feel like that was all I could be, there was something else there.[18]

To be successful residents and business owners in Provincetown, they all agreed, women needed to be much more than just "lesbians."

Even though these and other women moved to Provincetown because it was lesbian-friendly, once there they focused less on their identities as sexual minorities and more on developing identities that included but went beyond sexual orientation. The paradox is as follows:

The majority of Provincetown's consumers identified as gay, lesbian, bisexual, queer, or transgendered and visited Land's End because it was a gay and lesbian town. And most of Provincetown's gay and lesbian business owners and workers have decided to reside at Land's End also because it is a gay and lesbian town. In this way, sexual orientation has shaped Provincetown's demographic makeup. For many residents and visitors, however, the charm of Provincetown was that once at Land's End, they had the opportunity to play down their sexual identities, or in other words, they were able to let their sexual identities become less meaningful to them and others. Hence, even though they moved to or visited Provincetown because they could be openly gay or lesbian there without the dangers of homophobic harassment or discrimination, many wash-ashores and tourists once there felt freer to emphasize other aspects of their identities. When almost everyone in town was gay or lesbian, sexual orientation became less of a distinguishing characteristic.

The trajectory of women's economic, political, and cultural ascendancy in Provincetown was remarkably similar to that of their Portuguese neighbors and friends. They began by setting up their own businesses and carving out space for themselves in downtown Provincetown. Indeed, like Provincetown's other subcultural groups, even though lesbians recognized the value of assimilation, they also recognized the importance of acquiring space that they could call their own. The Ace of Spades, which catered to lesbians but welcomed all residents and visitors during the 1950s and 1960s, was one such place. Unlike the gay men's clubs, it had no dance floor—which was a moot point, since postwar state regulations criminalized dancing between same-sex couples—no professional "female impressionists" or drag performers, who also were "illegal," and no regularly scheduled sing-alongs. Gay women fondly recall the Ace of Spades as a small and dark but cozy bar with wooden barrels standing in as stools, a stench of stale liquor, and a sign-in book at the door. "It was mostly conversation," Lenore Ross noted. "People talked. They talked and drank." Pat Shultz remembered it as a place with "very colorful people," such as "Clayton Snow. He would come in with a Great Dane and he would order a daiquiri for himself and he would order a daiquiri for the Great Dane."[19]

The Ace of Spades encouraged women to congregate and socialize with other women, yet it also regulated women to the same degree that

The interior of the Ace of Spades Club ca. 1960. Postcard courtesy of Cape Cod Photo and Art, Orleans, Massachusetts.

all nightclubs and bars in the state of Massachusetts did at the time. During the 1950s and 1960s, local officials insisted that all nightclubs in Provincetown abide by members-only regulations. The "club" method for such establishments was two-sided. On the one hand, lesbian and gay patrons were reluctant to become club members because they did not want their names on any potentially harmful lists. On the other hand, restricting access to members and their guests allowed bar owners to throw out unruly or unwanted patrons. The rules also stipulated that no women could tend bar and that all women had to be seated before they could buy a drink. But still, the Ace of Spades offered women a place to express their desires for other women freely. And catering to gay women meant John and Frances Atkins could partake in Provincetown's increasingly profitable lesbian and gay tourist industry. Allegedly the longest continuously running lesbian bar in the United States, the Ace of Spades played a critical role in Provincetown's history as the first and, for many years, the only social institution at Land's End that catered specifically to women.

For more than four decades the Ace of Spades, which eventually became the Pied Piper, had only one brief challenge to its reign as Provincetown's only lesbian bar. This challenge came in 1974 when

Alice Foley and Mae Bush Stevens prompted Stan Sorrentino, owner of the Crown and Anchor Hotel, to open the Ms. Room, an upscale, fashionably decorated, women-oriented nightclub. Unlike the Ace of Spades, which attracted a working-class crowd and bore little resemblance to today's remodeled Pied Piper, the Ms. Room, which was located in the Crown and Anchor, appealed to a greater variety of lesbians from dark-skinned Cape Verdean and Native American entrepreneurs to young, white "baby butches." While the Ace of Spades paled in the face of the roaring seventies disco and feminist era, the more contemporary Ms. Room lured women from all socioeconomic backgrounds by offering entertainment, social mixers, and appetizers. Diane Corbo reminisced about being "in awe" of the older lesbians that she met at the Ace of Spades, including Beverly Spencer, Sandra Rich, Betty Villari, and Mae Bush, the last of whom "mesmerized" her because it was the first time that she had met a woman whom she considered "really powerful." But "women got dressed [up] to go" to the Ms. Room, Corbo recalled. "It was like wow" to see such a "cross-section of lesbian and gay culture."[20]

As a women-oriented space, the Ms. Room thrived, but when the lesbians running the nightclub demanded that Sorrentino, a gay man, allow them to make the Ms. Room for women only, it collapsed. Indeed, the marriage of convenience between Sorrentino and the lesbians running and patronizing the Ms. Room did not last long. After fewer than two seasons, Sorrentino decided to close it rather than succumb to the demands of separatist lesbians.

Whether the lesbians spearheading this separatist movement were asking too much of Provincetown's limited resources or whether Sorrentino was, in the end, a sexist entrepreneur is unclear. The answer most likely lies somewhere in the middle of these extremes. The most pressing issue seems to have been space: not gender-exclusive space, for there were a number of mostly male spaces at nightclubs like the A-House and the Crown, but women-only space. To justify his decision Sorrentino argued in the *Provincetown Advocate* that "designing bars for sexual preference is old fashioned and boring. It was 'in' five years ago when women's liberation was first an issue . . . people are seeking a mixed crowd now."[21] A Wellfleet resident articulated the view of many women when she disagreed with Sorrentino by stating that she knew of few, if any, gay people who opted for a "mixed" crowd. Sorrentino's decision, she added, simply convinced her that he cared about money more than people.[22] While there was certainly no love lost between the women who ran the Ms. Room and Stan Sorrentino, some lesbians suggested in retrospect that their insistence on a single-gendered space was detrimental to the prosperity of lesbian and gay cultures in a town that celebrated a cross-section of genders, ethnicities, sexualities, classes, and artistic sensibilities.[23]

Well before entrepreneurs in other towns targeted lesbians as potential customers, straight and gay townsfolk in Provincetown helped create this consumer group by capitalizing on the influx of gay women. Two decades after Sorrentino closed the Ms. Room, Donald Edwards, a straight Provincetown native, rebuilt the legendary Pilgrim House and decided to make the first floor into a large nightclub called the Vixen. Edwards already owned one of Provincetown's only straight bars, aptly named the Governor Bradford, and felt that Land's End already had enough gay men's clubs. What was missing, he decided, was a women's club that could compete with the successful Pied Piper. Shortly after the Vixen opened in the mid-1990s, it surpassed the Pied as the most popular women's bar in Provincetown and forced Susan Webster, the Pied's current owner, to begin catering to gay men as well as to lesbians. Webster responded with a brilliant marketing plan: she added (and copyrighted) an "after-tea tea dance" to the gay male "routine," thus guaranteeing the Pied a steady crowd and cash flow.

In addition to bars and nightclubs, lesbians also obtained space and power at Land's End by opening women's retail stores and guesthouses. These entrepreneurs and the women to whom they catered collectively changed Land's End from a gay male mecca into one of the only towns in the world that deliberately targets lesbians as well as gay men. A crafts store known as Womencrafts was the forerunner of these entities and is still a beacon for lesbians seeking affirmation, community, and women-oriented consumer goods in Provincetown. In 1976, shortly after the inception and closing of the Ms. Room, Alexea Pickoff and a woman who called herself Vashte XX opened the original Womencrafts store in Provincetown. It was named Womencrafts because during their first year, Alexea and Vashte sold furniture handmade and hand-painted by women, and at the time it was the only gender-specific retail store in town. Provincetown's visiting lesbian population appreciated the artistic wares that Womencrafts offered, and many women made the pilgrimage to Land's End just to visit Womencrafts. Few women, however, could afford to buy the expensive home furnishings. After eighteen months of peddling women's crafts, Alexea and Vashte phased out the pricey furniture items and focused instead on selling more affordable goods such as feminist jewelry that featured women's symbols like the labyris and lambda.

Womencrafts sparked the development of a gay consumer market that altered patterns of consumption in Provincetown. Carol Karlson and her partner, Jo Deall, two white working-class lesbians from Brooklyn, New York, share a migration history that closely resembles that of Diane Corbo. Like Corbo, Karlson and Deall spent most of their weekends and vacations in Provincetown during the 1970s. In order to make Land's End their home, they bought Womencrafts and moved to Provincetown in 1978. To Womencrafts' repertoire of jewelry, they added an array of feminist books, posters, records, and magazines. Recently, Karlson placed Womencrafts on Provincetown's growing list of "firsts" by revealing that although located out of sight down the alley at Pepe's Wharf for its first fourteen years, Womencrafts was nonetheless the first store in Provincetown to openly market lesbian or gay items. Other establishments, such as Sunsigns, had also sold feminist and lesbian-feminist jewelry in the late 1970s and early 1980s, but these stores placed their gay-related materials, like posters and pulp novels, into semihidden, poorly lit, X-rated sections, marking them, in effect, as illicit products.[24] Karlson and Deall were decades ahead of what scholars Amy Gluckman, Betsy Reed, and others have called the "gay marketing movement."[25]

In addition to initiating the then radical idea of marketing gay products, Karlson and Deall drew women to Provincetown by instilling a sense of pride in many lesbian patrons. They did this by selling an array of women-oriented goods and by offering all women a 10 percent lesbian discount. The lesbian discount, a marketing strategy that Alexea and Vashte invented, soon became infamous locally as a discriminatory price break. It was revolutionary during the late 1970s and 1980s, and the lesbian discount continued to influence Womencrafts' customers well into the 1990s. Karlson and Deall received numerous letters from women who insisted that Womencrafts and its lesbian discount changed their feelings about themselves and about Provincetown. In 1991, for instance, one patron penned the following: "Dear Womencrafts, You asked me if I wanted the Lesbian Discount. I said 'sure' and made some silly remark about how can you prove something like that."

After raising the popular and sometimes playful issue of "proof," she continued, "I want to thank you for that discount—not because of the two dollars I saved but because I left feeling proud and good. For once," she admitted, "being a lesbian gave me an advantage—a discount at a store. I had bought a book at your store to send to my mother in hopes she would want to read something about gayness and in hopes a book might break down some barriers. I was feeling very small when you gave me that lesbian discount but I left feeling wonderful."[26]

The lesbian discount provides an excellent snapshot of the way in which consumer purchases can help shape identities. In this way, the mechanics of capitalism helped form lesbian and gay identities, build lesbian and gay communities, and create lesbian and gay cultures. Womencrafts continues to offer women, especially those not interested in Provincetown's bars, a reason to visit Land's End. It also continues to encourage women to "come out" as lesbian in exchange for an economic reward and a certain amount of emotional or psychological approval. Consumer relationships based on sexual orientation created a tradition in Provincetown in which gay and lesbian tourists buy gay and lesbian consumer goods, such as rainbow flags (and now anything designed with the colors of the rainbow will do), freedom rings, and gay-specific greeting cards. The act of selecting and buying empowered gay men and lesbians as consumers and citizens, lent them at least a momentary and space-specific sense of pride in their alternative identities, and marked certain stores in Provincetown as gay spaces. But still, the creation of a gay market, as M. V. Badgett points out, has been blind to certain social inequalities, especially those regarding race and class.[27] If the aim is social justice, Badgett argues, wouldn't it be better to formulate an economic market that is inclusive rather than exclusive? Indeed, before long, Provincetown's gay market targeted a mostly white middle- and upper-class crowd and helped whiten and gentrify Land's End in the process.

Lesbians also established a women's presence at Land's End by providing accommodations. Provincetown's women-only guesthouses drew hundreds and, eventually, thousands of gay women to Provincetown each year, from the late 1970s until today, and continue to anchor Provincetown's lesbian culture. Before the 1970s, only a few maiden ladies and gay women opened guesthouses, like Ivy Ivans and Eleanor Bloomfield who took in boarders in the 1920s, Anne Kane who ran Room at the Top in the 1960s, and Marge Betzold who opened the Gull

Walk Inn in 1975. The Gull Walk Inn (now the Secret Garden) was a small women's rooming house just off the beaten track in the center of town between Commercial and Bradford Streets. While women innkeepers today agree that Betzold owned and operated the first women-only guesthouse, many nonetheless credit Laurel and Gabriel Brooke for opening Gabriel's, the first "official," publicized, "full-fledged," multiroom guesthouse for women in Provincetown.[28]

Gabriel Brooke differed from Provincetown's postwar female entrepreneurs in that she arrived in Provincetown with a certain knowledge of and experience in the lesbian-feminist movement. She eventually abandoned the movement because of its emphasis on middle-class privilege and its disparagement of working-class butches and femmes, but its momentum carried her forward nonetheless. When Brooke arrived at Land's End, she forged ahead with a firm sense of entitlement. "I came [to Provincetown]," she stated, "like a wild person where wildness was not a problem."[29]

Gabriel's sparked an entire movement in which lesbians publicly designated specific locations as women owned and for women only. The story of Gabriel's recounts a recurring "rags to riches" narrative. In 1979 Brooke, her late partner Laurel, and one other woman bought the decaying building known today as Gabriel's. The local housing inspector had condemned it just before it was put on the market, thereby making it affordable. Even though the house had been a family-style guesthouse, Laurel and Gabriel decided—despite the opinions of friends and fellow home owners who insisted that Provincetown was a gay male town—to remake the building into a women-only guesthouse with approximately ten units. Brooke remembered proudly in 1998 that many people discouraged her from opening a women-only establishment because they had no faith in women as consumers, especially in a male-dominated place like Provincetown. But Brooke instinctively felt that a market for women existed, and after opening Gabriel's, she noted fondly, "the women came."

After Karlson, Deall, Brooke, and Betzold proved to Provincetown residents and tourists that a profitable and relatively untapped market existed and that lesbians wishing to vacation in Provincetown were worthy of financial investments, about a dozen principally white middle- and working-class women followed their cue. The guesthouse sector illustrates this trend well. In the early 1980s, women's guesthouse own-

The exterior of Gabriel's illustrates part of the gentrification process. The top picture was taken when shortly after Gabriel bought the condemned house, and the one below was taken after she remodeled it in the 1990s. Photographs courtesy of Gabriel Brooke.

ers, including Diane Corbo of Ravenwood, Betty Adams of Windamar, Carol Whitman of the Dusty Miller Inn, Sandra Rich of the White Wind Inn, Angela Calamaris of Angels Landing, Dottie McKay and Diane Baines of the Check'er Inn, Jackie Kelly and Karen Harding of the Greenhouse, and Michael Wright[30] of Plums filled their rooms with lesbians from all walks of life. Virginia Allen, a lesbian from Staten Island, New York, who is part Cuban and part African American, stayed at a number of these guesthouses with a group of African American lesbians called the "we girls." Attracted mostly to Provincetown's ocean and beaches, Allen visited Land's End from the late 1960s through the mid-1990s and always returned, in her words, "rejuvenated" and "enriched."[31]

The guesthouse owner who attracted most of the women of color was Helen Brown, now Helen Caddie-Larcenia, an African American lesbian from Danbury, Connecticut, who owned the Aspasia Guesthouse with Bejay Prescott. Aspasia first was located at 98 Bradford before Caddie-Larcenia and a new partner, Julie Hamilton, moved it in 1983 to 31 Pearl Street. Caddie-Larcenia's clientele was primarily white when she opened Aspasia in the early 1980s, but by the time she moved to Maine in 1989, Aspasia had attracted large contingents of women of color, including such well-known black lesbians as the writer Barbara Smith, who founded the Kitchen Table: Women of Color Press with Audre Lord in 1981. Caddie-Larcenia recalled in 2000 that black women started coming to Land's End because the "word [had] spread" among black lesbians elsewhere "that there [was] a black woman that live[d] in Provincetown that own[ed] a guesthouse." Caddie-Larcenia was "joyously overwhelmed with this newfound place" and appreciated the townsfolk that, in her words, "welcomed me and accepted me and were like me."[32] She valued Provincetown for its "openness and freedom" and constructed a community of likeness that was based mostly on sexual and gender orientation, although for the women of color who stayed at her house, this likeness also included race. Together, Caddie-Larcenia, her co-owners, and the other women innkeepers transformed the tourist and resident landscape of Provincetown by renovating dilapidated houses, opening women-oriented guesthouses, and challenging gay men's exclusive claims to Land's End.

The women guesthouse owners soon came together as an economic and political bloc. Shortly after Michael Wright renovated an old Por-

Helen Caddie-Larcenia in front of Aspasia, ca. 1985. Photograph courtesy of Helen Caddie-Larcenia.

tuguese home in 1984, known until 1998 as Plums (now Seasons), this small and ambitious group of "women property owners" met first for social reasons at Corbo's Ravenwood. When Brooke returned to town, she organized the second meeting, perhaps still unaware that she had not been invited to the first meeting. These women formed a commanding political group whose goals were to create safe women-oriented spaces in Provincetown, advertise these spaces in lesbian and women's magazines nationwide, and assist one another in all ways possible, such as through referrals, to ensure the survival of their gender-specific presence at Land's End. Even though most of the original members sold their establishments in the 1990s and early 2000s, often but not always to men, the Women Innkeepers of Provincetown, "WIP" as they called themselves playfully, were and still are economically and politically influential.[33]

The Women Innkeepers influenced where and when lesbians vacationed at Land's End. Shortly after its inception, WIP set aside a three-day weekend in October to entertain and show appreciation for their faithful lesbian guests. "Women's Weekend," the economic brainchild of the Women Innkeepers, continues now in the form of "Women's Week" (an annual October event) to mark Provincetown, at least momentarily, as a women-oriented, rather than a gay male, resort. Although the designation of a period of time as belonging to women suggests that all other days and weeks of the year are reserved for men, Women's Weekend nonetheless introduced gay women to Provincetown and encouraged them to spend time and money there before, during, and after the summer season. The first Women's Weekend, in October 1984, attracted approximately two hundred women. It originated as a three-day event with a kick-off clambake party at the beach, open-house tours of women's guesthouses, and a number of women-only social events, including dances, performances, seminars, and, of course, softball games. Less than a decade later, visiting lesbians outgrew not only their designated three-day weekend but also their designated women-only guesthouses.

In 1992, the Women Innkeepers symbolically and literally extended their claims to Provincetown by transforming Women's Weekend into Women's Week. Objections, if any, were few and far between when WIP sent the overflow of women to neighboring male-owned guesthouses and hotels, many of which gladly changed their usually all-male spaces, which were mostly vacant during the off-season, into women-only spaces for the week. By the late 1990s, more than four thousand women were flocking to Provincetown during Women's Week—thereby transforming the town into something like a women-only commune—to enjoy artistic, social, and cultural women-oriented events. Although softball games still are popular, one of the most festive events of Women's Week is the "dyke drag brunch," which local lesbians use to showcase dyke "drag"—from women masquerading as women and looking like drag queens to women performing as men in the increasingly popular drag king tradition.

The Women Innkeepers expanded Provincetown's economic season and shaped Provincetown into a resort that increasingly welcomed

Figure 30: Festive participants pose at the annual Dyke Drag Brunch event during Women's Week, 1997. Collection of the author.

women as owners and consumers.[34] Women's Week, for example, prompted visiting women to patronize all of Provincetown's hotels, guesthouses, shops, and restaurants during its quiet off-season. Indeed, before Women's Week gave lesbians a reason to visit Provincetown in the off-season, most stores, restaurants, and accommodations had no reason to remain open after Labor Day. Although Fantasia Fair, a festival for cross-dressers and transgendered people, attracted visitors to Provincetown in October as early as 1975, it did not draw the numbers or the business that Women's Week did.[35] Fantasia Fair and Women's Week together, however, inspired other gay or gender-related interest groups to take advantage of Provincetown's off-season charms and low rates. Single Men's Weekend now lures male tourists and consumers to Provincetown in early November; Couples Weekend is scheduled in early June; and Holly Folly, organized for the first time in 1997, invites revelers to enjoy Land's End just before Christmas. After the success of Women's Week, the townspeople also began encouraging gay and lesbian vacationers to spend holidays like Thanksgiving, Valentine's Day, and New Year's Eve in gay-friendly Provincetown.

While extending Provincetown's economic reach so that the shoulder and winter seasons would become as profitable as the ten-week summer season, the Women Innkeepers did all they could to ensure that women-owned businesses would benefit as much as, if not more than, businesses owned by men. Although WIP promoted all of Provincetown to their guests during Women's Week, they compiled a separate list of women-owned businesses in Provincetown as particularly suitable and worthy. In 1985 this list contained approximately nineteen shops, restaurants, and fitness services, all of which offered a discount to registered Women's Weekend guests. By 1992, this list had expanded to almost seventy women-owned and women-operated businesses, from attorneys and bookstore owners to women-oriented sex-toy shops and "recovery" stores.

The Women Innkeepers also helped gentrify Provincetown by establishing an increasingly expensive and exclusive gay market, remodeling older homes, displacing natives, and inviting hordes of white middle- and upper-class women to enjoy Land's End. On the coattails of the original Women Innkeepers, for example, trailed a number of more financially solvent women, who, unlike their predecessors, already had the capital needed to purchase lucrative commercial properties and businesses in Provincetown.

The return of an international community of female artists, writers, and poets and the introduction of lesbian musicians and comedians bolstered the women's culture in Provincetown during the last quarter of the twentieth century. Not since the days of Maud Squire, Ethel Mars, Mary Heaton Vorse, Susan Glaspell, and Ada Gilmore had women's influence in the visual and literary arts at Land's End seemed so pronounced. From the late 1970s through the 1990s, Provincetown hosted a number of female artists, including painters such as D. Flax and T. J. Walton. Lesbian photographers such as Ariel Jones and Marion Roth, the last of whom cofounded a women's writing and photography school called Freehand with Rita Speicher, also worked at Land's End. Lesbian musicians and drummers, such as the late Laurel Brooke of the popular outdoor women's drumming corps, and Char Priolo of the Dyketones entertained audiences along Commercial Street. In the mid-1980s, lesbian writers and publishers like Susan Mitchell, Malu Nay Block, Sherry Dranch, Randy Turoff, and Jackie Lapidus published *Womantide: The Lesbian Magazine of Provincetown*.[36] And lesbian comedians, from Kate Clinton—the first woman to create a career for herself by entertaining audiences with amusing anecdotes about politics and lesbian culture—to Maggie Cassella, who weaves current political debates into witty but quaint lesbian humor, helped shape the lesbian culture at Land's End.

Besides transforming Provincetown's cultural and economic venues, lesbian and straight women established themselves politically at Land's End from the 1970s through the 1990s by taking advantage of Provincetown's accessible selectmen-plus-town meeting form of local government. Mary Jo Avellar, a Portuguese native, paved the way for women to become influential town leaders when she won a seat on the board of selectmen in 1976 and soon thereafter became the first woman to chair that board. With the exception of a seven-year respite from 1990 to 1997, Avellar has been a selectman since 1976 until today. Early in her career she, perhaps more than any other straight politician, fought to let gay men and lesbians enjoy Provincetown. "I resent any attempt to license morality," she argued in 1980 when other board members attempted to control gay men's public behavior.[37] A number of local straight women, including Betty Steele-Jeffers and Dolores deSousa, took Avellar's lead and won seats on the board of selectmen throughout the 1980s and 1990s.

Having straight women like Steele-Jeffers and Avellar on the board was important to a gender balance, but lesbians sought representation in town hall as well. By 1990, although the board of selectmen no longer acted as the licensing board, it still appointed townspeople to all the local government boards, including the licensing board. It also controlled the agenda at the annual town meeting and had considerable influence over all public policy issues. In 1990 Irene Rabinowitz became the fourth woman, second openly gay politician, and first open lesbian to win a seat on the board of selectmen. Jane Antolini, of Lady Jane's Inn, joined Rabinowitz in 1993, and both women eventually chaired the board. In 1997 Rabinowitz retired, but in 1998 Cheryl Andrews, a dentist and a lesbian, ran and won, as did David Atkinson, a gay male libertarian. The 1998 race shifted the balance of the board for the first time in Provincetown's history to a three-to-two gay majority, thereby ending half a century of uninterrupted Portuguese political power at Land's End. Although board members typically manage municipal issues that have little to do with gay life in Provincetown, they keep the local government in check regarding licensing and rule making in particular, and they send out a symbolic message that gay people now control the local political landscape at Land's End.[38]

Lesbians gained political ground on other levels as well. For instance, for nearly two decades, townspeople elected Roslyn Garfield to be the town moderator. Like that of the selectmen, Garfield's authority was symbolic as well as actual. From 1985 until her retirement in 2003, when Betty Steele-Jeffers stepped in, Garfield appointed members to the finance committee, which reviews all budget and fiscal policy matters and makes recommendations at the town meeting. Garfield moderated the town meeting, orchestrating the pace by letting certain debates linger while cutting others short. And she appointed committee members if the board of selectmen failed to do so within sixty days of a given opening. Throughout the 1990s, a number of lesbians served on various town committees, from the Zoning Board of Appeals to the Planning Board and Bicycle Committee.

Gay and straight women's move into town hall reshaped Provincetown's formal political territory by tipping the balance of power in terms of gender (fewer men), ethnicity (fewer Portuguese townspeople), and sexuality (fewer straight residents). In 1997, in addition to holding three of the five seats on the board of selectmen, women held 50 percent of all elected posts and 44 percent of appointed positions.[39] Men still held prominent jobs such as that of town manager and chief of police, but women's gains were evident in nearly all aspects of the local government. Similarly, gay wash-ashores seeking public office displaced a good number of Provincetown's Portuguese natives, many of whom were straight. Like Provincetown's other economic and political trends, the gay political movement mirrored the extent to which openly gay politicians came out and ran for office during the 1970s, 1980s, and 1990s around the United States.

Provincetown residents of all backgrounds responded defensively when they sensed that a new group or subculture might be encroaching on the limited resources at Land's End. In the early 1900s, Yankees attempted to assert their authority in the face of increasingly powerful Portuguese immigrants. During the 1950s, Portuguese and Yankee residents launched a full-scale moral panic when gay men took to their streets and nightclubs. And during the last quarter of the twentieth century, gay men and straight residents voiced concern over a perceived lesbian "takeover." Indeed, gay women's ascendancy in Provincetown (remember that categorically straight women lost ground during this time) was fraught with tension.

The main points of contention involved space, sex, and money. Successful lesbian entrepreneurs have incurred disproportionately large amounts of spite among gay male and straight townspeople. Joy McNulty is a case in point. With the help of her family, McNulty built a lucrative financial profile by buying and selling property while maintaining a first-rate dining establishment in the center of town. Many people criticize McNulty because she imports seasonal laborers from Jamaica and justifies her action by arguing that there is no "help" in Provincetown. McNulty is no stranger to these sentiments. In a 1997 oral history interview she admitted that people in Provincetown have never harassed her for being Jewish, a single mother, a lesbian, or a wash-ashore: "They hate me because I am successful in business," she complained.[40] Even though the Provincetown Chamber of Commerce estimated in 2004 that approximately 40 percent of all business owners rely on foreign-born seasonal workers under the H-2B or J-1 visa programs, McNulty often stands out as somehow more opportunistic than other entrepreneurs. In 2000 Helen Caddie-Larcenia spoke to a similar dynamic regarding prejudice in Provincetown: "I didn't feel any [racial tension] at all [when I ran Aspasia]. If anything, there was a little resentment amongst townspeople that so many gay people were coming to town and owning businesses."[41]

Tension specifically between gay men and lesbians erupted during the 1970s when lesbians started to become more visible and influential in Provincetown. A 1974 letter to the *Provincetown Advocate* provides a snapshot of the way women used the language of lesbian-feminism to debunk the myth of a monolithic gay community. Susan E. Cayleff, Susan J. Passino, and S. Lynn Rubin spoke for many lesbians when they responded to an article that the *Provincetown Advocate* published on gay pride and behavior:

> We personally cannot relate to the sagas or the joys of being left alone behind the Monument or on the beaches. This sadly is a manifestation of the gay male's culture. It is a vital oversight . . . [and] gross error to categorically describe the gay women and men's communities as one and the same.[42]

As opposed to being a gay male, which is often, Cayleff, Passino, and Rubin insisted, determined by the persons with whom one has sex, being a lesbian "is the culmination of socio-political and psycho-emotional convictions that have evolved through a continuous struggle with all forms of sexism that would have us relating heterosexually and riding the family train." Only when gay men and women come together to combat homophobia, sexism, racism, and labor exploitation, with an understanding that all these forms of oppression are linked inherently, they explained, will "Gay Pride . . . become a reality in Provincetown."[43] Although these lesbians contradicted their own case to end oppression by condemning men who participated in sexual activities that they could not understand, they still asked residents to consider the importance of differences—race, class, gender—other than sexual orientation. Although the "rift between the gay sexes," as the *Provincetown Advocate* called it, reached its pinnacle in the 1970s, tensions between gay men and lesbians over issues from misogyny—often played out by drag queens—to financial gain and public sex have festered just below the surface for decades.[44]

Lesbians slowly and consistently infiltrated Provincetown's economic, political, and cultural territories by following in the entrepreneurial footsteps of Portuguese and Yankee women and by aggressively securing positions for themselves in Provincetown's limited spatial, economic, and political arenas. They have not, however, come close to "taking over" Provincetown, and indeed, even though women hold roughly half of all municipal positions, lesbians are losing more economic ground than they are gaining. In 1992, for instance, women owned nearly seventy businesses in town, but five years later this number dropped to fifty. Similarly, most of the original Women Innkeepers sold their guesthouses to gay men within the past decade because the monetary rewards of selling were high and the work of owning a guesthouse was tiresome.[45]

Still, regarding women's perceived gains, townspeople have explained lesbian success in Provincetown using one of two narratives. One theme credits women directly for their efforts by focusing on their "rags to riches" achievements in business, politics, and the arts. The other attributes women's advancements to gay men's setbacks during the onset of AIDS. Indeed, one of the most common assumptions is that lesbians gained economic, political, and cultural ground in Provincetown only because the AIDS virus ended the lives of so many gay men so quickly. The importance of these explanations lies not in whether one is true and the other is not, for both are partly true, but in how each version attempts to explain and simplify the complicated history of lesbians at Land's End.

Attributing lesbian progress in Provincetown to the AIDS epidemic overlooks four key components. First, it does not take into account the nationwide increases in female entrepreneurs that took place during the 1980s and 1990s. Second, it neglects the gay men who remained healthy and continued to prosper at Land's End and elsewhere, and it excuses gay men from letting Land's End slip into the hands of women. Third, it fails to consider how the AIDS crisis affected lesbians both emotionally and financially when their friends, neighbors, and customers went through prolonged stages of illness and often died. And finally, arguing that the AIDS crisis cleared the way for women's advancements dismisses the hardworking and ambitious lesbians who secured space for themselves and other women in Provincetown before, during, and after the onset of AIDS.

The Horatio Alger "rages to riches" story of lesbians' ascent up Provincetown's economic ladder highlights the gay women who came to Provincetown with few resources but managed once there to establish lucrative businesses and, in some cases, financial empires. This version romanticizes the challenges lesbians faced as they often risked everything to invest in a resort town that focused principally on gay men. It also glosses over the ethnic and class displacements that lesbians ignited when they contributed to the gentrification of Land's End. In other words, by focusing on lesbian gains, on how they transformed dilapidated houses into women's guesthouses, it disregards the dire financial circumstances that led Portuguese natives to abandon the houses that previous generations had struggled to maintain. This version also alters typical "Horatio Alger" stories by placing women at the center of the "American Dream" of owning property and achieving financial success.

In 1986 Helaine Zimmerman explained how lesbians in Provincetown began linking their financial gains to their rights as American citizens. "I remember the days, not very long ago, when [gays and lesbians] owned nothing, controlled nothing, and had no political voice in Provincetown," she began in a letter to the editor of the *Provincetown Advocate*. But that changed in the 1970s, Zimmerman argued, when liberation movements transformed the expectations gay men and lesbians had as they moved from being "grateful that [they] could gather together and socialize in a place where [they] were not routinely arrested just for being together" to demanding their "inalienable rights" as citizens. "We, like our heterosexual counterparts, have the desire to be a part of the American dream. We too wish to buy houses and acquire real estate investments."[46]

Lesbians arriving in Provincetown during the last half of the twentieth century transformed the demographic, political, and cultural landscape at Land's End. They initiated market segmentation by marketing lesbian goods and spaces to lesbian consumers. And they extended Provincetown's economic season so that it reached well beyond the frame of ten weeks.

Although most of the lesbian entrepreneurs and their customers were white, the community of likeness that lesbians forged at Land's End was based primarily on sexual orientation rather than on being white or becoming white. Indeed, even though only a small percentage of women entrepreneurs were African American, Native American, or Cape Verdean, these women played key roles in Provincetown's social and economic arenas by setting up their own businesses, joining the Women Innkeepers, and attracting other women of color to Land's End. But still, lesbians in Provincetown contributed to both race stratification and gentrification by displacing Portuguese natives, tending to buildings in bad repair, and importing a racialized underclass of foreign-born workers. The gay world that lesbians and gay men forged at Provincetown ushered in new relationships of citizenship, new family structures, and new challenges to an already fragile sense of community.

7

"Gay World"

Only when one finally realizes that Provincetown is wholly a figment of somebody's imagination can its rhythms be properly understood. After all, could there actually be a town so lazily cozy, so placid to the eye and the ear, so impossibly drawn to the grape and hops, so given to truly byzantine politics, so enamored of the deadly game of realty purchase and sale, so benign in appearance in winters, boasting then a population no larger than 4,000 souls which, by some alchemy as yet unknown, transforms itself suddenly, come July 4 and thereafter for a couple of months, into the most sensuous place north of Rio, west of Paris, east of San Francisco, and under the North Star? Hardly! Logic tells us that Provincetown couldn't exist; logic is never wrong.
—David Brudnoy, *Provincetown Advocate Summer Guide*, 1975

IN 1971 the Provincetown selectmen removed the town hall benches one week before Independence Day. The benches, or "meat rack" as some referred to them, lined the entrance to town hall and offered a clear view of Commercial Street.[1] Portuguese townspeople rested on them, children played behind them, gay and straight visitors and residents cruised from them, and everyone from the East End to the West End of town marveled at the goings-on around them. The meat rack provided front-row seats to Provincetown's nonstop parade of eccentric characters. As the years passed, one was sure to see there the older woman from the "kingdom of Wellfleet" who wore a tiara, carried a plastic wand, and referred to herself as Princess Leia. Often "Popeye," an elderly man resembling the cartoon character of the same name, strolled by pushing his noisy shopping cart full of recycled bottles and cans. His contemporary, a homeless man answering to "Butch" (often causing much confusion among some lesbian bystanders), might saunter up and ask if you'd like to peer into his X-rated mini-viewfinder.

Although the benches were a magnet for residents and visitors of all backgrounds, Selectmen William White, John Bell, and Ernest Irmer removed them because, White insisted, they had become the habitual gathering spot of "undesirables" who were prone to commit "socially offensive acts" just short of fornication.[2] When pressed further, White and others raised the issue of class, defining the "undesirables" as unkempt "hippies" who camped in open spaces instead of renting rooms. Many residents and visitors were correct, however, as they learned fifteen years later, that "undesirables" also referred here to gay men and some lesbians.[3]

Those most dissatisfied with these guests lambasted Land's End for being a "dirty" town and cheered when the selectmen attempted to "clean up" downtown Provincetown by removing the benches. One Provincetown native, who had moved to Florida years earlier, congratulated the selectmen for eliminating the "'cancer'-type element from the heart of town." Joseph Cabral, a Portuguese fisherman, also supported the selectmen's decision by arguing that the "town dump is cleaner than our town hall." Robert Roman, a local motel owner, agreed, adding, "I, for one, dislike seeing the filth—not only the filth under the benches but the filth on top of the benches."[4]

But the selectmen's decision to police the area in front of town hall failed for the same reasons that the ten commandments had failed two decades earlier: a critical mass of townspeople overrode blatantly discriminatory regulations. Portuguese women, in particular, disagreed with the selectmen's terms regarding "undesirables" and insisted at a special hearing that they return the benches. Rose Pedro spoke for many Provincetown seniors who enjoyed watching people from the town hall benches and who had grown to value Provincetown's newest immigrants. "'I've seen those so-called undesirables move over and give [the elderly] a space," she argued. "And besides, I think they give color to the town." Mrs. Mary Perry, a Provincetown native, observed that "some characters sit out there" but that the native women enjoyed resting on the benches and "see[ing] the sights." "Who [are] the undesirables?" Frank Salles, a local fishermen, asked, "They could be you or me or anybody else."[5]

On July 22, in an editorial entitled "Property Owners and the 'Riffraff,'" the *Provincetown Advocate* questioned the selectmen's class bias by invoking Provincetown's heritage as a liberating outpost. "No wonder there are those who doubt that the Pilgrims landed here first," it stated flatly.[6] One week later, Sylvia S. Lazerow of Baltimore, Maryland, took issue with the selectmen's definition of undesirable: "After spending summer vacations and between $15,000 and $21,000 for rents, food, clothes, etc., in P-Town, I was informed over the 4th of July weekend that I was an 'undesirable.'"[7] Lazerow's sentiments were similar to those of many gay and lesbian tourists who began to wield economic leverage by demanding that townspeople recognize them as contributing citizens, as assets rather than liabilities. After a climactic open hearing, the residents' will prevailed over the selectmen's decision, and municipal workers returned the benches less than a month after they had removed them.

The town hall benches controversy provides a perfect window onto the challenges Provincetown's residents and visitors faced during the last three decades of the twentieth century. While Land's End tackled a host of complicated issues during this time, two interrelated themes stand out as bearing more weight than others: Provincetown's evolution from a Portuguese town into a gay mecca, and Provincetown's change from a vacation destination with economic diversity to a gentrified resort town. Class and sexual orientation took center stage as Provincetown became an exclusive town that housed a disproportionate number of gay and lesbian visitors and residents. Race, too, figured critically into Provincetown's latest incarnation as a middle- and upper-class resort that relied on foreign-born, seasonal laborers. Yet even while numerous residents and tourists continued to smooth Provincetown's transition into an affluent gay haven, just as many asked what kind of town Provincetown would become as gay and lesbian couples bought first and second homes there and as working-class residents and heterosexual families either chose or were forced to seek more affordable shores elsewhere.

Provincetown's gentrification process resembled the kind of refurbishing and remodeling that has taken place in popular vacation destinations and urban enclaves nationwide, from New York's Lower East Side to Colorado's Aspen ski resort and San Francisco's Castro district.[8] In Provincetown, an influx of full- and part-time property owners and renters created more demand than supply of available housing, prompting existing homeowners to winterize their cottages, build additions onto their houses, "finish" their basements and attics, and sub-divide their single-family homes into multiunit condominiums. New homeowners and developers staked out all available land, erected enor-mous houses (in developments like "Pilgrim Heights"), and made ex-tensive renovations to older homes that they bought from Yankee or Portuguese natives.

The shortage of houses and the inflated prices of those for sale drove real estate, rental, and tax values disproportionately high. The two-bedroom home of a retired Portuguese widow on Conant Street was assessed in 1946 at $4,500. Its value increased by 478 percent over the next four decades, but during the 1980s alone, its value increased by more than 400 percent, compared with the northeast regional average of 135 percent, and it was assessed in 1989 at $126,400. A larger water-front house at 47 Commercial Street with three small cottages in its backyard was assessed in 1970 at $36,800, and its owners paid $857.44 in property taxes. By 1994 its assessed value had appreciated by 1,352 percent, more than triple the average appreciation over the same period of time for existing single-family homes in the Northeast. Its new value was set at $534,400, with $5,878 in taxes billed to a retired couple living on a fixed income. From 1995 to 2001, home values in Provincetown ap-preciated by 106 percent, and the average single-family home tax bill increased by 31 percent. From 2000 to 2004 the median sales price for houses in Provincetown nearly doubled.[9]

The influx of money and gay people also changed the look of down-town Provincetown as most stores capitalized on the new gay market. These stores catered to an affluent gay culture decades before corpora-tions like Subaru and IBM and alcohol conglomerates like Anheuser-Busch and Absolut decided to court gay consumers and their "pink" dollars. Like Womencrafts, these shops sold books written by gay and lesbian authors like Rita Mae Brown and James Baldwin; music sung by gay and lesbian artists from Melissa Etheridge to Zoe Lewis; T-shirts with gay slogans like "I'm not a lesbian, but my girlfriend is"; and greet-ing cards or posters featuring lesbian and gay icons. Most stores also sold goods emblazoned with gay symbols and colors from triangle-shaped sun catchers to rainbow-color beach towels.

Over time, Provincetown became a hometown unlike any other as it allowed shops focusing on sex and sexuality to peddle goods along its main street rather steering them into marginalized "red-light" dis-tricts far from the center of town. Some residents and visitors found such blatant references to sex offensive and attempted unsuccessfully to limit the number of sex stores allowed in town and to relocate those already in town away from Commercial Street.[10] But entrepreneurs had no qualms about marketing sex, especially homosexual sex, up and down Commercial Street, as they opened sex and leather shops for both men and women. Along with its numerous gay-owned guest-houses, restaurants, and souvenir stores, these retail shops turned Provincetown's main commercial promenade into a gay shopper's paradise.

Provincetown's entertainment options joined its retail offerings in shaping Provincetown into a distinctly gay town. Like most resort towns providing after-dinner entertainment, Provincetown had its share of nighttime headliners, the only difference being that the actresses (and most performers were women by birth, sex change, or costume) celebrated gay sensibilities and focused on drag and humor. Drag queens toyed with gender ideals by performing as ultrafeminized women. Lesbian comedians poked fun at both straight and gay culture and politics in a way that affirmed gay and lesbian orientations. Provincetown's après-dinner lineup, moreover, forced nearly all performance-seeking visitors, regardless of class, ethnicity, age, or sexual orientation, to attend gay or lesbian shows. Only a fraction of Provincetown's visitors paid to see gay entertainment, however, because various kinds of drag were visible on Commercial Street at any time of the day or night.

As Provincetown became a gay haven, it also turned into a unique amusement park. Unlike most theme parks focusing on popular cartoon characters or death-defying roller coasters, Provincetown featured gender benders, risqué performers, and lesbian comics. It matured into what some called a Gay Disneyland, or, as one visitor put it, like Florida's "Sea World," Provincetown is "Gay World."[11] Drag queens became the sought-after, cartoonlike characters, who were willing, indeed even eager, to pose for voyeurs. Like those in the "real" Disneyland, the characters in Provincetown, meaning the drag queens like "Anna Chovi," "Ginger Vitis," and "Penny Champagne," saved their prime photo opportunities for children, who seemed just as thrilled or confused as if they were standing next to Minnie Mouse or Donald Duck. Most guests took part in Provincetown's queer charades simply by strolling down Commercial Street and brushing shoulder pads with the drag queens. Other visitors, dubbed "clingons" by the some locals, held

A nine-year-old tourist poses with "The B Girls" (above) before borrowing their fashion sense for the Saturday night "big dance" during "Family Week," August 2003. Collection of the author.

on tightly to their opposite-sex companions while gawking at rather than celebrating with Provincetown's more colorful street performers.

Provincetown's residents and visitors experienced its change into a gentrified gay resort in ways that were shaped largely by available forms of mobility and available amounts of space. In contrast to young tourists, Provincetown's resident children experienced their hometown's change into a gay town in a much more nuanced way. Aside from their familiarity and, indeed, boredom with the local drag scene, Provincetown's change into a tourist-driven economy and its emphasis on outsiders forced resident children to reorganize their social activities. Children's entertainment venues, like the aquarium and the bowling alley, for example, were turned into souvenir shops and fast-food joints as Provincetown blossomed into an adult-focused mecca into which children did not fit neatly.

Some children's activities did survive. During the summer months, the younger kids took sailing lessons at the West End Yacht Club, participated in organized activities like arts and crafts at the Community Center, or, if their families could afford it, took tennis lessons at the Provincetown Tennis Club. And when Provincetown lost sight of its adolescent culture, most children and teenagers filled this void with a variety of social and entrepreneurial activities. Teenagers congregated in places like the Pilgrim Memorial bas-relief and took part-time jobs as retail workers, while a handful continued the tradition of diving for coins when the Boston boat arrived. A few bought and sold drugs or engaged in paid sex work as a way to procure drugs or consumer goods.[12]

The Shadow Writing Project provided an alternative learning environment for kids interested in writing and publishing their own poetry. The project's founder and director, artist Kathe Izzo, edited two collections of her students' work: *Flicker* and *Flicker II: Fuel*.[13] Several teenagers also published their own "zine," *The Effects: Of Living on a Sandbar,* an angst-ridden collection that discusses typical adolescent challenges from understanding punk rock to processing death, mourning, and sadness. On the one hand, "the effects" of living in Provincetown seem like the effects of living in other similarly isolated, rural villages. "Carmen" sets the tone in an editorial on the second page of the zine:

> I hate my school; I really do. I don't like many of the kids because they
> are extremely rude, selfish, boisterous. . . . They make me ashamed of

who I am and where I come from. . . . I feel so trapped on this sandbar, in this sad excuse for a town, hence the title of this zine.[14]

On the other hand, *The Effects* seems to be a product of Provincetown's "artsy" and open climate, and publishing a zine of poetry and short essays fits well with Provincetown's creative literary traditions. In the zine, teenagers like Linsey Smith write about acceptance and difference: "The locals of Provincetown are very open-minded, but once we get out of our sheltered Cape Cod, it's a totally different world . . . whatever happened to unity and equality? It shouldn't matter what your color, religion, sexual preference [is]. . . . It should matter what you're like on the inside."[15]

Indeed, the presence of such a large gay contingent allowed local children to experience a part of the world that most of their peers elsewhere could only imagine (this was especially true before certain forms of gay life became popular on network television and on the Internet). Educational opportunities, in others words, complemented the distinct challenges of growing up in a gay town. When many of Provincetown's teenagers went to college, they learned not only that most people who had heard of their hometown associated it with a gay haven but also that most teenagers lacked the exposure and sophistication required to understand what lay behind gay sensibilities and difference.[16]

At the same time, Provincetown's reputation as a gay haven placed its children in awkward situations because their peers residing elsewhere often ridiculed them for living in a gay town. Before 1975, for instance, when school athletes traveled to "away" games, opposing teams and their fans often made fun of the Provincetown "Fishermen" by throwing dead fish onto the playing fields. But as Provincetown was becoming a gay town, other players began taunting the "Fishermen" by calling them "fags" and "dykes." According to the *Provincetown Advocate,* in 1987, students walked into another school's locker room to find a sign saying "Welcome Provincetown Faggots" taped to the door.[17] Provincetown's opponents also sometimes refused to shake hands with the "Fishermen," citing as an excuse their fear of contracting AIDS.

As Provincetown's gay culture became more pronounced, gay and straight visitors and residents reorganized both time and space at Land's End. During the summer season, many natives and year-round townspeople of all sexual orientations typically moved to the outskirts of town to avoid the tourists and the congestion on Commercial Street.

Some simply stayed home for most of July and August, and others rented their houses for the summer and headed to Maine or out West. Those who remained met with friends and neighbors at marginalized "townie" locations, like the Whaler Lounge at the Holiday Inn in the far East End of town, the Landing Lounge at the Provincetown Inn in the extreme West End of town, and the downstairs barroom at the Veterans of Foreign Wars ("Vets") building beyond the center of town near Route 6. Indeed, one of the only places natives coveted in downtown Provincetown was the old-fashioned soda counter in Adams Pharmacy on Commercial Street. Manuel "Cul" Goveia captured the status of most native townspeople during the summer in his weekly local history column, entitled *Endangered Species*.[18]

Provincetown's turn into a tourists' town also meant that residents looking for everyday household wares had to look much harder and farther as gay tourists replaced heterosexual families as the primary units of consumption. Because the businesses that made the greatest profits catered to tourists, those shops that served the resident community began to disappear. Stores that sold items like clothing, toiletries, groceries, and household goods, such as the New York Store, Cabral's Market, and Matheson's Clothing, gave way to ice-cream parlors, T-shirt stores, and sex-toy shops. In 1998 B. H. Dyer's Hardware store became an art gallery. For those people who came to Provincetown only occasionally, the gay tourist market posed few problems and many souvenir opportunities. But for the seasonal and year-round residents, especially those who were too old or young to drive an automobile, or too poor to own one, buying household staples became difficult. The nearest town that sold moderately priced household wares was Orleans, thirty miles up-Cape, and the nearest place to buy affordable clothing was in Hyannis, sixty miles up-Cape. A five-minute walk from the West End of town to downtown Commercial Street, in other words, became a half- or full-day preplanned excursion.

The new gay consumer and entertainment culture at Land's End also altered the visiting patterns of its more conservative tourists. When Provincetown's gay guests arrived downtown in the late afternoon and evening, after spending the day at Herring Cove, most of the day visitors escaped to more conventional towns like Wellfleet, Brewster, and Dennis. Indeed, progressive visitors aside, tourists split Provincetown in half: straight families and individuals frequented its streets and shops during the day when the environment seemed "safer," and gays took over during the evenings and nights. Straight families and individuals still visited Land's End to browse in its unusual stores, sunbathe at its stunning beaches, go on one of its whale-watching cruises, or gawk at its gender deviants. But whereas in the past these visitors spent a season, month, or week in Provincetown, by the turn of the twenty-first century, most were limiting their stays to a day, an evening, or a brief overnight trip. Once straight visitors found themselves overwhelmingly in the minority, in other words, many limited the kind of time they spent at Land's End.

Herring Cove Beach, at the far west of town, illustrates the ways in which visitors and townspeople of all sexual orientations altered Provincetown's geographic landscape. As they did in town, residents and visitors divided Herring Cove in half. Instead of East End versus West End, Herring Cove Beach was split into the north side and the south side. Straight tourists parked immediately to the north of the Cape Cod National Seashore (CCNS) bathhouse where the parking lot overlooks the ocean. Lesbian tourists monopolized the area just south of the bathhouse, and gay male tourists went even farther south on the "wild side," as many CCNS lifeguards call it.[19] The men closest to the ocean were typically those interested in sunbathing, swimming, and socializing. Those seeking public sex took a short walk from the ocean into the sand dunes. Natives and "townies" regardless of sexual or gender orientation escaped all tourists by going from the north end of the parking lot toward Race Point Lighthouse. Herring Cove Beach, in other words, reflected the structural divide of Provincetown as a whole. Tourists broke down into gay and straight camps and positioned themselves on either side of the Herring Cove bathhouse, with lesbians staking out one area and gay men congregating in another. "Townies" of all sexual orientations stayed clear of all tourists and relaxed off the beaten track near Hatch's Harbor (see map, p. 7).

As Provincetown became a gentrified resort town, residential mobility also became a critical issue for natives and longtime residents of all backgrounds. Because in-season rental prices often cost more than most workers made in a summer season, many year-round residents, including entire families, lived in affordable "winter rentals" during the off-season but scrambled every year to find a seasonal cottage or a room for the summer. Homeowners also had difficult choices to make. Some natives sold their aging houses in Provincetown and bought larger, newer ones in Truro, farther up-Cape, or in different parts of the

The Provincetown Business Guild's 1998 *Annual Guide* incorporates the usual language of freedom as well as scenes of the intersections among groups, this time between drag queens and lifeguards from the Cape Cod National Seashore, who are patrolling both the straight section and the "wild side" of Herring Cove Beach. Collection of the author.

state or country altogether. Provincetown native and bartender Jerome "Jerry" Lee Costa was born in the West End and lived in Provincetown until gentrification set in. Once he realized the profit he could make by selling his home in Provincetown, he did so immediately and built a large, contemporary home with ample yard, garage, and storage space in Truro. After his move, Costa claimed in a 1997 interview, he felt that he now had the best of both worlds: a quiet, wooded, spacious lot in Truro and, just ten minutes away, the hustle and bustle of what Brudnoy called "steamy" Provincetown. Although Costa's story ends well, other working-class natives have felt forced rather than free to leave their hometown and move to Truro. Marilyn Miller summed up this trend well in 1998 in an article entitled "Provincetown's Tired, Hungry and Poor Look to Truro: Gentrification, Loss of Diversity Hasten Outflow."[20]

In 1997 Kim Rilleau, a second-generation sandal maker, moved his wife and their family of three young children to Woodstock, Vermont. Before leaving, Rilleau explained, "You could say [we are leaving because of] the schools, that it's hard to make a living year-round or the [sense of] loss as a family town, but [our decision is] more than that." Not long after Rilleau moved, Katherine Witherstine Gilman and her husband, who owned a house on the water, decided to relocate because their real estate taxes had escalated beyond the already tight budget of their fixed income. They moved up-Cape to Brewster.[21]

Provincetown's process of gentrification was also a process of displacement, and it ushered in demographic shifts that fell along intersecting lines of sexual orientation, ethnicity, and class. The rising rental and real estate costs forced working-class artists to seek more affordable colonies elsewhere.[22] Rilleau was one of many artists, including Kathe Izzo, who moved to artistic communities in Vermont and New York State once they realized that Provincetown was no longer an affordable place to live or work. This was especially true when Provincetown's traditional art venues—its schools, collectives, and outdoor painting classes—became commercialized. With the exception of one or two summer art schools and the Fine Arts Work Center, onlookers found most "art" in expensive galleries.[23] For more spontaneous art, tourists might have caught a glimpse of one of Lois Griffel's classes from the Cape Cod School of Art on the beach or in their outdoor yard on Pearl Street or a lone painter at her easel along the east or west end of Commercial Street. To see performance art, tourists and residents might have attended a drag show or observed the exaggerated gender bending on Commercial Street. To be sure, Provincetown still hosted dozens of accomplished comedians, painters, sculptors, actors, musicians, and writers, like Mary Oliver, Harvey Dodd, Ron Fowler, Norman Mailer, Michael Cunningham, Eileen Miles, and Norma Holt. But for the most part, Provincetown's days as an affordable colony for artists were over.

Provincetown's influx of wealthy gay men and lesbians also displaced much of the town's working-class sector. Indeed, when less-expensive housing, especially that which was year-round, grew scarce, so did minimum-wage workers of all backgrounds. After all, who could afford to wash dishes in one of Provincetown's overpriced restaurants or sell T-shirts in retail stores that did not pay enough even to cover rental or mortgage debts? In 1999, for instance, the average annual income for workers in Provincetown was $23,322, and the median sale price for a single-family home was $290,000. Five years later, with workers making only slightly more, the median price tag for a single-family home in Provincetown had jumped to $630,000.[24]

The gentrification that followed Provincetown's turn into a gay resort, its status as a single-industry resort town, and its semi-isolated location meant that Provincetown was available to select residents and visitors only. While hundreds of gay men and lesbians would have liked to live in Queersville, U.S.A., most could not afford to because its seasonal service economy limited employment opportunities and its location limited commuter options. Those who could afford a life at Land's End either came to town with enough capital to set up their own businesses or made their money elsewhere. Many gay men and lesbians had permanent jobs up-Cape or had offices in Boston, New York City, Raleigh, or Atlanta and bought weekend or summer homes in Provincetown. One transgendered resident traveled from as far away as New Jersey (typically an eight-hour drive) every weekend just to be in Provincetown and call it home.[25] Other gay men and lesbians moved to Provincetown as soon as they retired.

The gentrification and displacement processes also had distinct racial implications as white business owners began importing black workers from Jamaica to do the menial jobs the remaining white workers turned down. When the twenty-first century arrived, Provincetown became, again, a two-tiered town divided by race.[26] This dynamic, whereby white owners assign the most menial and low-paying jobs to the darkest workers, re-created the stratified racial and class structure that shaped Provincetown less than a century earlier when white Yankees gave so-called dark-skinned Portuguese immigrants, Cape Verdeans, and African Americans the lowest-paying positions. Throughout the 1990s, dozens of Jamaican workers arrived in Provincetown by way of an H-2B visa seasonal work program.[27] By 2003, fifty-four of Provincetown's restaurants, hotels, and other businesses imported a total of 384 H-2B visa laborers, whose average wage was $10.12 per hour. Upon their initial visits, many Jamaicans were shocked once they realized that they had landed in a gay paradise. Some chose immediately to return home. Most, however, learned to tolerate, accept, or enjoy the preponderance of gays and lesbians and decided to return annually because, compared with Jamaica, Provincetown was a lucrative place to work.[28]

Provincetown's transformation from a working-class to a tourist town created financial winners and losers.[29] However, unlike some resort areas where wealthy white outsiders displaced nearly all the local residents, in Provincetown the winners and losers were not divided evenly according to place of origin, ethnicity, or sexual orientation.[30] Wealthy white couples and individuals, regardless of their sexual orientation, displaced many of Provincetown's working-class Portuguese natives. Yet alongside solvent wash-ashores stood a number of equally successful natives—both gay and straight—who stayed and prospered at Land's End.[31] Moreover, Portuguese natives did not necessarily depart empty-handed as many made enormous gains by selling older houses and buying larger, newer ones elsewhere. Similarly, wealthy wash-ashores did not displace only working-class natives. Working-class wash-ashores and artists of varying sexual orientations also chose or were compelled to leave town for financial reasons. Like their emigrating Portuguese counterparts, some left town with pockets full, while others left with pockets empty.

Provincetown's evolution into an exclusive gay resort, like its change from a Yankee seaport into a Portuguese fishing village, did not come about quietly or easily. Residents of all backgrounds continuously contested the terms of the gay "takeover," returning repeatedly to questions such as "who owns the Province Lands," what kinds of Pilgrims are welcome at Land's End, and under what terms can wash-ashores who are not full citizens elsewhere become full citizens in Provincetown. Both gay and straight residents expressed mixed reactions. Some gay and lesbian wash-ashores had moved to Provincetown during the 1950s, 1960s, and 1970s because it was a Portuguese fishing village and art colony that happened to be especially gay friendly, and they were disappointed to see it turning into a full-fledged gay resort mecca. Some straight residents were equally disappointed and often resentful when gay men and lesbians displaced their friends and relatives while making life in Provincetown an increasingly expensive undertaking. But Provincetown also had its share of straight residents who enjoyed the company of their new gay neighbors, who appreciated the efforts to fix up older homes, and who thrived as business owners in a lucrative gay market. While residents debated any number of issues while their hometown became a gay resort, they articulated their frustrations in terms of morality and citizenship, focusing most often on harassment, sex, religion, and the fate of Provincetown's children.

Some of Provincetown's teenagers seemed especially resentful of their gay neighbors and guests. Without access to formal political power, they asserted their rights to Land's End by using informal policing tactics and adding an element of physicality that the older residents avoided. From at least the 1930s, local teenagers and young adults had policed Provincetown's streets and beaches by harassing gay men.[32] For the most part, though, these attacks had gone unchecked until the summer of 1971 when gay men fought back by wielding their financial leverage. Less than two weeks before the selectmen decided to remove the town hall benches, a gay male visitor argued in the *Provincetown Advocate* that he spent "well over $5,000 [in Provincetown] per season. Now," he continued, "not only am I planning on not returning next summer but on leaving town now and summering elsewhere. . . . The reason is simple: I do not need to come to Provincetown to be beaten or to watch others being beaten."[33] In a new consumerized republic that was dependent on gay consumers, gay men began in the early 1970s to analyze their vacations in Provincetown in the context of market transactions. Because they were good consumers, they felt that they also were being good citizens and that Provincetown was therefore responsible for their safety, if not their happiness.

Indeed, inspired in part by the gay liberation and civil rights movements, gays and lesbians began in the early 1970s to demand that Provincetown live up to its promise as a unique gay haven or suffer financial consequences. The responses to this ultimatum, and to a supportive editorial that accompanied it, helped define Provincetown's late-twentieth-century social environment as one that shunned homophobic behaviors. The demand to stop Provincetown's tradition of youths harassing gay men inspired a local businessman to write an anonymous and homophobic letter to the editor. He argued first that "'beatin' up queers,' is nothing new here and has been a local past-time for years." The reason for this was that "there is a lot of local resentment among all generations to these swishy gay boys that strut up and down our streets in their exhibitionist fashions. For years, many of us who are here in business would much prefer less business if the alternative means catering to perverts." The "gay takeover" most infuriated the author, however, when he claimed that "some fairy" asked his son if he was gay. "As a local parent, I assure you my blood really boiled." Finally, he noted,

> As for the faggot whom you quoted at the Selectmen's meeting as saying, "I think if the gay crowd left Provincetown, it would pull up the sidewalks, and roll into the sea," and the other who wrote you that because he spends $5,000 in a summer in Provincetown that he is an asset to the town, I'm one businessman who would love to see 'em leave.

Apparently this man did not mind losing most of his business, for as he put it, "After you accept this dirty loot, you still have to sleep at night. In my book, these youth who rough up queers are local heroes."[34]

In its blatant disregard of the increasingly gay-friendly and gay-dependent direction in which Provincetown was moving, this diatribe helped reinforce the belief at Land's End that gay visitors would be accepted and homophobic residents would not. Indeed, the anonymous writer's extreme homophobia led to a wave of responses that began to turn the tide of legitimate phobias at Land's End.

The *Provincetown Advocate*, which published the letter, responded first. The editors of the local weekly told their readers that they had tried to persuade the businessman to admit to his bigotry. Despite his refusal, they printed his letter, "to show our readers the depths of prejudice and disrespect for the concept of equal protection under the law." They concluded by arguing that, "a gang of men who rough up (and 'rough up' in this case means kick and stab) vastly outnumbered other men are cowardly thugs. And in our book, businessmen who condone, and, indeed, encourage such beatings make the word 'thug' woefully inadequate."[35]

The numerous responses, which appeared for weeks afterward, revealed Provincetown's increasing intolerance of homophobic people and attitudes. A "local youth" wrote an anonymous letter admitting that he, too, disliked "queers" but that he also did not want "any sick businessman talking" on his behalf. "I think the real perverts," he added, "are the people who have to prove their manliness by beating up the gay community. And I think most of the local youth feel secure enough to not be bothered by the gay community." Representatives from the Homophile Assistance League of Provincetown concurred, calling the businessman a "moral coward, [a] spineless hypocrite, [and a] parasite." Several writers pointed specifically to the businessman's hypocritical stance of dismissing gay people's "dirty loot" yet fearing personal disclosure. One gay person contended that the businessman's "refusal to identify himself and his business show that he realizes just how much his profits depend upon our 'dirty loot.'" Mrs. May McClintock put it simply: "All he has to do is to come out in the open, say who he is, and I'm sure he'd be accommodated with 'less business' as he requests."[36]

Public discussions of gay harassment, which encouraged gay visitors and residents to demand equal rights as consumers and citizens, marked the summer of 1971 in Provincetown. Indeed, from this time on, gay men and lesbian women insisted that local officials and residents protect them from violent teenagers and adults. If Provincetown could not guarantee their safety, many gay visitors threatened to take their vacation money elsewhere. Although these conversations did not end gay harassment in Provincetown, they were a start. It took two more decades of negotiations before local violence came to a screeching halt under the careful watch of Provincetown's Hate Crimes Working Group.

By the early 1990s Provincetown had all but finished policing gays and turned instead to a municipal plan that recognized gay men and lesbians as consumers and rewarded them with greater citizenship status. Local officials called the institutionalized version of this official protection plan "community policing." After the police chief, James P. Meads, retired in 1992, both gay and straight residents worked with municipal employees, notably the new chief of police, Robert Anthony, and the town manager, Keith Bergman, to implement "the strong belief that Community Oriented Public Safety (COPS) should be the operational philosophy of the Provincetown Police Department."[37] Under the auspices of COPS, community leaders convened the "Hate Plan Working Group" and combined community action, education, law enforcement, and victim assistance to develop a "Plan to Overcome Hate Incidents."

This group focused on making Provincetown's environment as safe and welcoming as possible for gays and lesbians. They built partnerships with the judiciary, district attorney, and state attorney general, only the last of whom could obtain injunctions for civil rights violations in order to expedite the prosecution of hate crimes. When they discovered that a band of "troubled" high school students were committing most of the hate crimes in Provincetown, they asked the principal of the

Provincetown high school and town officials to better police, discipline, and educate juvenile offenders. Local officials introduced two intervention programs for "youth-at-risk." Provincetown's aggressive strategy for combating violence resulted in a 76 percent reduction in the number of hate crimes committed annually, prompting Governor William Weld's Task Force on Hate Crimes to give the Massachusetts Association Innovation Award to Provincetown in 1993.

Although it was meant to protect gays and lesbians, Provincetown's Plan to Overcome Hate Crimes also gave black residents and tourists more leverage against race-motivated offenses. In 1993 the working group helped obtain a restraining order for a racially motivated attack. Three years later, when a gay man led the Carnival Parade in an Aunt Jemima blackface costume, the working group drafted an official response that condemned racist actions. These incidents suggest once again how Provincetown's relationship to racial difference was complicated and far-reaching.[38]

As homophobic and racist acts became less acceptable and as gays and lesbians grew bolder and prouder, Provincetown's cultural climate changed as instances of heterophobia, not homophobia, increased. Anger at Provincetown's straight and working-class residents had distinct class components. In 1979 Josephine Johnson complained that "three homosexuals" had pushed her off the sidewalk on Commercial Street while they "shrilled, 'peasant.'"[39] Russell Pagliaro of Boston responded to Provincetown's early 1980 gay-bashing incidents by questioning the residents' intelligence: "For years I have refused to believe stories of the level of intelligence because of inbreeding, but could it be the drinking water" that causes local youth to harass gay men? "I hope for a fast turn-about," he added, "before the name townie, long spoken with arrogance, may be whispered in shame."[40] Perhaps the most popular term gay men and lesbians used to belittle straight couples, individuals, and families was "breeder." "Do you think there are special sidewalks for breeders?" two lesbians apparently asked after making way on Commercial Street's busy sidewalk for a young family.[41] The former administrative assistant to Provincetown's superintendent of schools, Clinton "Skip" Parker, complained in 1996 that the town's enforcement of tolerance was too rigid. Because Provincetown is dependent on gay tourists, if anyone even so much as speaks negatively about gays or the gay movement, Parker complained, "Everyone jumps on it.

. . . It's like for someone to holler shark in a community that lives off its nice beach. . . . I claim that kind of atmosphere is discriminatory."[42]

Overt displays of sexuality also concerned Provincetown residents of all sexual orientations, as a fraction of gay men enjoyed having sex in public spaces. Although local officials were persistent and at times ruthless regarding their policing tactics when it came to public sex, gay men were equally ambitious. In 1955, when local and state police squads raided Provincetown's most popular gay nightclubs, like the Atlantic House, and charged those engaging in public sex with "disorderly conduct" or "lewd and lascivious behavior," gay men merely moved outside or to less popular bars.[43] In 1970, when Cape Cod National Seashore Rangers entrapped gay men having sex at Herring Cove Beach under the guise of "erosion control," the gay men moved to the base of the Pilgrim Monument.[44] The police raided this area and marched the men, some with their pants around their ankles, across Bradford Street to the local jail, which was in the basement of town hall at the time. In 1974, when this humiliating response failed to discourage gay men from having sex at the monument, local officials put up a fence and illuminated the area with floodlights.[45] But once the lights went up, the men simply moved on to another ill-lit location, this time on the beach, dubbed the "dick dock." As the areas for gay male recreational sex shrank elsewhere in the United States, in Provincetown they survived.[46]

Gay men's persistence in holding on to locations for public sex also points to the ways in which townspeople drew and redrew boundaries for what they believed was appropriate behavior at Land's End. In the 1950s and 1960s the behavior that ruffled the most feathers was that exhibited by flamboyant gay men and female impersonators. By the last quarter of the twentieth century, however, natives and visitors took offense not at Provincetown's "boys" but at gay men who had sex in public.[47]

In this way, private homosexual sex moved from what anthropologist Gayle Rubin calls the "outer limits" of sexual behavior, which includes sadomasochism and bondage, to the "charmed circle" of sex acts, which encompasses monogamous heterosexual sex, sex for procreation, and "vanilla" sex.[48] In other words, as long as gay residents and visitors stayed close to their new niche in the "charmed circle" of sex acts by keeping their sex lives private and, better yet, engaging in monogamous partnerships, gay and straight townspeople approved. But as soon as gays, queers, and lesbians moved from the "charmed circle" toward the "outer limits" of sexual behavior by engaging in casual public sex, townspeople of varying sexual orientations removed them at once from the local community of likeness. As Peter Hardaway put it in 1985, Provincetown is a place of tolerance, however, "public, sexually-intensive behavior is unacceptable."[49] Others concurred with language reminiscent of Provincetown's early-twentieth-century colonial revival: "Tolerance and total license are not the same thing . . . this is a hometown community with standards," one editorial argued in 1977, while another stated flatly, "Everything doesn't go in Provincetown."[50]

In 1989 gay and straight residents in Provincetown jumped at the opportunity to reinforce these sentiments and to exclude the gay community's more radical fringe when ACT UP (AIDS Coalition to Unleash Power) marched in the local pride parade. At the front of the procession, an unidentified member of ACT UP carried out the organization's strategy of being confrontational by waving a sign to and fro that stated something to the effect of "Legalize Butt Fucking."

The "sign," as the incident came to be called, rocked the already shaky balance between Provincetown's gay and straight communities as few events had before or have since. Gay and straight townspeople alike vented what seemed to be years of rage toward the bearer of the sign and all that he represented: in-your-face, nonmonogamous, public homosexuality, on the one hand, and aggressive gay politics, on the other. The anger generated by the straight community, however, differed from that of the gay community. Straight residents and visitors expressed unfocused outrage toward gays and lesbians in general, whereas gay men and lesbians lashed out more specifically at the disruptive tactics of ACT UP because they felt that this strategy was unnecessary in the tolerant climate that had taken decades to cultivate at Land's End. In this way, gay men and lesbians in Provincetown narrowed their community of likeness and excluded the gay movement's more radical participants. Gay and lesbian residents expected their gay guests to conduct themselves with a certain amount of decorum.

The message of Provincetown's gay population was clear: do not come here and ruin it for the rest of us. One lesbian remembered the exact moment she saw the sign: "I was shocked," she wrote in a letter to the *Provincetown Advocate*, "What about all these kids? What about community rapport? . . . Then I was livid! . . . The past two days," she lamented, "I've spent focusing on what energy all of us in the gay/lesbian population who remain here in Provincetown have to generate to clean up the unsavory, unacceptable mess that was dumped on us by a handful of irresponsible agitators."[51] This response was indicative of the political conservativeness that many local gay men and lesbians fell into once they took up residence in a gay-friendly enclave, away from queer struggles elsewhere.

The President of the Provincetown Business Guild (PBG), Philippe D'Auteuil, published a similar warning. In "an open letter to ACT UP," D'Auteuil charged the group with doing a "great disservice" to the PBG because of the fallout associated with the "sign." The PBG, D'Auteuil stated, had worked persistently for more than a decade to promote gay tourism in Provincetown and to make Land's End into a gay-friendly vacation spot. "We are active, contributing citizens. As such, we have enjoyed a greater degree of freedom, not just tolerance, than is afforded to gay people living in most places in this country," he asserted. Local townspeople, D'Auteuil argued, have blamed the PBG for the "obscene" sign, which in turn had "alienated friends and given bigots a focus for their hatred." "This is what you have done to us," D'Auteuil continued. "We now face great hostility as we try to rebuild trust, to apologize for your excess, and to do so while maintaining pride in who and what we are."[52]

A number of writers took up the issue of citizenship and homophobia more explicitly and registered their irritation with the intensity of the responses to the sign. "The wording of the sign was offensive," James Bella of Provincetown agreed, but "it is also offensive when, in most states, gay men and women cannot love one another in the privacy of their own homes without being in violation of a criminal law or statute." Rene LeBlanc agreed, adding, "It is every citizen's right to express him or herself as each chooses fit even if that opinion is only his alone."[53]

Just as Philippe D'Auteuil predicted, many straight townspeople and visitors used the ACT UP sign as an excuse for unchecked outbursts of homophobia. After vacationing at Land's End for fourteen years, William T. Henderson of Morristown, New Jersey, decided not to return. After watching "your gay parade with their filthy signs, obscene dress, etc. we can't handle it any longer," he claimed. "We were starting to get tolerant of their lifestyle, but they have gone too far. . . . Your town has become 'sin' city." Vida Wongola of Provincetown stated that she was "shocked, saddened, and, yes disgusted by [the] March of Filth, as I like to call it." Others were more subdued. "If gays want to march or parade, fine," A. J. Souza explained, "but please keep it at a decent level" for the sake of observant children.[54]

The sign controversy illuminated two aspects of Provincetown's complicated political landscape. First, it revealed the fragility of Provincetown's community of likeness as a single person holding one sign prompted straight residents to distinguish themselves immediately from their "filthy" gay guests. Second, it clarified how resident gays and lesbians prioritized assimilation and aimed to make peace with local townspeople by criticizing gay visitors outside Provincetown's "charmed circle."

In the absence of pivotal events like "the sign," disgruntled residents often invoked the innocence of children to register their dissatisfaction and frustration with Provincetown's openness regarding sex and sexuality. Helen Souza, a native of Provincetown, spoke for many when she exclaimed: "I am disgusted and offended by the gays who carry on on the bay beach and publicly do things people used to do behind closed doors. . . . This is right smack in the middle of playing children who can't help but notice their disgusting antics."[55] Dolores M. deSousa was outraged when her eleven-year-old daughter returned home from shopping on Commercial Street with a T-shirt featuring two elephants in the act of fornication above the caption, "Elephants never forget." "Parents wake up!" she exclaimed. "Open homosexuality, drugs, and pornography, it's all a part of the moral decay of Provincetown's children."[56]

Tourists also used children to scold Provincetown for allowing itself to become a gay haven. In 1979 Marjorie Osborne Whorf of Hingham, Massachusetts, was "appalled" to learn that the Provincetown Business Guild supported the town's Little League baseball teams. "Isn't it enough that these kids are forced day after day to witness the bizarre behavior of homosexuals?" she asked. "I raise my hand in protest at the very mention of this homosexual organization daring to infiltrate the sweet hope of a young boy with his bat and glove going out to prove his mettle."[57] After spending her vacations in Provincetown every year for thirty years, Whorf decided not to return, owing to what she called the "takeover." In 1986 Albert S. Johnson, a summer visitor, rebuked Provincetown for being tolerant of the "abnormal actions" of gays and lesbians. Perhaps its residents would reconsider their positions, he observed, if they put themselves "in the shoes of the parent who is trying to raise a normal offspring in an environment which, to say the least, is not normal according to the opinion of the majority of our country."[58]

In addition to moral arguments regarding children, some visitors and residents used religion to launch potentially (financially) harmful homophobic outbursts. In December 1985 a heated dialogue that continued for nearly a year erupted over the issue of homosexuality and religion. Kate Barnett of Provincetown helped fuel this bitter debate by arguing, "I for one am sick and tired of hearing that we have to be tolerant and have to accept acts that are immoral. I'm also equally tired of hearing about 'gay rights.' . . . Any way you look at it, God still created Adam and Eve, and not Adam and Steve." Anette Dalpe of Naples, Florida, agreed and invoked specific passages from the Bible (Leviticus 18:22, 20:13; Corinthians 6:9–10; Romans 1:22–27) to contend that a rise in homosexuality pointed to nothing less than a society's "last stages of decay."[59]

Outbursts like these prompted a number of residents and visitors to take part in the "current Chapter and Verses Sweepstakes," to use resident Will Walker's phrase. Walker urged readers to consider the First Epistle General of John 2:9, "He that saith he is in the light, and hateth his brother, is in the darkness even until now." Sally Price of Provincetown responded specifically to Barnett by asking her not to play God, stating, "If in your standards our happiness and freedom are degrading, then my heart breaks for you." Mrs. Henry Morgan of New York City concurred and accused Barnett of having "the judgmental attitude that creates the leper mentality and that deliberate ignorance that breeds fear."[60]

Finally, in the tradition of Provincetown's early Yankees, some townspeople also looked to the *Mayflower* Pilgrims to restore Land's End to a safe yet financially lucrative heterosexual order. Provincetown, they reminded their guests and fellow residents, was the landfall of this country's forefathers and was not meant to be a place where alternative sexualities, genders, and behaviors predominated. In 1972 Catherine B. Cadose, chairman of "Women for Decency," a local affiliation of the Catholic Daughters of America, asked "Provincetownians" to pay more attention to "decency" and "Moral Laws." "We certainly don't want lawbreakers in this historic town, the first landing place of the Pilgrims," she stated. Nine years later Frank W. Adams of Provincetown reflected the thoughts of many: "The Pilgrims would blush with shame to see what is being shown in the streets of this town. . . . May God forgive us all."[61]

Many writers appropriated the same language to call not for more "decency" but for an increase in their rights as citizens of Land's End. For decades, they argued, Provincetown had promoted itself as an oasis for the persecuted and would do well to live up to that reputation. In 1986 Danny Barillo railed against homophobia and censorship by hoping that "maybe someday in my lifetime Provincetown will really be the town that we say it is: The Birthplace of American Freedom."[62] One year later Sidney Wordell spoke out against Provincetown's policing tactics in an angry letter to the editor: "Visit historic Provincetown, Birthplace of American Democracy. . . . Gaze at the gentle, unspoiled scenery, but don't pause. You may be arrested! . . . Provincetown's credo: we want your money. We don't want you."[63] In these ways gay visitors and residents hitched their rights as citizens to their financial investments and to Provincetown's legendary beginnings.

These aforementioned debates were heated and demonstrated how freedom of speech and acts of dissent—how democracy—works in small communities. But they also suggest that Provincetown dealt with an unusually large amount of strife as it evolved into a gay resort. Some might ask whether a sense of community existed in a town trapped between dueling factions of residents and tourists. In many ways Provincetown was, and continues to be, unique; its status as one of the most popular gay resort destinations in the world guarantees that it has faced and will continue to face challenges that other hometowns and even other resort towns have not encountered. But like that which took place in other hometowns and resort towns, when the dust settled after townspeople aired their disputes, Provincetown remained occupied with the municipal tasks that were needed to make it a safe and prosperous place to live and visit. From manning its volunteer fire stations to raising money for its charities, Provincetown's residents remained dedicated to their town and to one another. The question, then, is not *did* a sense of community exist in Provincetown but, rather, *how* did Provincetown function *as* a community.

Provincetown's demographic and socioeconomic shifts prompted residents to reexamine its municipal strategies and institutions. The number of tourists taxed the environment, which already was unstable, for Provincetown had seemed to forget that it was hosting thousands of people on a tiny spit of land lacking the facilities, like a central sewer system, to manage such a dense population. The selectmen discussed wastewater management as much as, if not more than, any other issue as Provincetown approached the new millennium, aside from the perennial debates over what to do with the town-financed Cape End Manor (assisted-living facility) and over how to create more affordable housing.[64] Local institutions, like the public school system and the volunteer fire department, staples of most New England villages and towns, suffered significantly as natives left town and part-time residents or retired gay wash-ashores replaced them.[65] School enrollment declined sharply when young families and heterosexual couples left town and gay couples with either few or no children replaced them as seasonal and year-round residents.[66] In 2002 Provincetown recorded only one birth. What will Provincetown look like as a "Town without Children"? one local paper asked.[67]

Residents also paid special attention to the health and well-being of their friends and neighbors. Provincetown became a town where seasonal depression, alcoholism, and drug abuse soared as year-round businesses gave way to seasonal shops that left nearly half of all workers jobless for six months or more.[68] Residents made sure daily "recovery" groups were available for those seeking a different way to live. They wholeheartedly supported organizations like the Provincetown AIDS Support Group and Helping Our Women. And unlike some communities that rely on foreign-born laborers, Provincetown established a Human Rights Resolution Working Group that counsels foreign-born workers and attempts to oversee their labor and housing conditions.

Provincetown has acted like a community that cares about its members especially during annual celebrations and unexpected tragedies.[69] When the Moors Restaurant burned to the ground in May 1956, residents of all sexual orientations worked together to rebuild it in time for the upcoming summer season. Forty years later, when one of the buildings in the Maushope Apartment Complex, which houses many of Provincetown's senior residents, went up in flames, straight townspeople like those manning the volunteer fire department raced there immediately to put out the conflagration, while gay residents who owned restaurants and guesthouses pitched in with food, clothing, and hous-

MUSTY CHIFFON
In a Benefit Concert for the
Provincetown Public Library Internet
and Driskel Studio

plastic   surgery

Benefits like the one in 1998 advertised above brought together a cross section
of residents, including the public library staff, resident children, and a drag
queen called Musty Chiffon. Collection of the author.

ing.[70] Similarly, benefits raising money for Provincetown's nonprofit organizations also attracted residents of all sexual and gender orientations. The predominantly straight Provincetown Fire and Rescue De-
partments, for example, sponsored an annual drag show called "Holly-
wood Night" to benefit local rescue squads. It was held at a popular gay
club, and drag queens entertained a mixed gay and straight audience.

In addition to benefits, Provincetown's numerous annual festivals
also attracted crowds of varying backgrounds and interests. Straight
Portuguese natives produced the Blessing of the Fleet ceremony and the
Portuguese Festival in late June, yet both gay and straight businesses
supported it, and gay and straight residents and visitors participated in
it. Similarly, during the Provincetown Business Guild's Carnival parade
in late August, the streets are filled with drag queens while spectators
of all ages, ethnicities, and sexual and gender orientations line the sidewalks. Moreover, it is not unusual for Carnival parades to honor one or
more of Provincetown's straight residents. For instance, one of the legendary Town Criers, Gene Poyant, and one of Provincetown's most
revered Portuguese immigrants, Grace Goveia Collinson, were the
grand marshals of the 1985 Carnival parade.[71] In addition to these pub-

lic entertainment venues, semipublic locations such as the Whaler Lounge at the Holiday Inn, which offers free movies nightly, drew, and continues to draw, a hearty mix of gay and straight residents.

Besides coming together in the face of tragedy or in the name of entertainment, gay and straight townspeople have fostered relationships at work as well. Until the end of the twentieth century, for example, gay men owned and ran Fat Jack's Café and employed gay men, lesbians, bisexuals, and straight or "questioning" residents to serve gay, straight, queer, and transgender townspeople and visitors. Municipal employees and local town boards have included a mix of gay, straight, and queer representatives. The town clerk's office, for instance, was overseen for several years by a native Portuguese woman, "Babe" Silva, and a gay male wash-ashore, Stephen Nofield. These common grounds allowed Provincetown to become a gay resort, albeit with a complicated racial, economic, and demographic history. They also allowed residents, like Constance Black, to utter these words in 1988: "But we still have a sense of community here, which is very precious and rare in the modern world."[72]

Edging closer to the new millennium, gay men and lesbians expanded their authority in Provincetown by becoming increasingly active citizens and consumers. They accessed Provincetown's local governing bodies, spoke out in favor of rights for gay residents and visitors, and continued to dominate the real estate sector. They ultimately succeeded in transforming Provincetown into a unique consumerized republic by demanding that Land's End give gay people a decent return in the form of freedom on their increasingly heavy-handed financial investments. Concurrently, Provincetown's late-twentieth-century changes ushered in new forms of discrimination as residents and visitors of dissimilar backgrounds clung tightly to Provincetown as their hard-won home.

Provincetown is indeed a precious and rare place, but it is also a town like any other that has been embroiled in the latest twists, turns, and inequities bound up in global capitalism. While attempting to re-create a sense of togetherness as residents and tourists come and go at Land's End, townspeople must not allow the romance of community to cloud the ways in which oppression and power have shaped and continue to shape working and vacationing experiences in Provincetown. Indeed, if Provincetown continues to re-create itself as a place of liberation and freedom, it needs to ask itself which kinds of residents and which kinds of visitors have access to full or even partial citizenship at Land's End. And if it wants to change the direction of its expanding inequities in housing and labor, it needs to work even harder on issues like affordable housing and the maintenance of a diversified workforce. Beginning in this way, Provincetown can continue to distinguish itself as a unique harbor of democracy.

Conclusion

Cape Queer?

ONE OF THE CHALLENGES of writing this book has not been figuring out where to begin but deciding when to end. In no way have Provincetown's shifting landscapes and seascapes settled. Real estate and rental prices continue to soar, and working-class residents of all ethnic, sexual, and gender backgrounds continue to seek more affordable housing elsewhere. As a consequence, residents have responded by turning once again to foreign-born laborers in order to fill the working-class void. The decisions Provincetown's residents make to stay or leave, rent or buy, build affordable houses or luxury condominiums, hire native or foreign-born workers, and become year-round or seasonal dwellers continue to shape the experiences of those who visit, live, and work at Land's End.

Just last year, in 2004, two events made a significant impact on Provincetown's success as a gay resort town. In March the U.S. Department of Homeland Security stopped issuing H-2B visas for foreign-born seasonal workers because the annual cap had been reached, and in May the Massachusetts state legislature gave city and town clerks permission to issue marriage licenses to gay and lesbian couples. While both events concerned tourism, labor, and citizenship, the first meant Provincetown would have to scramble for workers in order to satisfy the labor needs of its summer vacation communities, and the second meant Provincetown could expect even more tourists than usual as it evolved almost overnight into a gay and lesbian marriage altar and honeymoon suite.

"Save Summer Act of 2004" was the term lobbyists and employers used to describe the labor crisis lapping at the shores of the northeastern seaboard in March of the same year.[1] From Maine to Virginia, summer resorts like Boothbay Harbor, Nantucket, and Provincetown panicked not because gasoline prices had escalated, not because U.S. military troops were embroiled in Iraq, and not because in Massachusetts alone 173,600 residents were counted as unemployed.[2] Rather, the H-2B annual visa cap for foreign-born seasonal workers set at 66,000 had been reached, and the Department of Homeland Security, in an unprecedented move, refused all additional requests.[3] Hundreds of employers from those owning restaurants and inns to boat builders and transportation agencies had come to depend on the seasonal importation of Jamaican workers and European students (with J-1 visas) to fill menial labor positions from dishwashing to bus driving.[4]

Businesses on Cape Cod, Martha's Vineyard and Nantucket received approximately 5,500 H-2B visas during its 2003 summer season. After a bill cosponsored by Maine Senators Olympia Snowe and Susan Collins and Massachusetts Senator Edward Kennedy to raise the 2004 cap from 66,000 to 106,00 visas was defeated, it became clear that at least 1,100 of Cape Cod's previous total would remain unfilled.[5] Paula St. Pierre of Cape Cod's Chatham Boat Company helped set the tone: "We're panicking; we really are," she told the *Boston Globe* on April 1.[6]

The summer of 2004 predicament pivoted on questions of labor and citizenship as business owners sought desperately to satisfy American consumer needs. Why not hire unemployed U.S. citizens or native-born high school and college students instead of importing foreign-born laborers, many onlookers asked. "'So many people don't understand, they think it's a way of getting cheap labor,'" explained Provincetown native Napi Van Derek, owner of Napi's Restaurant.[7] Another entrepreneur called the process "a necessary evil" but stated that students' schedules cannot accommodate the increasingly busy "shoulder seasons" in late spring and early fall.[8] Peter Matell, owner of the Wesley Hotel on Martha's Vineyard, claimed that he hasn't "had an American girl apply for a chambermaid job in eight years."[9] Cape Cod Chamber of Commerce chief executive officer Wendy Northcross admitted that many employers prefer foreign-born laborers to U.S. workers because they believe the former by and large have better work attitudes than the latter. "There's a real disconnect between the currently available jobs and the currently unemployed American[s]," she told the *Boston Globe*.[10]

Some entrepreneurs like Lori O'Connell of the twenty-eight-room Chatham Highlander Motel resolved the problem by importing foreign-born workers who have U.S. citizenship status. O'Connell hired a labor broker from the enterprising firm Workers on the Move, which opened its doors just this spring in response to the labor shortage. Workers on the Move recruits laborers that have U.S. citizenship status from the U.S. Virgin Islands, thus conveniently avoiding the H-2B and J-1 visa entanglements while taking advantage of the Caribbean's off-season (summer) labor market.[11]

Filling U.S. labor needs with an assortment of foreign-born workers raises far more problems about global capitalism than this book can detail. Still, regarding Provincetown specifically and labor importation more generally, several implications stand out. First, because of the H-2B cap, Jamaicans who have worked in the United States for years and who have come to depend on a seasonal U.S. income are suffering financially and finding class mobility impossible.[12] Writing from Jamaica, Philip Dinham called the H-2B program a "newfound avenue to mobility" for hundreds of Jamaicans who have exhausted ways to get ahead back home.[13] Second, locating yet another external pool of laborers skirts the local issues that are preventing U.S. citizens from taking or wanting working-class jobs. Affordable housing and class diversity are cases in point. While arguing that native-born U.S. citizens do not want menial labor positions, employers still readily admit that college students and other working-class residents can no longer afford the rental or real estate prices that most summer resorts like Provincetown and Martha's Vineyard now demand. Class displacement and exclusion in these vacation destinations is widespread, and importing an underclass of foreign workers rather than exacting strict measures to create affordable housing remains the prevailing solution.

Finally, this particular aspect of global capitalism fuels troubling race and gender patterns. Hundreds of H-2B visa laborers are women who have left children and families behind for roughly six or more months each year. Thus, as Christine G. T. Ho has argued, on the one hand, the international division of labor allows certain women more economic independence; on the other hand, it has weakened labor conditions in the Caribbean and has forced women either to work at home under oppressive conditions or to leave their families and work in the United States in similarly oppressive jobs. Like their Latin American counterparts who work for white U.S. families as nannies, Jamaican women leave unpaid housework in Jamaica for paid housework in the United States.[14]

This transnational exchange of black women's labor relegates Jamaican women in both places to domestic work and forces them to abandon the same families they mean to support. Indeed, the importation of black Jamaicans and their placement in low-paid, unskilled jobs perpetuates America's long-standing history of relegating women and people of color to the most menial labor positions. With race and gender equity in mind, the H-2B visa "crisis" might be recast as a history of repeating oppressions. White Yankees imported "dark-skinned" Portuguese seamen in the mid- to late nineteenth century because American sailors found greater opportunities onshore. A full century later, white gay entrepreneurs and white Portuguese residents are mobilizing a similar dynamic by importing an underclass of black and, to a lesser degree, white foreign-born seasonal laborers rather than creating housing and labor possibilities for working-class Americans. Yet unlike most Portuguese immigrants, who were able to become both white and American, Jamaicans' and Eastern European students' opportunities for joining Provincetown's communities of likeness have been foreclosed. Neither group has categorical access to American citizenship, which would facilitate, although not guarantee, financial progress. And Jamaicans face the additional obstacle of gaining access to whiteness, another key to prying open the doors to upward mobility.

In contrast to the first event affecting the 2004 tourist season, the second involved native-born residents who migrated to Provincetown in order to cash in on an increase rather than a decrease in their rights to U.S. citizenship. On May 17, 2004, Massachusetts became the first state in the United States to issue marriage licenses to gay and lesbian couples. And Provincetown entrepreneurs, linked to a long-standing history of capitalizing on shifts in the tourist industry, started gearing up for newlyweds as soon as the Massachusetts Supreme Judicial Court ruled in November 2003 that it was unconstitutional to deny gay and lesbian couples access to the institution of marriage.

By February 2004 local businesses were ready with "gay" wedding packages and planners. Volunteers from the Provincetown Business Guild had agreed to help couples process their paperwork while donning lavender golf shirts emblazoned with the message "Ushering in a New Equality."[15] Even though gay and lesbian couples had migrated to Provincetown in the past for "union ceremonies" not recognized by any state, by May 2004 room and restaurant reservations had skyrocketed during Provincetown's typically quiet and brisk late May and June shoulder season as entrepreneurs took advantage of a new form of gay citizenship and of the gay community's annual $54 billion travel industry.[16] Couples, friends, family members, and newscasters swarmed Land's End on May 17 to partake in the festivities. And again Provincetown added another "first" to its roster of pioneering achievements. "We're becoming literally a gay Niagara Falls," Provincetown director of tourism Patricia Fitzpatrick exclaimed on May 18, when gay and lesbian newlyweds selected Land's End despite the summer of 2004 labor crisis.[17]

Provincetown's evolution into a gentrified enclave, panicking over how many laborers from Jamaica it can import while sanctioning lesbian and gay marriages, raises questions about Provincetown's future as a progressive outpost. Will its subversiveness depend on whether other states allow or ban gay marriage? Can it continue to re-create itself as a landfall of freedom or as a queer enclave if it lacks race and class diversity? What is Provincetown becoming and how can residents influence where it is going? These are the questions that Provincetown has to ask itself as it moves forward in the new millennium.

Provincetown's history demonstrates how successful marketing campaigns can yield unanticipated results. Portuguese and Yankee residents responded to Provincetown's declining fishing industry by switching with ease from an independent, agrarian community to a town dependent on tourists and a seasonal, service economy. Entrepreneurs of all backgrounds reaped hefty financial rewards from Provincetown's status as a birthplace of freedom and from its importation of foreign-born workers.

But the switch from fishing village to resort town eventually led to unforeseen transformations in familial and recreational patterns.[18] Portuguese and Yankee residents who could afford to remain at Land's End witnessed the creation of new family structures as gay and lesbian couples and individuals began to outnumber nuclear families as residents and consumers. Throughout town, tea dances replaced bowling alleys; gift shops and art galleries stood in the place of stores that once sold household staples; and social entities like bars, restaurants, and guesthouses took the place of civic institutions like churches, schools, and fire stations.

Similarly, it didn't take long for Provincetown's reputation as a white gay mecca to push its local community to the margins. Cultural events, such as the Blessing of the Fleet, once integral to Provincetown as an annual Portuguese religious ritual, have become showcase tourist festivals meant to celebrate Provincetown's alluring ethnic past in the face of its diminishing ethnic present. And residents who once enjoyed the taverns and restaurants along Commercial Street now feel more comfortable socializing with other locals in the basement bar of the VFW building.

Even Provincetown's reputation as a Gay Disneyland has been thrown into jeopardy as only certain kinds of people can afford to enjoy Land's End: those with money. An even smaller number can reside there seasonally or year-round. Provincetown is a fantasy many will never realize because they don't have the means to get to or stay at Land's End, and, once there, they have few ways to engage politically with local residents or other tourists.

Still, townsfolk remain committed to the ideals of freedom, democracy, and equality that have characterized Provincetown's noteworthy past. For instance, residents have formed a number of committees to address affordable housing and foreign-born laborers' employment and housing conditions. Several groups such as the Provincetown Human Rights Resolution Working Group, the Provincetown/Truro Interfaith Coalition of Congregations, and the Provincetown Tourism Department have worked together to attend to the needs—from filing employee complaints to dealing with domestic abuse—of Provincetown's Jamaican and European-student laboring communities.[19] One committee, the Community Development Working Group, is charged specifically with developing a "community vision" that takes into account affordable housing, space and resource protection, transportation, and economic development. In April 2004 Selectman Mary Jo Avellar articulated the frustrations of many during the annual town meeting when she argued, "We need affordable housing and we need it now!"

In addition to valiant efforts in the arena of formal politics, a number of residents have also taken to the streets and the stage in order to protest both the commercialization of Provincetown and the fantasy that Provincetown "is for everyone."[20] Part drag artist, part clown, Ryan Landry and his "booger drag" cast of Gold Dust Orphans produce play adaptations at Land's End each year and have generated a cult following of gay men and lesbians. In 2003 Landry wrote *The Gulls,* a spoof on Provincetown using Hitchcock's narrative from *The Birds.* Remarkably similar to the original, *The Gulls* sets loose a scathing critique of class and race politics shaping Provincetown in the new millennium. During the same summer he disrupted a well-meaning fund-raiser at town hall by rolling out a "Stanley Petunia, Mayor of Provincetown" routine. Donning a too-tight, old-fashioned, baby-blue tuxedo, Landry's new mayor exposed—in a snappy ten-minute rant—a corrupt police department, dirty politics in town hall, ineffective affordable-housing policies, racial discrimination in the context of Jamaican laborers, and Provincetown's false promises of freedom.

Like the hopeful efforts put forth by Landry and Provincetown's community working groups, this book sheds a piercing light on the promises and perils of gay enclaves and global capitalism. It has shown, ultimately, how the making of a gay resort town cannot be divorced from the economic and demographic shifts—both local and global—preceding the emergence of modern gay identities and communities. As this book has demonstrated, the landfall of the *Mayflower* Pilgrims meant Yankees and others could refashion Provincetown into an outpost of freedom, a reputation gay men and lesbians would later turn to their advantage. The decline of seafaring endeavors prompted Yankee and Portuguese residents to build a replacement service industry and to welcome gay men and lesbians into their homes and markets. And under economic duress during the Great Depression, townsfolk opened their doors even wider to white middle- and upper-class tourists just in time for America's mass "coming out" movement.

Nor can Provincetown's evolution into a gay town be separated from the tensions around ethnicity, gender, and economic struggle that have shaped American landscapes. At the turn of the last century, Anglo-European anxieties about race and immigration enabled Yankees to characterize Provincetown's Portuguese residents as exotic but tame and to bill Provincetown as distinctly American but with foreign tendencies. At about the same time, Portuguese immigrants learned the value of whiteness and endeavored to become white Portuguese Americans and to build relationships with other white people, including white gay men and lesbians. Excluded from fishing trips, Portuguese women in Provincetown made the most of their homebound stations by setting up cottage industries and forming relationships with gay men

Portuguese natives with less consumer power than wealthy gay wash-ashores distance themselves from local and national forms of citizenship, 2003. The sign in the top photograph reads, "Bergman and His Puppet Chief of Police Endorse Hate." Collection of the author.

and lesbians. By the middle of the twentieth century, these relationships —based on perceived racial likeness, economic need, and familial affection—withstood the onslaught of McCarthy-era politics.

What will happen as competing groups continue to press for space in Provincetown, only time will tell. In the meantime, both residents and tourists would do well to consider the realities that shaped Land's End against the fantasies that they expect from it. They might also consider the memories of people like Amelia Carlos, who minimized the gap between unlikely bedfellows by means of wit and charm.

On a winter day in 1998, I ventured over to Amelia Carlos's house on Creek Road to conduct an oral history interview with her. During our time together, I kept trying to explore Provincetown's past, but she, obviously more adept than I, kept us focused on the present, telling me stories about her relationships with gay neighbors and tenants. One man in particular, John Hines, was special: she treated him like a son, and he, according to Amelia's grandson, "loved [her] deeply and quickly."[21] In a significant and not unusual Provincetown exchange, Amelia sold her house to John Hines well below the market rate, and in return, Hines allowed Amelia to continue living there until she died.

Amelia's family members were both surprised and delighted by her friends. Seated at her kitchen table, she smiled wryly while telling me the following tale: A nephew of hers, or perhaps her grandson, was chiding her:

> He told me one day that all my friends are homosexual. I said I'm glad to have them. They're wonderful friends. They're caring friends. Anything that they can do for me they will gladly do, so why should I look down on them? Who am I? That took care of that argument.[22]

She finished this story with a righteous but still playful expression before launching, after a sip of tea, into her excitement about the upcoming summer season. According to Amelia, during the summer, "the young people move in, and they're wonderful, and I look forward to seeing them every spring. They're so nice." Relationship building, though, is a year-round job in Provincetown. And Amelia seemed to be an expert. "I have a boy that came in across the street this winter," she said with a quick glance out the window, "and at Christmas time he brought me a tin full of homemade cookies that he had made. And he said this is for you and have a happy Christmas. And I was so pleased by that I always give him banana bread. I pound on the window and tell him to come get banana bread when I make it."

In 1995 Gordon Wood wrote the following: "The American people are ill-informed, cynical, and directionless. They are atomized and unconnected, a mere collection of strangers, with little sense of community."[23] Provincetown may be in danger of slipping into Wood's fatalistic commentary on community, but with thoughtful engagement of neighbor and guest, the spirit of Amelia Carlos and the countless others who have made Provincetown extraordinary can live on.

Notes

NOTES TO THE INTRODUCTION

1. Amelia Carlos, interview by author, audiotape recording, Provincetown, Mass., February 8, 1998, Provincetown Oral History Project (hereafter POHP), Provincetown Public Library (hereafter PPL), Provincetown, Massachusetts.

2. Dan Scroggins, telephone conversation with author, December 13, 2003.

3. John Carbone, interview by author, videotape recording, Truro, Mass., January 27, 1997, POHP, PPL.

4. Kathleen Scroggins, telephone interview by author, audiotape recording, Durham, N.C., December 19, 2003.

5. See Automobile Legal Association, *Automobile Green Book: Road Reference & Tourist Guide—New England Stages, Canada, and Trunk Lines West & South* (Boston: Scarborough Motor Guide Co., 1927), 31; in reference to Queersville, USA, see Michael Cunningham, "Social Studies: Out Town," *Out*, June 1995, 83.

6. *Provincetown Advocate*, August 24, 1916; quoted in part in Leona Rust Egan, *Provincetown as a Stage: Provincetown, the Provincetown Players, and the Discovery of Eugene O'Neill* (Orleans, MA: Parnassus, 1994), 156.

7. The only community history of Provincetown was written by Mary Heaton Vorse and published by Dial Press in 1942. See Mary Heaton Vorse, *Time and the Town*, 1942, reprint edited by Adele Heller and with a foreword by Daniel Aaron (New Brunswick, NJ: Rutgers University Press, 1991). Citations are to the Rutgers edition. Norman Dunnell's "The Province Lands: A Social and Economic History of Provincetown to 1900" (master's thesis, Northeastern University, 1993), offers a comprehensive account of Provincetown's geographical history and development to 1900. Most books about Provincetown focus on its famous art colony or the Provincetown Players. See Egan, *Provincetown as a Stage*; Adele Heller and Lois Rudnick, eds., *1915 The Cultural Moment: The New Politics, the New Woman, the New Psychology, the New Art, and the New Theater in America* (New Brunswick, NJ: Rutgers University Press, 1991); and Cheryl Black, *The Women of Provincetown, 1915–1922* (Tuscaloosa: University of Alabama Press, 2002). Studies focusing for the most part on present-day Provincetown include David R. Gleason, "Becoming Dominant: Shifting Control and the Creation of Culture in Provincetown, MA" (Ph.D. diss., University of Pennsylvania, 1999); Michael Cunningham, *Land's End: A Walk in Provincetown* (New York: Crown, 2002); Peter Manso, *Ptown: Art, Sex and Money on the Outer Cape* (New York: Scribner, 2003); and Sandra Faiman-Silva, *Courage to Connect: Sexuality, Citizenship and Community in Provincetown* (Champaign-Urbana: University of Illinois Press, 2004). Any number of novels have also been written about

Provincetown from Normal Mailer's well-known *Tough Guys Don't Dance* (New York: Random House, 1984) to the more obscure novella by John Preston, *Franny, Queen of Provincetown* (New York: St. Martin's Press, 1983). Frank X. Gasper's *Leaving Pico* (Hanover, NH: University Press of New England, 1999) is a novel about Azorean experiences and politics in Provincetown.

8. Dona Brown, *Inventing New England: Regional Tourism in the Nineteenth Century* (Washington, DC: Smithsonian Institution Press, 1995), 8–9. Michael Kammen refers to a similar hunt for national landmarks during the Progressive Era and calls it "innovative nostalgia" and the "heritage syndrome." See Michael Kammen, *The Mystic Chords of Memory: The Transformation of Tradition in American Culture* (New York: Knopf, 1991), 146, 271, 626.

9. This book attempts to expose the "romance of community," as Miranda Joseph puts it, by detailing not *if* community has worked at Land's End, but *how* it has worked. In Joseph's words, communities still function as "sites of hope in a difficult world." Yet "fetishizing community only makes us blind to the ways we might intervene in the enactment of domination and exploitation." See Miranda Joseph, *Against the Romance of Community* (Minneapolis: University of Minnesota Press, 2002), ix.

10. Katherine Dos Passos, *Down Cape Cod: The Complete Guide to Cape Cod* (New York: Dodge, 1936), 3.

11. Massachusetts Department of Commerce and Development, *Town of Provincetown Monograph* (Boston, 1968, 1970, 1980), Nickerson Local History Collection, Cape Cod Community College (hereafter CCCC-NC).

12. These minor exceptions, which are all beyond the downtown area, include the mid-twentieth-century construction of Route 6, which wraps around the back side of Provincetown and is now the main thoroughfare leading into town; Route 6A, which used be the only entrance to Land's End and which once included a bridge over East Harbor, now Pilgrim Lake; the main roads leading to the Cape Cod National Seashore's Herring Cove Beach and Race Point Beach; and the new neighborhoods in the West End of town that include high-income single-family homes and condominiums.

13. For documentation of the Portland Gale, see the Cape Cod Pilgrim Monument and Provincetown Museum Archive (hereafter CCPMA) collection of shipwreck histories. Provincetown also experienced an economic depression in the 1890s; see Massachusetts Historical Commission, *Reconnaissance Survey Report* (hereafter MHCRS), 1984, 3, Massachusetts State Archives (hereafter MSA).

14. See "KKK" folder, miscellaneous records box, CCPMA.

15. Reed Woodhouse, "Provincetown," in *Hometowns: Gay Men Write about Where They Belong*, ed. John Preston (New York: Dutton, 1991), 127, 226, emphasis original. See also Paul Monette, *Halfway Home* (New York: Crown, 1991); John Howard, *Men Like That: A Southern Queer History* (Chicago: University of Chicago Press, 1999).

16. See Lizabeth Cohen, *A Consumers' Republic: The Politics of Mass Consumption in Postwar America* (New York: Knopf, 2003); and Lizabeth Cohen, "From Town Center to Shopping Center: The Reconfiguration of Community Marketplaces in Postwar America," *American Historical Review* 101 (October 1994): 1050–1081.

17. Richard O. Davies, *Main Street Blues* (Columbus: Ohio State University Press), 1998.

18. Provincetown Business Guild, *Guide to Our Town* (Provincetown: Provincetown Business Guild, 1997), 1.

19. Cindy Aron, *Working at Play: A History of Vacations in the United States* (New York: Oxford University Press, 1999), 2.

20. On the relationship of citizenship to tourism and to economic modes of production and consumption, see Cohen, *A Consumers' Republic*, 8–9; Marguerite S. Shaffer, *See America First: Tourism and National Identity, 1880–1940* (Washington, DC: Smithsonian Institution Press, 2001); and John Sears, *Sacred Places: American Tourist Attractions in the Nineteenth Century* (New York: Oxford University Press, 1989), 5.

21. I am grateful to Jocelyn Olcott for raising the term *community of likeness*. For an informed discussion of women and citizenship, see Jocelyn Olcott, *Revolutionary Women in Postrevolutionary Mexico* (Durham, NC: Duke University Press, forthcoming). Olcott builds on the importance of boundaries and likeness set forth by Sheldon Wolin in "Fugitive Democracy," in *Democracy and Difference: Contesting the Boundaries of the Political,* edited by Seyla Benhabib (Princeton, NJ: Princeton University Press, 1996), 6. Wolin argues, "Both as container and as excluder, boundaries work to foster the impression of a circumscribed space in which likeness dwells, the likeness of natives, of an autochthonous people, or of a nationality, or of citizens with equal rights. Likeness is prized because it appears as the prime ingredient to unity. Unity, in turn, is thought to be the sine qua non of collective power." See also Joan B. Landes, "The Performance of Citizenship" in Benhabib, 295–313.

22. Elizabeth Kennedy and Madeline Davis faced a similar problem of terminology. See Elizabeth Kennedy and Madeline Davis, *Boots of Leather, Slippers of Gold: The History of a Lesbian Community* (New York: Routledge, 1993), and Elizabeth Kennedy, "Navigating the Slippery Slopes of Sex, Bodies, and Identities in History" (paper, "Queer Studies Queer Activism," Smith College, Northampton, Massachusetts, November 7, 1998). George Chauncey Jr. identifies several pre-WWII terms for gay men in New York City; see George Chauncey Jr., *Gay New York: Gender, Urban Culture, and the Making of the Gay Male World, 1890–1940* (New York: Basic, 1994), 13–21, 105.

23. Numerous scholars have expounded on the meanings and uses of the term "queer." See Teresa de Lauretis, "Queer Theory, Lesbian and Gay Studies: An Introduction," *differences: A Journal of Feminist Cultural Studies* 3/2 (Summer 1991; special issue): iii–xviii; Eve Kosofsky Sedgwick, *Epistemology of the Closet* (Berkeley: University of California Press, 1990); Eve Kosofsky Sedgwick, *Tendencies* (Durham, NC: Duke University Press, 1993); Judith Butler, "Against Proper Objects," introduction to "More Gender Trouble: Feminism Meets Queer Theory," *differences: A Journal of Feminist Cultural Studies* 6/2–3 (Summer-Fall 1994; special issue): 1–26; Lisa Duggan, "Making It Perfectly Queer," *Socialist Review* 22 (1992): 11–31; Lisa Duggan, "Theory in Practice: The Theory Wars, or, Who's Afraid of Judith Butler?" *Journal of Women's History* 10/1 (Spring 1998): 9–19; "The Queer Issue: New Visions of America's Lesbian and Gay Past," *Radical History Review* 62 (Spring 1995; special issue); William B. Turner, *A Genealogy of Queer Theory* (Philadelphia: Temple University Press, 2000); Michael Warner, "Introduction," in *Fear of a Queer Planet,* ed.

Michael Warner (Minneapolis: University of Minnesota Press, 1993); and Moe Meyer, "Introduction," in *The Politics and Poetics of Camp*, ed. Moe Meyer (New York: Routledge, 1994), 1–3. See Scott Bravmann, *Queer Fictions of the Past: History, Culture, and Difference* (New York: Cambridge University Press, 1997), 31–32, for a compelling discussion of "comic," meaning linear, heroic, or glossy descriptive histories. This book heeds Bravmann's and other queer theorists' calls to read and write history as a performative retelling not of a truthful past—of what "really" happened— but of one laced with complexities surrounding race, gender, class, and sexuality.

24. Doug Fraser, "Gay/Lesbian Enclave or Diverse Community?" *Provincetown Advocate*, October 27, 1995.

25. This book benefited from the gay and lesbian community histories that scholars published just as I began to research this project. These works include George Chauncey's *Gay New York;* Madeline Davis and Elizabeth Kennedy's *Boots of Leather, Slippers of Gold;* Marc Stein's dissertation "City of Sisterly and Brotherly Love," now published in book form as *City of Sisterly and Brotherly Loves: Lesbian and Gay Philadelphia, 1945–1972* (Chicago: University of Chicago Press, 2000); and Esther Newton's *Cherry Grove, Fire Island: Sixty Years in America's First Gay and Lesbian Town* (Boston: Beacon Press, 1993). See also William G. Hawkeswood, *One of the Children: Gay Black Men in Harlem*, ed. Alex Costley (Berkeley: University of California, Press, 1996); Katharine Gilmartin, "The Very House of Difference: Intersections of Identities in the Life Histories of Colorado Lesbians, 1940–1965" (Ph.D. diss., Yale University, 1995); Nan A. Boyd, *Wide Open Town: A History of Queer San Francisco to 1965* (Berkeley: University of California Press, 2003); Howard; and Brett Beemyn, ed., *Creating a Place for Ourselves: Lesbian, Gay and Bisexual Community Histories* (New York: Routledge, 1997).

NOTES TO PART I

1. James Gifford, "Address Delivered at the Opening of the Old Colony Railroad to Provincetown," July 23, 1873, box 1, document 10, Research Club Collection, CCPMA.

2. On the economic impact of the railroad see William Cronon's *Nature's Metropolis: Chicago and the Great West* (New York: Norton, 1991). On the railroad bolstering tourism, see Aron, 45–53.

3. Quoted in Robert H. Farson, *Cape Cod Railroads Including Martha's Vineyard and Nantucket* (Yarmouth Port, MA: Cape Cod Historical Publications, 1993), 40.

4. Farson, 40.

5. Aron, 19.

6. "Provincetown as a Watering Place," *Banner and Cape News*, Vol. 1, No. 1, June 1856.

7. Provincetown Board of Trade, "The Tip End of Cape Cod, One of the Oldest Towns of the New World," 1897, Heritage Museum Archive (hereafter HMA).

8. Ibid.

9. See *Provincetown Resident Directory*, 1899, 1902, CCPMA; and Clive Driver, "Looking Back: The Ocean View Sanitarium," *Provincetown Banner*, October 16, 1997.

10. Edmund J. Carpenter, "Provincetown: The Tip of the Cape," *New England Magazine* 22 (July 1900): 533.

11. On the distinction among vacationers, tourists, and other travelers, see Aron, 127–128.

12. See Aron, 130, 144; Kammen; Shaffer; Sears; Karen Dubinsky, *The Second Greatest Disappointment: Honeymooning and Tourism at Niagara Falls* (New Brunswick, NJ: Rutgers University Press, 1999); and William Irwin, *The New Niagara: Tourism, Technology and the Landscape of Niagara Falls, 1776–1917* (University Park: Pennsylvania State University Press, 1996).

13. Aron, 144.

14. Dean MacCannell, *The Tourist: A New Theory of the Leisure Class* (New York: Schocken, 1976); quoted in Aron, 145.

15. Brown, 47–48, 57; Shaffer, 12–13.

NOTES TO CHAPTER I

1. See Clive Driver, "Looking Back: Visits by Early Explorers to Provincetown," *Provincetown Banner*, November 20, 1997; Margaret Mayo and Peter Carter, "The History of Provincetown," in *Provincetown: 250 Years* (Provincetown: Provincetown Historical Association, Inc., 1977), 3, 33; MHCRS, 3; C. Keith Wilbur, *New England Indians* (Chester, MA: The Glove Pequot Press, 1978), 11, 74; Francis P. McManamon, ed., *Chapters in the Archeology of Cape Cod, III* (Eastham, MA: Eastern National Park and Monument Association, 1990), 37; Howard S. Russell, *Indian New England Before the Mayflower* (Hanover, NH: University Press of New England, 1980), 23; Mellen C. M. Hatch, *The Log of Provincetown and Truro* (Boston: Industrial School for Crippled Children, 1939), 25; Dunnell, 8.

2. See http://www.gis.net/~baron/history.htm (accessed January 19, 2004); http://capecodhistory.us/Deyo/Provincetown-Deyo.htm (accessed January 19, 2004).

3. John Smith, www.mayflowerhistory.com/History/BiographyTisquantum .php (accessed January 19, 2004); Dunnell, 15.

4. In Edmund J. Carpenter, *The Pilgrims and Their Monument* (New York: D. Appleton, 1911), 30.

5. "Cape Cod Pilgrim Memorial Open at Provincetown for its 32nd Season," *Cape Cod Standard Times*, April 3, 1942, quoting speech in early 1900s made by Captain J. Henry Sears, President of Cape Cod Pilgrim Memorial Association; on "prolific parent" see "Landing of the Pilgrims (written in 1880)," Research Club box, document 25, CCPMA.

6. H. H. Sylvester, *Provincetown* (n.p., 1882), quoted in J. H. Hogan, *The First Resident Directory of Provincetown, Massachusetts: Containing Also a Complete Business Directory, Churches, Schools, Societies, Town Offices . . .* (Massachusetts: W. F. Richardson and Co., 1886), 21. See also Carpenter, *The Pilgrims*, 55.

7. Dwight B. Heath, ed., *Mourt's Relation* (Cambridge, MA: Applewood Books, 1963), 18–19; quoted in Dunnell, 4. See also Henry David Thoreau, *Cape Cod* (New York: Penguin, 1987), 297–298.

8. Sylvester, quoted in Hogan, 21.

9. Some local historians believe Prence bought all the Cape land from, more specifically, the Nipmucks, a subdivision of the Wampanoags, www.iamprovince-town.com/timeline.html (accessed August 12, 2004). George F. Willison, *Saints and Strangers* (Orleans, MA: Parnassus Imprints, 1971), 6–7; quoted in Dunnell, 16.

10. Thomas Smyth, *Who Owns the Provincelands?* (Boston: Massachusetts Historical Society, 1890), 4, 7–8; quoted in Dunnell, 22.

11. Shebnah Rich, *Truro—Cape Cod, or Land Marks and Sea Marks* (Boston: D. Lothrop and Co., 1883), 85.

12. William Kittredge, *Cape Cod: Its People and Their History*, 2d ed. with Post-epilogue by John Hay (Boston: Houghton Mifflin, 1958), 93.

13. Simeon L. Deyo, *History of Barnstable County, Massachusetts* (New York: H. W. Blake and Co., 1890), 962; quoted in Dunnell, 29.

14. Rich, 84; Dunnell, 29.

15. Deyo, 963; quoted in Dunnell, 30.

16. Ibid.

17. Deyo, 964–965; quoted in Dunnell, 37.

18. Deyo, 965; quoted in Dunnell, 37.

19. Deyo, 965; Kittredge, 104; Dunnell, 41, 46; Frederick Freeman, *The History of Cape Cod, Annals of the Thirteen Towns of Barnstable County* (Boston: W. H. Piper and Co., 1869), 634; Herman Jennings, *Provincetown or Odds and Ends from the Tip End* (Provincetown: Peaked Hill Press, 1975), 21, 196.

20. Rich, 108; Hatch, 28–30; quoted in Dunnell, 54.

21. Kittredge, 185–186; Edith Ferguson, *The 1790–1840 Federal Censuses, Provincetown, Barnstable County, Massachusetts* (Bowie, MD: Heritage Books, 1983), 1–5; Dunnell, 54.

22. Freeman, 641; Everett Ladd Clarke, "Provincetown," *New England Magazine* 46 (1912): 70; Dunnell, 58.

23. Freeman, 642; quoted in Dunnell, 59.

24. Commonwealth of Massachusetts, Joint Committee on Harbors, "Evidence on the Condition of Cape Cod Harbor, at Provincetown and the Plans for Its Protection and Preservation" (1898); quoted in Dunnell, 59.

25. Donald R. Hickey, *The War of 1812* (Chicago: University of Illinois Press, 1990), 171; also quoted in Dunnell, 60; Rich, 357.

26. Hatch, 42; Nancy W. Paine Smith, *The Provincetown Book* (Brockton, MA: Tolman Print, 1922), 50–51; Jennings, 11, 36; Timothy Dwight, *Travels in New England and New York* (Cambridge, MA: Belknap Press, 1969), 55; and Dunnell, 68. For a visual of the windmills, see Major James D. Graham, *Chart of the Extremity of Cape Cod* (Washington, DC: U.S. Corps of Topographical Engineers, 1836).

27. See CCPMA permanent exhibit on Long Point.

28. See Mayo and Carter, 3, 33; U.S. Census Reports, 1960, Table 81, volume 23, page 246; Dunnell, 81; See the November 10, 1830, issue of the *Barnstable Patriot*, quoted in Jason M. Cortell and Associates, Inc., *Final Environmental Impact Statement* (United States Coast Guard First District, October 1975), 16.

29. Robert G. Albion, William A. Baker, and Benjamin W. Labaree, *New England and the Sea* (Mystic, CT: Mystic Seaport Museum, 1972), 115; Hatch, 70; Dunnell, 148.

30. Clifford Ashley, *The Yankee Whaler* (New York: Dover, 1966), 39, 42; Samuel Eliot Morison, *The Maritime History of Massachusetts, 1783–1860* (Boston: Northeastern University Press, 1979), 146; Alexander Starbuck, *History of the American Whale Fishery* (Secaucus, NJ: Castle Books, 1989), 240–372; Dunnell, 62–63.

31. George Bryant, "The Port of Provincetown 1776–1900" (n.d., n.p., photocopy), 8–10, HMA. See Dunnell, 78–83, on wharf industry records for Atwood & Freeman Company and others.

32. Edward Kendall, *Travels through the Northern Parts of the United States in the Years 1807 and 1808*, Vol. II (New York: I. Riley, 1809), 154; quoted in Dunnell, 71.

33. *Harper's Magazine*, 1875, quoted in "Cape Cod Impressions in 1875," in *Your Weekly Guide to Cape Cod* 3 (June 19, 1948): 33.

34. On wharf industries see Bryant; Hatch, 46–47; Smith, *Provincetown*, 82–87; and Dunnell, who provides detailed descriptions of items bought, sold, and borrowed on the wharves, 78–82. See also Gaylon Harrison, *One Hundred Years of Growing with Provincetown* (Provincetown: First National Bank, 1954), 1.

35. Dunnell, 136; Bryant.

36. www.iamprovincetown.com/timeline.html (accessed August 12, 2004).

37. Dunnell, 90, 101, 114–115, 132; Bryant; Hatch, 69.

38. Quoted in Bryant, 15.

39. See Dunnell, 101, 112; Hatch, 72–73.

40. On Yankee exodus and new fishing boats see Bryant, 11; Nancy Paine Smith, *Book about the Artists: Who They Are, What They Do, Where They Live, How They Look* (Provincetown: n.p., 1927), 32. On greater opportunities inland see Alfred Chandler Jr., *The Visible Hand: The Managerial Revolution in America* (Cambridge, MA: Harvard University Press, 1977), 411–415, 464.

41. See Reverend Elias Nason, *A Gazetteer of the State of Massachusetts with Numerous Illustrations on Wood and Steel* (Boston: B. B. Russell, 1874), 422–423.

42. John Wesley Hanson, *Biography of William Henry Ryder* (Boston: Universalist Publishing House, 1891), 11.

43. See Brown, 193–204. Brown argues that only Provincetown and Hyannis had any appeal prior to 1900.

44. See Brown, 184.

45. See Article no. 578(b) sheet 276, List B, and List I, HMA.

46. For a brief history of the Research Club which refers to the founders as "ladies of Mayflower lineage" see "Research Club Started in Small Way to Become Important Asset to Town," *Provincetown Advocate*, November 3, 1938. For reference to the ladies as "aristocrats of New England," see unsorted box, Ladies Research Club file, CCPMA. Ironically, even though many of Provincetown's Yankees were allegedly descendants of Stephen Hopkins, visitors and residents rarely accused Yankees of inbreeding—a derogatory suggestion grounded in class prejudice. On the other hand, townsfolk and guests repeatedly degraded working-class Portuguese residents by referring to them as inbreds. See Russell Pagliaro, letter to the editor, *Provincetown Advocate*, December 23, 1982. See also letters by mid-Cape resident Bob Dunham. In September of 1986 Dunham wrote: "I am definitely against flaming gays—the lispers, swishers, lip pursers, and cruisers." Yet regarding the recent gay bashings, it may be because "some lizard . . . slinked off the meat rack looking for a

tender morsel to play with," yet there are as well "a few town-toughs and local dim-bulbs/in-breds who need some discipline and restraining." Bob Dunham, letter to the editor, *Provincetown Advocate*, September 25, 1986; Bob Dunham, letter to the editor, *Provincetown Advocate*, July 16, 1981.

47. Reba Bush Lawrence, "Colonial Music," in file "Research Papers," Research Club's unsorted files, CCPMA.

48. "Research Club Started"; see also the Research Club uncatalogued collection boxes, CCPMA. After the Research Club folded in 1956, due most likely to its declining membership, it transferred its collection of artifacts to its brother-institution, the Pilgrim Monument, which opened its adjacent Provincetown Museum in 1965.

49. On Yankee women who crossed class and ethnic divisions by intermarrying, see Marguerite Beata Cook, interview by author, videotape recording, Provincetown, Mass., January 22, 1997, POHP, PPL; Mary Ruth O'Donnell, interview by author, videotape recording, Provincetown, Mass., January 22, 1997, POHP, PPL; Susan Leonard, interview by author, videotape recording, Provincetown, Mass., January 15, 1997, POHP, PPL; John "Powerful" Patrick, interview by author, videotape recording, Provincetown, Mass., January 29, 1997, POHP, PPL—all of whom were either in or were the offspring of mixed marriages. On white women beyond Provincetown who were Progressive Era reformers seeking to diminish class and race divides, see Anne Firor Scott, *Natural Allies: Women's Associations in American History* (Chicago: University of Illinois Press, 1991); Nancy Cott, *Bonds of Womanhood: "Women's Sphere" in New England, 1780, 1835* (New Haven: Yale University Press, 1977); Mary Ryan, *Cradle of the Middle Class: The Family in Oneida, New York, 1890–1865* (New York: Cambridge University Press, 1982); Mary Ryan, *Women in Public: Between Banners and Ballots, 1825–1880* (Baltimore: Johns Hopkins University Press, 1990), 8; Nancy Hewitt, *Women's Activism and Social Change: Rochester, New York, 1856–1872* (Ithaca, NY: Cornell University Press, 1984); and Lori Ginsberg, *Women and the Work of Benevolence: Morality and Politics in the Northeastern United States, 1820–1865* (New Haven: Yale University Press, 1990). On the overlap between the Research Club and the KKK see Ku Klux Klan file in Miscellaneous Box at CCPMA, as well as Research Club Membership Lists also at CCPMA.

50. For an excellent narrative of the building of the Pilgrim Monument see Edmund J. Carpenter, *The Pilgrims and Their Monument* (New York: D. Appleton, 1911). See also *The Cape Cod Pilgrim Memorial Association*, a leather-bound booklet that CCPMA board members distributed to solicit money, Article 88, Sheet 39, File B, 3, HMA.

51. Edwin A. Grozier, ca. 1920, in "The Pilgrim Monument: Marking the First Landing Place of the Pilgrims Fathers at Provincetown, Ma, November, 11, 1620," HMA, argues, "For many years in histories, in school books, in popular literature, historical injustice has been done to Provincetown." See also WPA, RG 69, FWP Guide, Carton 8, Box 48, Folder Provincetown, National Archives (hereafter NA), where one writer reports, "Provincetown, which rightly claims the first coming of the Pilgrims has always looked with somewhat lofty scorn at the prominence given her mainland neighbor."

52. Carpenter, *The Pilgrims*, 38–61.

53. From Cape Cod Pilgrim Memorial Association booklet, 7, HMA.

54. Ibid, 13, 16; Professor William Marshall Warren declared that the monument will serve to mark Provincetown as "a place of pilgrimage for those to whom our national life may appear shallow and sluice-drawn."

55. Ibid, 16.

56. Ibid.

57. "Getting Ready for Provincetown's Great Day," *Boston Sunday Post,* June 30, 1907, included a full front page article with panoramic pictures of Provincetown and its harbor.

58. "Provincetown All Dressed Up for Its Distinguished Guests," *Boston Journal,* August 20, 1907. See also *Boston Sunday Globe,* August 11, 1907, August 21, 1907, and August 6, 1910; *Boston Sunday Post,* August 18, 1907, August 21, 1907, and August 6, 1910; *Boston Traveler,* August 20, 1907, and August 6, 1910; *Boston American,* August 20, 1907, and August 6, 1910; *Boston Herald,* August 21, 1907 (a.m. and p.m. editions), *Boston Herald,* August 30, 1907; "Throngs Listening to President Roosevelt at Provincetown," *Boston Daily Globe,* August 21, 1907; and "President [Taft] Dedicates Great Monument: Many Thousands Are Present at Impressive Exercises," *Boston American,* August 5, 1910.

59. "Eyes of the Nation on Provincetown Today: Mighty Warships Gather, Distinguished Guests Arrive, Whole Town a Blaze of Color for Dedication of Great Monument," *Boston Post,* August 5, 1910.

60. Before cameras became popular and accessible, tourists often bought and sent postcards. Souvenir china, too, especially cobalt blue (popular from 1890 to 1910) and aluminum ashtrays, saucers, cups, salt and pepper sets, thimbles, and plates that depicted Provincetown's looming monument or grand hotels reminded visitors, or the recipient of such gifts, of a pilgrimage to the landing of the Pilgrims and of Provincetown's status as a historic Yankee landmark. Souvenir china information from Lawrence Williams, "Souvenir China" (lecture, Pilgrim Monument and Provincetown Museum, Spring 1997). See CCPMA souvenir permanent collection.

61. Josef Berger [Jeremiah Digges], *Cape Cod Pilot* (Provincetown: Modern Pilgrim's Press, 1937), 269–270.

62. Leonard, interview.

63. See Research Club Collection, Box 2, CCPMA, for samples of annual programs.

64. Provincetown Business Guild, *The Gay and Lesbian Guide Book to Provincetown* (Provincetown: Provincetown Business Guild, 1999), 1.

NOTES TO CHAPTER 2

1. Kammen, 225, 258.

2. For analyses of other resort destination that offer alienated leisure, see Martha K. Norkunas, *The Politics of Public Memory: Tourism, History and Ethnicity in Monterey, California* (Albany: State University of New York Press, 1993); Dubinsky; Maria Montoya, "The Roots of Economic and Ethnic Division in Northern New Mexico: The Case of the Civilian Conservation Corps," *Western Historical Quarterly* (1995): 26; Sarah Horton, "Maintaining Hispano Identity through the Santa Fe Fiesta: Reappropriating Key Symbols and Resisting Anglo Dominance," *Kiva* 66 (2000):

249–265; Annie Gilbert Coleman, "Call of the Mild: The Rocky Mountain Ski Industry" (paper, American Historical Association Annual Meeting, New York City, January 4, 1997).

3. Agnes Edwards, *Cape Cod: New and Old* (Boston: Houghton Mifflin, 1918), 151, 163.

4. On the utility of "othering" as a cultural process that complicates the interplay between desire and identification across races, ethnicities, and bodies, see Stuart Hall, "New Ethnicities," in *Black Film/British Cinema I* (London, 1988), 29; and Eric Lott, "'The Seeming Counterfeit': Racial Politics and Early Blackface Minstrelsy," *American Quarterly* 43 (June 1991): 227.

5. Arthur Tarbell, *Cape Cod Ahoy! A Travel Book for the Summer Visitor* (Boston: A. T. Ramsay and Co., 1932), 233.

6. Katherine Dos Passos, *Down Cape Cod: The Complete Guide to Cape Cod* (New York: Dodge, 1936), 24.

7. Nancy P. Smith, "How to Amuse Yourself in Provincetown," *The Provincetown Guide Book* (Provincetown: Provincetown Art Association, 1931), 69.

8. See "Provincetown Harbor Scenes Change with Passing Hours," newspaper clipping in Scrapbook I, PPL.

9. See M. Estellie Smith, "Portuguese Enclaves: The Invisible Minority," in *Social and Cultural Identity: Problems of Persistence and Change*, ed. Thomas K. Fitzgerald (Athens: University of Georgia Press, 1974); Leo Pap, *The Portuguese-Americans* (Boston: Twayne, 1981); Donald Taft, *Two Portuguese Communities in New England* (New York: Arno Press and the New York Times, 1969); Francis Rogers, "The Portuguese Experience in the United States," *Journal of the American Portuguese Society* 10 (Spring 1976); Alec Wilkinson, *The Riverkeeper* (New York: Knopf, 1986); Eduardo Mayone Dias, ed., *Portugueses na América do Norte* (n.p.: Peregrinação, 1983); Carlos E. Cortes, ed., *Portuguese Americans and Spanish Americans* (New York: Arno Press, 1980); Edward W. Crane, "Sons of the Azores on Cape Cod," *Travel* (September 1937); Jeremiah Digges, *In Great Waters: The Story of Portuguese Fishermen* (New York: Macmillan, 1941); Clarke, 60–65.

10. Maria Ioannis Benis Baganha, *Portuguese Emigration to the United States, 1820–1930* (New York: Garland, 1990), 264–265, 372–379. See also Urban Tigner Holmes Jr., "Portuguese Americans," in *Our Racial and National Minorities*, ed. Francis J. Brown and Joseph Slabey Roucek (New York: Prentice Hall, 1937), 394–404; Pap, 39–40; Seth Rolbein, "Selling Ms. Sandy," *Yankee Magazine* (December 1990): 90; and Sandra Wolforth, *The Portuguese in America* (San Francisco: R & E Research Associates, 1978), 1–18.

11. Baganha, 372–379.

12. Pap, 39–40, 58; Holmes, 396; Marsha McCabe and Joseph D. Thomas, eds., *Portuguese Spinner: An American Story* (New Bedford, MA: Spinner, 1998); Henry R. Lang, "The Portuguese Element in New England," *Journal of American Folk-Lore* 5 (1982): 9–18; Taft, *Two Portuguese*, passim; Dorothy Ann Gilbert, *Recent Portuguese Immigrants to Fall River, Massachusetts: An Analysis of Relative Economic Success* (New York: AMS Press, 1989); Wenona Giles, *Portuguese Women in Toronto: Gender, Immigration and Nationalism* (Buffalo, NY: University of Toronto Press, 2002).

13. James H. Gill, *A History of the Azores* (Menlo Park, CA: n.p., 1972), 26–28.

14. Alice D. Kelly, "Portuguese Fisherman," Works Progress Administration (WPA), Box A714, Folder "WPA Folklore Project, Massachusetts, Alice Kelly," Library of Congress (hereafter cited as LC).

15. "Reminiscences of Provincetown: Collinson, An Immigrant Record," *Provincetown Advocate*, July 10, 1975. On conflict between the Azoreans and Lisbons see Mary "Lil" Russe, interview with author, videotape recording, Provincetown, Mass., February 15, 1997, POHP, PPL; Gaspar, *Leaving Pico*.

16. Josef Berger, "Relationships of Racial Groups," 1–2, RG 65, New Bedford File, NA.

17. Bela Feldman-Bianco and Donna Huse, "The Construction of Immigrant Identity," in McCabe and Thomas, 64.

18. See especially Russe, interview; Florence Corea Alexander, interview with author, videotape recording, Provincetown, Mass., November 9, 1996, POHP, PPL; John Patrick, interview; Jerome Lee Costa, interview with author, videotape recording, Truro, Mass., May 6, 1997, POHP, PPL. See also Alice D. Kelly, "Captain Joseph Captiva of the Elmer S," 4, WPA Box A714, Folder "WPA Folklore Project," LC.

19. Pap, 36–37. See also Jerry Williams, "Where Are They Now? Location Characteristics of Portuguese Americans," in Dias, 15–28; Maria Angelina Duarte, "Luso-American Literature—Then and Now," in Dias, 170; Nancy T. Baden, "America, the Promise and the Reality: A Look at Two Portuguese Immigrant Autobiographies," in Dias, 191–205; Raul d'Eca, "The Portuguese in the United States," in Cortés, ed., *Portuguese Americans*, 365–369; Mary Heaton Vorse, "The Portuguese in Provincetown," in Cortes; Henry R. Lang, "The Portuguese Element," 9–18.

20. Baganha, 7, 9.

21. Samuel Morison, *The Maritime History of Massachusetts, 1783–1860* (Cambridge, MA: Riverside Press, 1961), 353; quoted in Baganha, 21. See also M. Estellie Smith, "Portuguese Enclaves," 84; Pap, 18–20; Mark A. Nicholas, "Mashpee Wampanoags of Cape Cod, the Whalefishery, and Seafaring's Impact on Community Development," *American Indian Quarterly* 22 (March 2002).

22. See Nancy W. Paine Smith, *Provincetown*, 98; Hatch, 72–73; and "Pirate Captive First Portuguese Settler," September 4, 1937, newspaper clipping in scrapbook, "Portuguese," 5, CCPMA.

23. Jennings, 101.

24. See Pap, 39–40. See also Scott Corbett with Manuel Zora, *The Sea Fox: The Adventures of Cape Cod's Most Colorful Rumrunner* (London: R. Hale, 1957); "Collinson, An Immigrant Recorded"; Florence Corea Alexander, interview; Clement Silva, interview by author, audiotape recording, Truro, Mass., November 24, 1997, POHP, PPL; Russe, interview; Manuel "Cul" Goveia, interview by author, videotape recording, Provincetown, Mass., March 6, 1997, POHP, PPL. See also Kelly, "Captain Joseph Captiva," 4.

25. "Collinson: An Immigrant Recorded."

26. Located in Abbie Cook, Putnam scrapbook, CCPMA. Reverend Harris also argued that "one of our greatest weapons is the rapidity with which the foreigner is Americanized." See also the *Provincetown Advocate*, January 23, 1913, on advice to American boys to stay in school so that their immigrant neighbors don't pass them by.

27. Jeanne Petit, "The Polar Opposite of Our Pioneer Breed: Manliness, Race, Citizenship, and the Immigration Restriction League" (paper, the American Historical Association Annual Meeting, New York City, January 3, 1997).

28. See Noel Ignatiev, *How the Irish Became White* (New York: Routledge, 1995); and Karen Brodkin, *How Jews Became White and What That Says about Race in America* (New Brunswick, NJ: Rutgers University Press, 1998).

29. Taft, 18–43. See especially p. 43 where he reproduces tables from "Ships Docking at Providence in 1920."

30. "Drudgin," *New England Magazine* XLI (Jan. 1910): 671.

31. Ibid., 669.

32. Vorse, *Time and the Town*, 161.

33. My arguments on *becoming* Portuguese American draw upon George Sanchez's *Becoming Mexican American: Ethnicity, Culture and Identity in Chicano Los Angeles, 1900–1945* (New York: Oxford University Press, 1993).

34. See Oscar Handlin, *The Uprooted: The Epic Story of the Great Migrations That Made the American People* (New York: Grosset and Dunlap, 1951); John Bodnar, *The Transplanted: A History of Immigrants in Urban America* (Bloomington: Indiana University Press, 1985); James Grossman, *Land of Hope: Chicago, Black Southerners and the Great Migration* (Chicago: University of Chicago Press, 1989). See also Lawrence H. Fuchs, *The American Kaleidoscope: Race, Ethnicity, and the Civic Culture* (Hanover, NH: Published by University Press of New England [for] Wesleyan University Press, 1990).

35. See Wolforth, 12–16.

36. Edward Alsworth Ross, *The Old World in the New: The Significance of Past and Present Immigration to the American People* (New York, 1914), 179, emphasis original; quoted in Wolforth, 36–37.

37. Hatch, 72.

38. Wolforth, 35–37.

39. See Alice D. Kelly, "Record of Interviews," 2, 5; "Drudgin," 665–666; Russe, interview; Arthur Costa, interview by author, audiotape recording, Provincetown, Mass., May 6, 1997, POHP, PPL; Florence Corea Alexander, interview; Ursula Silva, interview by author, audiotape recording, Truro, Mass., November 25, 1997, POHP, PPL; Elena Hall, interview by author, audiotape recording, Provincetown, Mass., February 6, 1998, POHP, PPL; Charlotte Matta, interview by author, audiotape recording, Provincetown, Mass., March 1998; Alice D. Kelly, "Captain Joseph Captiva," 17.

40. See Josef Berger, "Cuisine," 1, RG 69, New Bedford File, NA.

41. See Montoya, "Ethnic Division," 26, on the importance of naming; "Fishermen Celebrate Old World Feast," Scrapbook I, PPL; Alec Wilkinson, *The Riverkeeper* (New York: Knopf, 1986), 4; Josef Berger, "Racial Cultural Heritage," 1–2, RG 69, WPA Massachusetts Guide, FWP, Folder Provincetown, NA; Josef Berger, "The Portuguese in Massachusetts," RG 69, FWP, WPA, NA; Josef Berger, "Customs," 2 RG 69, New Bedford File, NA; Taft, *Two Portuguese*, 87; Russe, interview; Rolbein, 90–92, 130.

42. Town Hall Meeting Minutes, September, 30, 1937, Provincetown Town Hall Archives (hereafter PTHA).

43. *Provincetown Annual Town Report* (Provincetown: Year Ending December 31, 1943), 192, 213.

44. Alice D. Kelly, "Record of Interviews with Portuguese Fishermen, to date, from notebook (unrevised) Dec. 14, 1938," WPA Box A714, 3; Alice D. Kelly, "Captain Joseph Captiva of the Elmer S.," 7. See also newspaper clipping December 24, 1937, in Scrapbook, "Portuguese," 13, CCPMA, which states, "years ago nearly every Provincetown home had a Menino Jesus Altar depicting the Nativity at Christmas time. Although the custom has died out to a large extent, investigation today led to the discovery of a few, and one of the best this year . . . [was] at the home of Mr. and Mrs. John Russe on Standish St."

45. For histories of the Blessing of the Fleet, see "The History of the Blessing of the Fleet," *The 15th Annual Blessing of the Fleet Ceremony Program* (June 24, 1962); Betty V. Costa, "Retrospective," in *The 35th Annual Blessing of the Fleet Ceremony Program* (June 27, 1982), 2; Gregory Katz, *Provincetown Advocate*, June 30, 1977; *The 46th Annual Blessing of the Fleet Ceremony Program* (June 22, 1993); Elsa Allen, "The Blessing of the Fleet," *Provincetown Magazine* (June 24, 1993), 13. See also programs for the Blessing Ceremonies located in HMA.

46. *Provincetown Advocate*, June 29, 1950.

47. Leonard, interview. Almost every oral history interview in the Provincetown Oral History Collection contains information on the Blessing of the Fleet ceremony.

48. On the Blessing losing its religious significance, see Summer Guide, *Provincetown Advocate*, June 27, 1985. See also "Blessing Is Low Key This Year," *Provincetown Advocate*, June 29, 1989; "Blessing Quiet This Year but Not Gone," *Provincetown Advocate*, July 4, 1996.

49. Editorial, *Provincetown Advocate*, July 4, 1996.

50. On the chamarrita see "Customs of Old Portugal to Feature Artists' Ball," August 9, 1938, scrapbook, "Portuguese," 5, CCPMA. For reference to Portuguese being spoken on the streets, Christmas traditions, and business traditions see "Cape Tip Story Told by Radio: Mrs. Marion Blakeman and Alice Silva Relate History and Customs," scrapbook, "New Jerseyite," book one, CCPMA.

51. See Provincetown Business Guild, *Guide to Our Town*, (Provincetown, 1997), emphasis original.

52. Vorse, *Time and the Town*, 161.

53. See Hatch, 72–73; Josef Berger, "Racial Groups," 5–6; Josef Berger, "Transportation," n.p., RG 69, WPA Massachusetts Guide, NA; Vorse, "The Portuguese," 71; "Portuguese Among First to Land Here: Town Has Produced Distinguished Works of Art: Once Richest Town: Portuguese Come with Whaling Ships," September 4, 1937, in scrapbook, "Portuguese," 8, CCPMA; Phyllis Duganne, "The Coast Guard," in *The Provincetown Guide Book* (Provincetown: Provincetown Art Association, 1931), 40.

54. Goveia, interview. Scott Corbett and Manny Zora put forth a similar interpretation in the *Sea Fox* when they wrote, "The Portuguese . . . were walled in by the language barrier and by the resentment of the outnumbered Yankees against the encroachments of any outsiders, especially foreigners. Time, however, was on the Portygee's side." Corbett and Zora, *Sea Fox*, 66.

55. The CCPMA elected its first Portuguese American President, Ernest Carriero, in 1997. See Wolforth, 121–123, on what she calls a weak political awareness among Portuguese immigrants.

56. Alice D. Kelly, "Record of Interviews," 3.

57. Ibid.

58. Ibid.

59. *New Deal Minstrel*, Presented by the Catholic Daughters of America and the Knights of Columbus, January 10, 1934. For a set of blackface minstrel programs see Article No. 578(b), Sheet 276, List B, HMA. See also *National Minstrels*, Provincetown Town Hall, April 30, 1913, in photograph collection, CCPMA. *Holy Name Minstrels* (program), Article No. 578(b), Sheet 276, List B, HMA. See same location for programs for Provincetown Lion's Club, *On the Levee* minstrel show produced in 1937; Veterans of Foreign Wars Lewis A. Young Post No. 3152, *The Second Annual Variety Minstrels*, 1950; and St. Peter's Holy Name Society *Minstrels*, 1955.

60. Roediger, 117.

61. Alice D. Kelly, "Record of Interviews," from notebook (unrevised), 1.

62. "Reminiscences of Provincetown." Some narrators from the Provincetown Oral History Project noted, much more blatantly, that Yankees were prone to call Portuguese residents "black Portygees." See especially Marguerite Beata Cook, interview; and Clement Silva, interview.

63. Joseph Berger, "Racial Elements," 2, RG 69, FWP, Folder "Provincetown," NA.

64. For an excellent analysis of Cape Verdeans as betwixt and between races and ethnicities, and of Cape Verdeans' tendencies to distance themselves from African Americans, see Marilyn Halter, *Between Race and Ethnicity: Cape Verdean American Immigrants, 1860–1965* (Chicago: University of Illinois Press, 1993), xi–xv, 5–17, 46, 120, 145–166. Halter argues that the politics of race in the New World were learned well before Cape Verdeans stepped foot in the United States, as whaling captains and other transportation hierarchies taught them the value of being white. She also contends that "the 'white' Portuguese, chiefly from the Azores and Madiera, disassociated themselves from" the Cape Verdeans. Cape Verdeans on Cape Cod and especially in factory towns like New Bedford and Fall River were excluded from Portuguese parishes, social clubs, and neighborhoods. Cape Verdeans, she finds, "quickly perceived the adverse effects of racism on the upward mobility of anyone considered nonwhite in this country," 7. See also Wolforth, 12, 129.

65. Lucy Ramos, "Black, White, or Portuguese? A Cape Verdean Dilemma," in *Spinner: People and Culture in Southeastern Massachusetts* (New Bedford, MA: Spinner, 1980).

66. See H. Jerusa Korim, "Provincetown Reclaims Native Son," March 27, 1995, in Vertical Files, "Douglas Roach," PPL.

67. See Edward S. Roach, letter to the editor, *Provincetown Advocate*, March 10, 1949.

68. Ed Dahill, letter to the editor, *Provincetown Advocate*, March 17, 1949.

69. Mildred Greensfelder, letter to the editor, *Provincetown Advocate*, March 17, 1949.

70. Editorial, "Ban All Discrimination," *Provincetown Advocate*, March 17, 1949.

71. Edward S. Roach, letter to the editor, *Provincetown Advocate*, March 24, 1949.

72. Beatrix Faust, letter to the editor, *Provincetown Advocate*, April 7, 1949.

73. *Provincetown Advocate*, March 5, 1949.

74. See James Baldwin, "On Being 'White' . . . and Other Lies," in *Black on White: Black Writers on What It Means to Be White*, ed. David R. Roediger (New York: Schocken, 1998), 177–180; David R. Roediger, "Introduction," in *Black on White*, 20–22; James Baldwin, *The Price of the Ticket: Collected Nonfiction, 1948–1985* (London: M. Joseph, 1985).

75. The idea that in some places and at some moments race matters more than sexual orientation is not new. See, for example, Hawkeswood, *One of the Children*; Reverend Chester McCall, "Spirituality in the African-American LGBT Community" (lecture, Duke University Mary Lou Williams Center for Black Culture, Durham, N.C., March 9, 2000).

NOTES TO CHAPTER 3

1. Brown, 47–48, 57.

2. William H. Evaul Jr. and Tony Vevers, *The Beginnings of the Provincetown Art Association and Museum* (Provincetown: Provincetown Art Association and Museum, 1990), 3–6 (catalogue essay). Waterman quoted by I. H. Caliga in an interview with Lawrence Dame, *Boston Herald*, August 11, 1914.

3. Although Provincetown marks 1899 as the birth of its art colony (it celebrated the centennial in 1999 with town-wide festivities), a number of artists and writers, some famous (including Henry David Thoreau) and some lesser known, visited and resided in Provincetown four to five decades before Hawthorne's visit.

4. Egan, 165.

5. "Biggest Art Colony in the World at Provincetown," *Boston Globe*, August 27, 1916.

6. For histories of Provincetown's eclectic art colony see Egan; Ross Moffett, *Art in Narrow Streets: The First Thirty-Three Years of the Provincetown Art Association* (Falmouth, MA: Kendall, 1964); Heller and Rudnick; Edwin Robinson, *The Beachcombers* (Provincetown: Advocate Press, 1947); Josephine Couch Del Deo, *Beginnings: The History of the Fine Arts Work Center, 1964–1969* (Provincetown: n.p., 1986); Tony Vevers, *The Beginnings of the Provincetown Art Association* (Provincetown: Provincetown Art Association and Museum, 1990); Nyla Ahrens, *Provincetown, the Art Colony: A Chronology and Guide* (Provincetown: Provincetown Art Association and Museum, 1997); Deborah J. Minsky, "Provincetown: A Sense of Place" (master's thesis, California State University, Long Beach, 1984); Louis Andrew Eisenhauer, " 'Our Kind': Art, Society, and the Cultural Radical of the 1910s in the Plays of the Provincetown Players" (master's thesis, University of Maryland, 1994); Ronald A. Kuchta and Dorothy Gees Seckler, *Provincetown Painters, 1890s–1970s* (Syracuse, NY: Everson Museum of Art, 1977).

7. Moffett, 40–69.

8. Carpenter, "Provincetown," 533. See also Clarke, 60–65; Edwards; Smith, *Provincetown Book*; and Isaac Morton Small, *Just a Little about the Lower Cape* (Truro, MA: n.p., 1926).

9. Nancy Paine Smith, *Book about the Artists*, 3.

10. Hatch, 57.

11. "Beach-Combers Ball at the Tip of the Cape, Gayest, Largest, Liveliest Ever," August 1, 1924, clipping from "Scrapbook of Mrs. Cora C. Fuller"; "Provincetown Ball Gay and Satiric," August 21, 1939, clipping from scrapbook, PPL; "Town Crier's Daughter Enlivens Provincetown Ball—Kubik Protests Masquerade Act during Gay Annual Artists' Costume Revels," August 19, 1916, clipping from scrapbook, PPL. One article even reported that "tonight's affair would be unusually 'gay' and 'nude'"; see "Burlesque Cannes Act at Artists Costume Ball," August 20, 1937, clipping from scrapbook, PPL.

12. "Artists Are Queer Ducks," n.d., newspaper clipping, scrapbook, PPL.

13. "Beachcombers Ball Is Rich in Gayety and Color," August 23, 1923, clipping from "Scrapbook of Mrs. Cora C. Fuller," Research Club Collection, box 2, CCPMA.

14. Chauncey, 14.

15. In addition to those mentioned already, visual artists who worked in Provincetown included Edwin Dickinson, Paul Burlin, Fritz Bultman, Adolph Gottlieb, Helen Frankenthaler, Myron Stout, Mark Rothko, Robert Motherwell, Claes Oldenburg, Milton Avery, Max Bohm, Lucy L'Engle, Harry (Heinrich) Pfeiffer, Tod Lindenmuth, Philip Malicoat, Peter Busa, Leo Manso, Kahlil Gibran, Anton Van Derek, Edwin Reeves Euler, Bruce McCain, Ada Raynor, Fritz Fulgister, Agnes Weinrich, Charles Heinz, Lee Krasner, Jackson Pollock, and Jack Tworkov. See Moffett for a more comprehensive list. And writers that worked at or visited Land's End included Henry Thoreau, John Dos Passos, Stanley Kunitz, Norman Mailer, and Alan Dugan. This is by no means an exhaustive list, but is meant instead to give an indication of Provincetown's popularity as an artists' haven.

16. See William Evaul, interview by author, videotape recording, Truro, Mass., February 12, 1997, POHP, PPL; William H. Evaul, "Whiteline Woodblock Prints Provincetown 1914," *Cape Cod Antiques and Arts* (Feb. 1988); and Janet Flint, *Provincetown Printers: A Woodcut Tradition* (Washington, DC: Smithsonian Institution Press, 1983).

17. The story of the Provincetown Players has been told a number of times. See especially Egan; Rudnick and Heller; Vorse, *Time and the Town*. See also Allen Churchill, *The Improper Bohemians: Greenwich Village in Its Heyday* (New York: Dutton, 1959); Christine Stansell, *American Moderns: Bohemian New York and the Nation of a New Century* (New York: Metropolitan Books, 2000); Ross Wetzsteon, *Republic of Dreams: Greenwich Village, The American Bohemia, 1910–1960* (New York: Simon and Schuster, 2002); Susan Glaspell, *The Road to the Temple* (New York: Stoke, 1927); Hutchins Hapgood, *A Victorian in the Modern World* (New York: Harcourt, 1939); Edmund Wilson, *The Twenties* (New York: Farrar, 1975); and Edmund Wilson, *The Thirties* (New York: Farrar, 1975).

18. Egan, 14.

19. The Sixes and Sevens was a "coffeehouse" that was open every evening from 8:00 to 11:00. Ross Moffett notes that it was "filled every evening . . . with artists and others of the intelligentsia. Among the patrons were also staid vacationers, curious to take home some observation of life with the artists." Moffett, 39.

20. Egan, 4–5, 152.

21. Wallace Nutting, 22.

22. Alice Foley, interview by author, videotape recording, Provincetown, Mass., January, 30, 1997, POHP, PPL.

23. For a similar argument about a later period of time, see William Evaul, *The Provocative Years, 1935–1945: The Hans Hofmann School and Its Students in Provincetown,* August 3 to October 28, 1990, catalogue (Provincetown: Provincetown Art Association and Museum [hereafter PAAM]).

24. Houghton Cranford Smith, *The Provincetown I Remember,* edited and compiled by Florence Cranford Smith Shepard in 1991, copyright Laura Cranford Smith, 1991 (n.p., 1963), 6; Ahrens.

25. Houghton Cranford Smith, 6–7, 15, 16–17.

26. Moffett, 11.

27. "Town Crier's Daughter Enlivens Provincetown Ball—Kubik Protests Masquerade Act during Gay Annual Artists' Costume Revels," August 19, 1916, clipping from scrapbook, PPL.

28. See "Beach-Combers Ball at the Tip of the Cape, Gayest, Largest, Liveliest, Ever," CCPMA.

29. Artists staged at least one and possibly several blackface minstrel shows. See Houghton Cranford Smith, 7; Egan, 196. Provincetown writers also belittled Portuguese and by extension Yankee residents by suggesting that native townsfolk were incapable of appreciating "art" or their own aesthetic surroundings before the artists arrived. Local writer, artist, and well-known Yankee Nancy Paine Smith argued in her *Book about the Artists* that "the natives saw only the desolation of the sand hills, till the artists and the poets taught them their majesty." Smith, *Book about the Artists,* 12–13. Similarly, in 1915 the *Provincetown Advocate* noted that the Art Association's first public exhibition was "helping the townspeople, especially, to appreciate art." *Provincetown Advocate,* August 12, 1915; quoted in Vevers, *Beginnings,* 10.

30. See Marsden Hartley, "Summer Art Colonies," MSS, in "Laughter of Steel and Journal Entries," Hartley-Berger Collection, Yale Collection of American Literature, Beinecke Rare Book and Manuscript Library, Yale University (hereafter cited as YCAL).

31. Quoted in Allen Churchill, 25.

32. George Chauncey refers to this as "Anglophilia." See Chauncey, 106.

33. Whether other bohemians liked both men is debatable. Demuth seems to have been more popular, while Hartley, according to Leona Rust Egan and others, did not make friends as easily. See Egan, 174.

34. Marsden Hartley, "Farewell, Charles," MSS, Hartley-Berger Collection, 3–4, YCAL, quoted in part in Emily Farnham, *Charles Demuth: Behind a Laughing Mask* (Norman: University of Oklahoma Press, 1971), 75. It is possible this meeting took place in 1913. See also Townsend Ludington, *Marsden Hartley: The Biography of an American Artist* (Ithaca, NY: Cornell University Press, 1992), 77, who notes: "Subsequently they would sit together at the Thomas and take pleasure in observing the characters who passed in front of the restaurant, such as . . . 'the very manly Georges Banks,' who looked so much like Oscar Wilde that Hartley and his friends called her 'Oscar Wilde la Seconde.' This sort of thing was 'tres exagere of course.'"

35. Helen W. Henderson, "Charles Demuth" (paper read before the Junior

League of Lancaster Pennsylvania, Nov. 10, 1947), from Weyland Scrapbook No. II, 158–161; quoted in Farnham, 79. See Ludington, 9.

36. See George Biddle, Response to Questionnaire #1, Farnham Collection, YCAL, where he notes that Demuth was a "homosexual, 'fin de siecle.'" Others remembered that Demuth, although elegant, was also quite social and visible in Provincetown. Demuth, they recalled, often traveled "way up along" or "down along" Commercial Street (Commercial Street was two-way then) on the popular "Accommodation" (open-air) bus, chatting with the driver and waving to friends and passersby along the way. During the evening hours, he often walked the length of Commercial Street to converse with friends or frequent one of the local drugstores. John Francis, a local Portuguese "native," for example, rented rooms to Eugene O'Neill and Charles Demuth in Francis' Flats. See also Harry Kemp, *Love among the Cape-Enders* (New York: Macauley Co., 1931), a "fictional" work on the bohemian "Cape-Enders"—remarkably similar to the Provincetown Players—who rented rooms from and had relationships with Portuguese "natives." See Moffett, 25, for a short list of women who rented rooms to artists.

37. Susan Watts Street, interview by Emily Farnham, January 21, 1956, New York, in Emily Farnham, "Charles Demuth: His Life, Psychology and Works" (Ph.D. diss., Ohio State University, 1959), 975; quoted in Jonathan Weinberg, *Speaking for Vice: Homosexuality in the Art of Charles Demuth, Marsden Hartley, and the First American Avant-Garde* (New Haven: Yale University Press, 1993), 48.

38. Demuth's unconventional appearance was not lost on his contemporaries. Charles Daniel, Demuth's art dealer, remarked, for example, "Ah, Demuth. He was a rare one. I can tell you this right now—he wore the most beautiful neckties in New York. . . . He was very vain; and wore unusual colors." Charles Daniel, interview with Emily Farnham, New York, 1956, in Farnham, "His Life, Psychology, and Works," 990–991; quoted in Weinberg, 47.

39. Stuart Davis, interview by Emily Farnham, January 20, 1956, New York, in Farnham, *Laughing Mask*, 82.

40. Most evidence, including postmarked letters and postcards, date Hartley's visit to Provincetown as 1916, yet in his unpublished essay "That Great Provincetown Summer" he notes that the visit was in 1915. See Hartley-Berger Collection, YCAL, specifically No. 26 (19); and "Marsden Hartley 1916," letters to Alfred Stieglitz, Stieglitz Collection, YCAL.

41. See Marsden Hartley to Mabel Dodge, MSS, Hartley-Berger Collection, YCAL.

42. See Marsden Hartley, "Somehow a Past," YCAL; Ludington, 33.

43. Hartley's enthusiasm for costume balls began as early as 1912 in Paris and continued throughout his life. See Ludington, 33; Weinberg, 206; Tony Vevers, *Provincetown Arts Magazine* (April 1991): 111; Barbara Haskell, *Marsden Hartley* (New York: Whitney Museum of American Art, with New York University Press, 1980).

44. On artistic communities, like the Beats, being both homophobic and gay-friendly, see Boyd, 123–124. See G. Frank Lydston, "Sexual Perversions, Satyriasis, and Nymphomania," *Medical and Surgical Reporter* 61, no. 10 (Nov. 1889): 253–258, who argues, "'There is in every community of any size a colony of male sexual perverts; they are usually known to each other, and are likely to congregate together. At

times they operate in accordance with some definite and concerted plan in quest of subjects wherewith to gratify their sexual impulse.'" Quoted in Weinberg, 6–18.

45. Catherine Ryan, *Très Complémentaires: The Art and Lives of Ethel Mars and Maud Hunt Squire* (New York: Mary Ryan Gallery and Susan Sheehan Gallery, 2000). See also "Ethel Mars," vertical file, PAAM.

46. Dorothy Squire to Robin Squire, February, 1986; quoted in Ryan, 5.

47. Taped interview with Ethel Mars's heir, 2000, quoted in Ryan, 5.

48. Hapgood, *A Victorian,* 474. See also Ada Gilmore to Hutchins Hapgood, October 11, 1939, Hapgood Collection, YCAL.

49. Taped interview with Mars's heir, 2000, quoted in Ryan, 5. In Vence, Mars and Squire dined with Marsden Hartley and associated with other eccentric artists such as Fred Marvin. See Hapgood, 474. This is not to say, however, that they were popular; it seems from Gilmore's letter to Hapgood that Ethel Mars, in particular, offended several other queer artists.

50. Gertrude Stein, "Miss Furr and Miss Skeene," MSS, 1908–1912, Stein Collection, YCAL. Published in *Vanity Fair* (July 1923): 55; and Gertrude Stein, *Geography and Plays* (Boston: Four Seas Co, 1922). The editor in *Vanity Fair* wrote, "it will be seen that the style, though queer, is exactly suited to the subject." That Miss Furr and Miss Skeene refer to Ethel Mars and Maud Squire is clear from references in personal letters as well as Ethel Mars's reference to herself and Squire as "Miss Furr and Miss Skeene." See Ethel Mars calling card signed "Miss Furr + Miss Skeene," Stein Collection, YCAL. See also Stendahl on de-coding of Stein's pieces. See Ryan for further analysis and "sing-song" quote.

51. See Evaul, "Whiteline Woodblock Prints," 10. On Gilmore's meeting with Mars in France see *Woodblock Prints of Ada Gilmore Chaffee* (Kalamazoo Arts Institute, November 8 to December 9, 1979), catalogue in "Gilmore" vertical file, PAAM. On the property they held see Provincetown Assessor's Records, 1920–1940, Provincetown Town Hall Archive (hereafter cited as PTHA).

52. See *Blanche Lazzell: A Modernist Rediscovered* (Archives of American Art, New York Regional Center Exhibition, June 25 to September 20, 1991), in Lazzell vertical file, PAAM; Robert Bridges and Kristina Olson, *Blanche Lazzell: The Hofmann Drawings* (Morgantown: West Virginia University Press, 2004); *Blanche Lazzell: American Modernist* (New York: Michael Rosenfeld Gallery, 2000); Barbara Stern Shapiro, *From Paris to Provincetown: Blanche Lazzell and the Color Woodcut* (Boston: Museum of Fine Arts, Boston, 2002).

53. Ryan, 6. On Hartley's heterosexual affairs see Ludington, 29, 36–37, 125; Weinberg, 126–127. And on Demuth's bisexuality see Weinberg, 76–81; Farnham, "Charles Demuth," 81, 127–128.

54. Smith, *I Remember,* 7–8.

55. Oliver Chaffee to Hutchins Hapgood, n.d., Hapgood Collection, YCAL. See also Fred Marvin to Hutchins Hapgood, July 13, 1935, and Fred Marvin to Mrs. Hapgood, February 10, 1936, Hapgood Collection, YCAL. Marvin and Cesco apparently lived at 211 Bradford Street.

56. "A Village within a Village," July 14, 1982, in Vertical File "Peter Hunt," PAAM. See also Mary Jo Avellar, interview by Denise Gaylord, videotape recording, Provincetown, Mass., February 12, 1998, POHP, PPL.

57. Anna Hall [pseud.], interview by author, audiotape recording, Provincetown, Mass., September 10, 1997.

58. Eleanor Bloomfield and Ivy Ivans, *A Tale of the Ship's Bell* (Dayton, OH: Lowe Brothers Company, n.d.), 5. From the *Provincetown Valuation Records, 1919–1921*, PTHA, it is clear that Bloomfield purchased the land on Allerton Street in 1920, then had the house moved there in 1921.

59. Ibid., 14–15.

60. Ibid., 23.

61. Ibid., 24.

62. Antoinette Quinby Scudder, *East End, West End* (New York: Henry Harrison, 1934), 12–14.

63. See Judy Grahn, *Another Mother Tongue, Gay Words, Gay Worlds* (Boston: Beacon Press, 1984), 83, regarding Lesbos as a place "'where the women bonding are sisters—*and more than sisters,*'" as well as her notes on Sappho resonating as a distinctly white and not necessarily "liberatory" text for all lesbians. Quoted in Bravmann, 51–54.

64. See Carroll Smith-Rosenberg, *Disorderly Conduct: Visions of Gender in Victorian America* (New York: Knopf, 1985), 286; Esther Newton, "The Mythic Mannish Lesbian," *Signs* (Fall 1984): 557–575; and Lisa Duggan, "The Trials of Alice Mitchell: Sensationalism, Sexology and the Lesbian Subject in Turn-of-the-Century America," *Signs* (Summer 1993): 791–814.

65. Josef Berger, "Racial Groups," 1.

66. Smith, *I Remember*, 14.

67. Harry Kemp, "Provincetown Torn by Strife of Art Schools," *New York Herald Tribune*, August 7, ca. 1927, scrapbook, HMA.

68. See Berger, *Cape Cod Pilot*, 230. Besides exploring all of Cape Cod, Berger intended specifically to show how and why visitors should "appreciate [the] hardy, muscular set of decorations that the town's art colony has."

69. "Accident Changed 'Johnny Kitty' from Fisherman into Able Artist," n.a., n.d., Scrapbook 1, PPL. For an example of Yankees asserting themselves as artists, see Henry Lincoln Clapp to Mr. Putnam, April 5, 1919, where he writes, "In 1863 there were no artists colonies [in Provincetown]. But Barber Atkins, Mitchell, and Johnny Hilliard, were there, each an artist in his line. Atkins put the artistic contour and shine on my hair; Mitchell could adjust a hair spring to a hair; and Johnny made me an artistic instrument out of ebony wood." Research Club Collection, CCPMA.

70. Lecture delivered at Provincetown Art Association and Museum, Summer 1995, Provincetown, Mass., audio recording, PPL.

71. "Coming out" for gay natives after WWII presented entirely new challenges and options. See Clement Arthur Silva, interview by author, videotape recording, April 25, 1997, Provincetown, Mass., POHP, PPL; Leonard, interview; Joseph J. Trovato, III, "Growing Up Gay in Provincetown," *Provincetown Advocate*, November 13, 1997.

72. Frances Alves, telephone conversation with author, Provincetown, Mass., November 15, 1997; Mary Ruth O'Donnell, conversation with author, Provincetown, Mass., October 15, 1997.

73. Peter Hand, interview with Michael Orlando, videotape recording, Provincetown, Mass., 1990, Provincetown Historical Commission, PPL.

74. Florence Alexander, interview.

75. Hand, interview.

76. Clement Silva, interview.

77. Moffett, 9–10, 44; Vevers and Evaul, 15, 120.

78. Moffett, 40.

79. Nancy Paine Smith, *Provincetown Book*, 146.

80. Ray Hues, "White-Line Woodblock Prints," at http://www.mcbride-gallery.com/whiteline_woodblock.html (accessed August 22, 2004). See also Kathryn Lee Smith, "Down the Line," www.provincetownpocketbook.com/articles/downtheline.htm; and Reva Kern, "History of the Provincetown Print," http://www.jvarnoso.com/co/exlibris/reva1.html (accessed August 22, 2004), who calls white-line woodblock printing "a uniquely American art form."

NOTES TO PART II

1. *Provincetown Advocate*, January 27, 1938.

2. All the facts about the S-4 disaster are from Robert Loys Sminkey, "Submarine USS-S-4 (SS-109)," http://www.subvetpaul.com/USS-S-4.htm (accessed March 12, 2004); Jim Coogan and Jack Sheedy, "The S-4 Disaster," in *Cape Cod Companion*, http://www.barnstablepatriot.com/cccompanion/chapter4.html (accessed March 12, 2004); and Vorse, *Time and the Town*, 226–234. See also Laurel Guadazno, "S-4 Disaster," *Provincetown Banner*, December 9, 1999; and Liz Winston, "Submarine Tragedy Still Resonates," *Provincetown Banner*, December 7, 2000.

3. Sminkey.

4. Vorse, *Time and the Town*, 228.

5. Ibid., 234.

6. Barbara Melosh, *Engendering Culture: Manhood and Womanhood in New Deal Public Art and Theater* (Washington, DC: Smithsonian Institution Press, 1991), 1.

7. See Lizabeth Cohen, *Making a New Deal: Industrial Workers in Chicago, 1919–1939* (New York: Cambridge University Press, 1990); Studs Terkel, *Hard Times: An Oral History of the Great Depression* (New York: Avon Books, 1971).

8. See Florence Alexander, interview.

9. Russe, interview; Anthony Joseph, interview by author, audiotape recording, Provincetown, Mass., April 12, 1997, POHP, PPL; Joe Lazaro [Manuel "Cul" Goveia], "Endangered Species," *Provincetown Magazine*, September 16, 1993, July 29, 1993, August 19, 1993, and August 8, 1993. On local grocers' accounts see Provincetown Board of Selectmen Meeting Minutes, January 27, 1939, PTHA. On freezer strike see Joseph Berger, "Social Institutions," File D-672, WPA-FWP New Bedford, RG 65, NA; and Kelly, "Portuguese Fishermen," 21.

10. On changes in leisure trends see John A. Jackle, *The Tourist* (Lincoln: University of Nebraska Press, 1985), 1; William R. Eadington and Valene L. Smith, "Introduction: The Emergence of Alternative Forms of Tourism," in *Tourism Alternatives*, ed. Eadington and Smith (Philadelphia: University of Pennsylvania Press,

1992), 1; and Juliet B. Shor, *The Overworked American: The Unexpected Decline of Leisure* (New York: Basic, 1991). On resorts being segregated by race see Aron, 213–223.

11. For information on Amphibian Airways or Provincetown–Boston Airline see CCPMA collections and exhibits, as well as "A Brief History of Provincetown–Boston Airline, Inc.," http://airline-online.com/PBA/history.html (accessed March 5, 2003); see also Laurel Guadazno, "Provincetown–Boston Airline," *Provincetown Banner,* November 2, 2000.

12. Vevers, interview; Harvey Dodd, interview by author, videotape recording, Provincetown, Mass., February, 27, 1997, POHP, PPL.

13. To provide a summary of this period I consulted the following texts: Estelle Freedman and John D'Emilio, *Intimate Matters: A History of Sexuality in America* (New York: Harper and Row, 1988); Allan Bérubé, *Coming Out under Fire: The History of Gay Men and Women in World War Two* (New York: Plume, 1990); John D'Emilio, *Sexual Communities, Sexual Politics: The Making of a Homosexual Minority in the United States, 1940–1970* (Chicago: University of Chicago Press, 1983); Elaine Tyler May, *Homeward Bound: American Families in the Cold War Era* (New York: Basic, 1988); Joanne Meyerowitz, ed., *Not June Cleaver: Women and Gender in Postwar America, 1945–1960* (Philadelphia: Temple University Press, 1994); and Marjorie Garber and Rebecca L. Walkowitz, eds., *Secret Agents: The Rosenberg Case, McCarthyism, and Fifties America* (New York: Routledge, 1995). I also relied on the following letters and interviews: Donald Windham, ed., *Tennessee Williams' Letters*; Roslyn Garfield, interview by author, audiotape recording, Provincetown, Mass., June 18, 1998, POHP, PPL; Carbone, interview; Murray Wax, interview by author, videotape recording, Provincetown, Mass., February 13, 1997, POHP, PPL; Barbara Stevens, interview by author, videotape recording, Provincetown, Mass., January 9, 1997, POHP, PPL; Lenore Ross and Pat Shultz, interview by author, audiotape recording, Provincetown, Mass., December 16, 1997; Jack Richtman, interview by author, audiotape recording, Provincetown, Mass., May 28, 1997, POHP, PPL; Foley, interview; Catherine Janard, interview by author, audiotape recording, Provincetown, Mass., March, 5, 1997, POHP, PPL; Beverly Spencer, interview by author, audiotape recording, Provincetown, Mass., December 8, 1997, POHP, PPL; and Miriam Hapgood DeWitt, letter to the editor, *Provincetown Advocate,* July 18, 1981.

14. Freedman and D'Emilio, 288.

15. Ibid., 293.

NOTES TO CHAPTER 4

1. Margaret Roberts, interview by Joyce Johnson, videotape recording, 1990, Provincetown, Mass., Provincetown Historical Commission, PPL.

2. Harrison, 24.

3. Florence B. Brown (Mrs. Harold Haven Brown) to Eleanor Roosevelt, June 15, 1938, WPA State Files, Massachusetts, RG 65, NA.

4. *Provincetown Advocate,* December 8, 1938. Whether this was a typical "white flight" movement, whereby white people leave towns or urban areas as soon as a critical mass of nonwhites have moved in, is unclear. See Bryant Simon, "New York Avenue: The Life and Death of Gay Spaces in Atlantic City, New Jersey, 1920–1990,"

Journal of Urban History (March 2002): 300–327, for a history of the white flight from Atlantic City during the 1970s and 1980s, which made room for the area to become a gay resort.

5. *Provincetown Advocate*, November 17, 1939.

6. Vorse, *Time and the Town*, 287.

7. See Carol Stack, *All Our Kin: Strategies for Survival in a Black Community* (New York: Harper and Row, 1974), xii, 33, 43, 54, on working-class communities that rely on gift exchange or swapping economies. On subsistence living via family economies, see also Kathy Peiss, *Cheap Amusements: Working Women and Leisure in Turn-of-the-Century New York* (Philadelphia: Temple University Press, 1986). For references to an "over-the-back-fence economy" see Goveia, interview; and Napi Van Derek, interview by author, videotape recording, Provincetown, Mass., December 12, 1997, POHP, PPL.

8. See Marguerite Beata Cook, interview; Corbett with Zora, *The Sea Fox*.

9. Florence Alexander, interview.

10. O'Donnell, interview; Goveia, interview; Florence Alexander, interview.

11. Goveia, interview; Anthony Joseph, interview by author, audiotape recording, Provincetown, Mass., April 12, 1998, POHP, PPL; Joe Lazaro [Manuel "Cul" Goveia], "Endangered Species," *Provincetown Magazine*, September 16, 1993, July 29, 1993, August 19, 1993, and August 8, 1993, newspaper clippings in Vertical Files, "Local History," PPL; and Berger, "Social Institutions," 1.

12. Clement Silva, interview. See also Florence Alexander, interview; Carlos, interview; Clement Arthur Silva, interview.

13. Hand, interview; Florence Alexander, interview; Clement Arthur Silva, interview; Clement Silva, interview; Carlos, interview; Carbone, interview.

14. Kelly, "Record of Interviews," 19. See also "Cape's Lucrative Fishing Industry Changes Drastically as Years Pass: Few Boats Go Far Today: Banks Are No Longer Source of Profit," *Standard-Times*, May 31, 1938, in Scrapbook Collection, "Fishing," CCPMA.

15. See town meeting warrants in *Town of Provincetown Annual Report*, 1936–1940.

16. See Josef Berger et al., RG 65, WPA Massachusetts Files, NA.

17. See Berger, *Cape Cod Pilot*; and Federal Writers Project, *Massachusetts: A Guide to Its People and Places* (Boston: Houghton Mifflin, 1937).

18. Lisa Beade, "A Portrait of Singular Style: Provincetown Painter Ross Moffett," *Arts-By-The-Sea* (n.p., 1996), 37.

19. Joyce Johnson, "WPA: Federal Arts Project" in *WPA Artists*, May 23–June 16, 1997, catalogue (Provincetown: Provincetown Art Association and Museum), exhibit curated by M. M. Batelle and Joyce Johnson. See also Joan Saab, "Painting the Town Red (and White and Blue): Art and Politics in 1930s New York City," (Ph.D. diss., New York University, 1999).

20. See Josef Berger et al., RG 65, WPA Massachusetts Files, NA. Provincetown artists paid by the FAP included George Yater, Bruce McKain, Blanche Lazzell, Philip Malicoat, Karl Knaths, Charles Heinz, Charles Kaesslau, Tod Lindenmuth, Fritz Fuglister, Fritz Pfeiffer, Vollian Rann, Robert Rogers, and supervisor Vernon Smith (Orleans).

21. *Provincetown Advocate,* December 10, 1936.

22. Vernon Smith quoted in Tony Vevers, "The Federal Art Project on the Lower Cape," in Batelle and Johnson, *WPA Artists,* 5.

23. Katherine Witherstine Gilman, interview by author, audiotape recording, Provincetown, Mass., April 2, 1997, POHP, PPL.

24. Patricia Zur, conversation with author, Provincetown, Mass., September 11, 1997.

25. *Provincetown Advocate,* November 17, 1939.

26. Joseph Captiva, interview by Alice Kelly, WPA Project on Living Lore in New England/Living Folklore, "Portuguese Fisherman—Joseph Captiva," February 15, 1939, from "The WPA Life Histories Collection" website, http://memory.loc.gov/ammem/wpaintro/wpahome.html (accessed March 22, 2002).

27. Shirley Pell Yater, interview by author, audiotape recording, Truro, Mass., February 28, 1997, POHP, PPL.

28. See *Provincetown Advocate,* January 12, 1939, and March 7, 1940.

29. Aron argues that tourism in fact escalated during even the early years of the Depression. See Aron, 238–241.

30. *Provincetown Advocate,* August 27, 1936.

31. Vorse, *Time and the Town,* 293.

32. Katherine Dos Passos and Edith Shay, *Down Cape Cod* (New York: National Travel Club, 1947), 186–189. See also Hatch; Federal Writers Project, *Massachusetts: A Guide;* Berger, *Cape Cod Pilot;* Eleanor Early, *And This Is Cape Cod!* (Boston: Houghton Mifflin, 1936). See especially Early, 144, where she notes that half the town "rents rooms, and the other half serves meals."

33. Paul Smith, *A Modern Pilgrim's Guide to Provincetown* (Provincetown: Modern Pilgrim Press, 1934–1937), 25.

34. "Burlesque Cannes Act at Artists Costume Ball," August 20, 1937, newspaper clipping from scrapbook, PPL.

35. Headline from August 21, 1939, clipping in scrapbook, PPL.

36. Lawrence Dame, *The Boston Herald,* ca. 1939, scrapbook, PPL.

37. *Provincetown Advocate,* July 15, 1937.

38. Provincetown Board of Trade, *Constitution and By-laws,* adopted February 4, 1911, revised February 1, 1936, Article I, HMA. See *Provincetown Advocate,* September 30, 1937, and March 14, 1940.

39. Arthur Costa, the main dune-taxi business owner in Provincetown today, was one of Nunes's drivers. See Joseph Nunes, interview by Alice Joseph, audiotape recording, Provincetown, Mass., February 2, 1975, PPL; and Arthur Costa, interview.

40. Josef Berger, "Transportation," RG 65, File D-500, 1–3, 294, NA.

41. Vorse, *Time and the Town,* 294.

42. Josef Berger, "Social Institutions," RG 65, File No. D-676, 1, NA.

43. Vorse, *Time and the Town,* 293.

44. Joseph Captiva, interview by Alice Kelly; Alice Kelly, "Record of Interviews."

45. *Provincetown Advocate,* July 6, 1939.

46. "Ten Years Ago, March 16, 1939: Shorts Ban Fails to Pass," *Provincetown Ad-*

vocate, March 17, 1949; John Clifford Snow, letter to the editor, *Provincetown Advocate*, March 23, 1939; "Yours for Shorter Shorts," Virginia Dale, letter to the editor, *Provincetown Advocate*, March 9, 1939.

47. *Provincetown Advocate*, August 12, 1937.

48. *Provincetown Advocate*, September 30, 1937.

49. Ibid.

50. *Provincetown Advocate*, September 8, 1938.

NOTES TO CHAPTER 5

1. Tennessee Williams to Donald Windham, Provincetown, July 1944, in *Tennessee Williams' Letters to Donald Windham*, edited by Donald Windham (New York: Holt, Rinehart & Winston, 1977), 137–138.

2. Ibid., 139, 142. "Gayflower Set" quote from *Hush-Hush*, November 1955, 24.

3. See Boyd, 121, 129, 133.

4. Windham, 134.

5. "Art Town, 1958," *Time* (August 18, 1958). See also John Canaday, "Provincetown UP: Cape Cod's Summer Art Capital Shows Improvement after a Decline," July 9, 1961, in Book Four, "Arts and Artists," 97, CCPMA.

6. See Jarie Stedman, "Cabral Benefit Show for FAWC," *Provincetown Advocate*, July 6, 1989.

7. Carbone, interview; Wax, interview.

8. Reginald Cabral, talk delivered at the Provincetown Heritage Museum, recorded from Joyce Johnson's weekly radio program, "The Sands of Time," on WOMR, December, 1996, Provincetown, Mass.

9. See *Days Lumberyard Studios: Provincetown 1914–1971* (Provincetown: Provincetown Art Association and Museum, 1978); *The Sun Gallery: An Exhibition at the Provincetown Art Association and Museum* (Provincetown: Provincetown Art Association and Museum, 1981); Dr. Thomas and Marika Herskovic, *New York–Provincetown: A '50's Connection* (Provincetown: Provincetown Art Association and Museum, 1994), especially Tony Vevers, "Abstract Expressionism in Provincetown."

10. See Bérubé; D'Emilio; Windham; Garfield, interview; Carbone, interview; Wax, interview; Stevens, interview; Ross, interview; Shultz, interview; Richtman, interview; Foley, interview; Janard, interview; and Spencer, interview. See also Miriam Hapgood DeWitt, letter to the editor, *Provincetown Advocate*, July 18, 1981.

11. See Selectmen's Meeting Minutes, August 15, 1958, and October 6, 1958, PTHA; John C. Snow, letter to editor, *Provincetown Advocate*, August 21, 1952; *Provincetown Advocate*, July 30, 1952, August 27, 1953, July 23, 1959, July 30, 1959, and August 6, 1969.

12. Foley, interview.

13. Richtman, interview.

14. Napi Van Derek, personal conversation with author, Provincetown, Mass., December 12, 1997; Florence Alexander, interview; and Russe, interview. In some reports Baoine is referred to as Bayonne.

15. Richtman, interview.

16. Richtman, interview. The material for the gay routine also stemmed from a

panel of gay men and lesbians who spoke about Provincetown's gay past at the Provincetown Heritage Museum in the summer of 1997. Panelists included Jack Richtman, Richard Snell, and Roslyn Garfield. See also Cook, interview; Ross and Shultz, interview; Florence Alexander, interview.

17. Richtman, interview; Stevens, interview; Sonny Shanis, interview by author, audiotape recording, Provincetown, Mass., January 14, 1997, POHP, PPL; Joel Newman, interview by author, audiotape recording, Provincetown, Mass., January 14, 1998, POHP, PPL; Spencer, interview; Richard Hornak, "Lynne Carter Was Not a Female Impersonator," *Provincetown Advocate*, January 17, 1985.

18. Russe, interview.

19. Anthony Joseph, interview.

20. Florence Alexander, interview.

21. Cook, interview. For a list of patrons and performers at the popular Weathering Heights Club see "Club Opening Is Huge Success," *Provincetown Advocate*, June 5, 1952, and "'Evening in Paris,' Weathering Heights Event of Week," *Provincetown Advocate*, August 14, 1952.

22. See Peter Stallybrass and Allon White, *The Politics and Poetics of Transgression* (Ithaca, NY: Cornell University Press, 1986), 5, where they argue that carnivalesque events like impersonator shows make "socially peripheral" characters "symbolically central."

23. Wax, interview.

24. Esther Newton, *Mother Camp: Female Impersonators in America* (Englewood Cliffs, NJ: Prentice Hall, 1972), 109.

25. See Moe Meyer, "Introduction," in *The Politics and Poetics of Camp*, ed. Moe Meyer (New York: Routledge, 1994), 5, where he notes that "this piggy-backing upon the dominant order's monopoly on the authority of signification explains why Camp appears, on the one hand, to offer a transgressive vehicle, yet, on the other hand, simultaneously invokes the specter of dominant ideology within its practice, appearing in many instances to actually reinforce the dominant order." Meyer builds and challenges theories posited by Michel Foucault, Andrew Ross, Susan Sontag, and others.

26. "Cape Cod and the Vineyard," *Mademoiselle*, September 1949; reprinted in part in "Of Ill Report," *Provincetown Advocate*, September 22, 1949.

27. Ibid.

28. On the nature of moral panics see Stanley Cohen, *Folk Devils and Moral Panics* (New York: Routledge, 1972); and Stuart Hall et al., *Policing the Crisis: Mugging, the State, and Law and Order* (London: Macmillan, 1978).

29. "Of Ill Report," *Provincetown Advocate*, September 22, 1949.

30. "Many Encourage Influx of 'The Boys,'" *Provincetown Advocate*, December 14, 1950.

31. "Chamber to Ponder 'The Boys' Influx," *Provincetown Advocate*, December 7, 1950.

32. "The 'Queer' Question," *Provincetown Advocate*, February 2, 1951.

33. "Selectmen Clamp Down on Gay Spots with New Regulations to Curb Evils," *Provincetown Advocate*, June 5, 1952.

34. See Selectmen's Meeting Minutes, June 15, 1959, April 14, 1961, and July 10, 1961, PTHA.

35. "Traveler Applauds Cape End Stand," *Provincetown Advocate,* June 19, 1952; emphasis original.

36. S. Osborn Ball, letter to the editor, *Provincetown Advocate,* June 19, 1952.

37. L. A. Martin, letter to the editor, *Provincetown Advocate,* July 10, 1952.

38. Cook, interview.

39. "An Appeal to All Decent People in the Town of Provincetown," *Provincetown Advocate,* August 7, 1952.

40. See Selectmen's Meeting Minutes, May 1960–July 1960, PTHA; and *Provincetown Advocate,* June 1, 1960.

41. Selectmen's Meeting Minutes, June 15, 1959, PTHA.

42. Ibid.

43. Ibid.

44. Ibid. For accounts of the Weathering Heights controversy, see the following: *Provincetown Advocate,* May 26, 1960, and July 21, 1960; *Provincetown Beacon,* May 25, 1960, and July 20, 1960; *The Cape Cod Times,* July 19, 1960. See also Selectmen's Meeting Minutes, July 18, 1960, PTHA; ABCC Correspondence File, 1958–1969, PTHA.

45. On July 5, 1955, Charles Harrington of the Bridgewater State Police, John Farrell of South Yarmouth Police Department, and Francis Marshall and Frank Veara of Provincetown arrested fourteen men for lewd and lascivious speech and behavior, twelve men for drunkenness, a handful for rude and disorderly conduct, and Reggie Cabral for "keeping and maintaining a building where lewdness occurred." Cabral faced a two-week suspension for these infractions plus fines of $200 from the district court and $500 from the Barnstable Superior Court. See Barnstable Second District Court Docket #'s 20624–20638, July 5, 1955, Orleans District Court House. See also Steven Schwadron, "Selectmen Revoke A-House License," *Provincetown Advocate,* August 25, 1977.

46. "Fat Jack," conversation with author, Fat Jack's Cafe, Provincetown, Mass., May 7, 1999.

47. "Shopkeeper's Plea Puzzles Selectmen," *Provincetown Advocate,* July 28, 1960.

48. "Folks Want Cheer in Vacation Town," *Provincetown Advocate,* July 21, 1960.

49. See Amy Gluck and Betsy Reed, "The Gay Marketing Movement," in *A Queer World: The Center for Lesbian and Gay Studies Reader,* ed. Martin Duberman (New York: New York University Press, 1997), 519.

50. Thorstein Veblen (1934), quoted in M. V. Lee Badgett, "Thinking Homo/Economically," in Duberman, 470.

51. "Selectmen Commended for Recent Actions," *Provincetown Advocate,* August 10, 1960; Thomas Hennessey, letter to the editor, *Provincetown Advocate,* July 28, 1960.

52. See *Provincetown Advocate,* April 13, 1961, and August 29, 1961.

53. Helen Davis, "Taxi Operator Hits Beach Indecencies, Four Restaurants Here Branded Unfit," *Provincetown Advocate,* September 14, 1961.

54. "Police Break Up Gang Crime Wave," *Provincetown Advocate,* August 14,

1949; Manuel Patrick (pseud.), interview by author, videotape recording, Provincetown, Mass., 1997.

55. Richtman, interview.

56. Wax, interview.

57. On Provincetown's "Gestapo" postwar environment, see also Miss Adrienne Schnell, letter to the editor, *Provincetown Advocate*, July 23, 1953; "A Powder Keg," *Provincetown Advocate*, July 23, 1953.

58. Cohen, 8.

59. A. Hammond, S. Broudy, and J. C. Ackerd, letter to the editor, *Provincetown Advocate*, July 14, 1960; "Citizens Dispute Racial Bias at Open Hearing," *Provincetown Advocate*, March 20, 1969; Stevens, interview; Stacy Williams (pseudo.), interview by author, audiotape recording, Provincetown, Mass., 1998; and Laura J. MacKay, "Retaining Order Issued After Racial Attack in Provincetown," *Cape Codder*, June 22, 1993.

NOTES TO PART III

1. Diane Corbo, interview by author, audiotape recording, Provincetown, Mass., September 26, 1997, POHP, PPL.

2. Randy Shilts, *And the Band Played On: Politics, People and the AIDS Epidemic* (New York: St. Martin's Press, 1997), xxi, xxii.

3. See Foley, interview; Jeanne Braham and Pamela Paterson, *Starry, Starry Night: Provincetown's Response to the AIDS Epidemic* (Cambridge, MA: Lumen Editions, 1998); Lisabeth Lipari, "Elderly Fear AIDS Patients," *Provincetown Advocate*, March 30, 1989; "Courses Are Not a Cure-All for Anti-Gay Prejudice," *Provincetown Advocate*, April 2, 1987; Frank Reeves, "AIDS Play Opens at Universalist," *Provincetown Advocate*, May 29, 1987; "Doctor Tells Public: Learn Facts about AIDS Crisis," *Provincetown Advocate*, June 26, 1986; Joyce Johnson, "State Issues School Guidelines on AIDS," *Provincetown Advocate*, October 3, 1985; Preston Babbit Jr., letter to the editor, *Provincetown Advocate*, August 7, 1986; Peter Steele, "Angry Crowd Confronts Selectmen," *Provincetown Advocate*, August 28, 1986; George Petras, "Benefit for AIDS Support Group," *Provincetown Advocate*, August 29, 1987; John Van Arsdale Sr., letter to the editor, *Provincetown Advocate*, September 25, 1986, where Van Arsdale complains about gay rights then states, "Probably in the long run AIDS will solve the problem"; response by Richard Rogers, letter to the editor, *Provincetown Advocate*, October 2, 1986, "Van Arsdale Sr. sure as hell didn't refuse gay money for his rinky-dink airline"; *Provincetown Advocate*, October 29, 1989, announcement by town nurse and the Provincetown Aids Support Group on new column about AIDS appearing in weekly paper; Peter Steele, "AIDS Numbers Are Misleading," *Provincetown Advocate*, June 2, 1988; and "AIDS Discussion Planned at St. Peter the Apostle," *Provincetown Advocate*, June 2, 1988.

4. Mark Doty, *Heaven's Coast: A Memoir* (New York: HarperCollins, 1996), 173–174, 179, 207.

5. Material on the growth of small businesses in the 1980s and women's businesses in particular is vast. See Candida Brush, Sara Gould, and Kathryn Keeley, *Enterprising Women: Local Initiatives for Job Creation* (Paris: Organization for Economic

Cooperation and Development, 1990); Muriel Orhan and Don Scott, "Why Women Enter Entrepreneurship: An Explanatory Model," *Women Management Review* 16 (2001): 232–244; Carmen Brown, "Black Women on the Rise," *Network Journal* 6 (March 1999): 30; Beverly Brooks, "Women Change the Face of Small Business Ownership," *Journal of the American Society of CLU & ChFC* 51 (May 1997): 10–13; Sandra Maltby, "Banks and the Woman Business Owner," *Vital Speeches of the Day* 62 (January 1996): 186–189; Dorothy Moore and E. Holly Buttner, *Women Entrepreneurs: Moving Beyond the Glass Ceiling* (Thousand Oaks, CA: Sage Publications, 1997); Jeannette M. Oppedisano, *Historical Encyclopedia of American Women Entrepreneurs: 1776 to the Present* (Westport, CT: Greenwood Press, 2000); Loraine Edwards and Midge Stocker, eds., *The Woman-Centered Economy: Ideals, Reality and the Space in Between* (Chicago: Third Side Press, 1995); and Robert Fairlie, *Ethnic and Racial Entrepreneurship* (New York: Garland, 1996).

    6. Brush et al., 39.

    7. Maltby, 186; Brooks, 10.

    8. Brush et al., 3.

    9. Tourist attractions, like Niagara Falls, New York, Steamboat Springs, Colorado, Monterrey, California, and Santa Fe, New Mexico, bore witness to similar processes as their working-class, ethnic enclaves became resort destinations. See Coleman, 1997; Dubinsky, 2000; Horton, 2000; Norkunas, 1993. Countless urban and rural locations such as Manhattan's Lower East Side and Virginia's Loudoun County have struggled under similar strains of gentrification. See C. Mele, "Globalization, Culture and Neighborhood Change: Reinventing the Lower East Side," *Urban Affairs Review* 32 (1996): 3–22; D. Spain, "Been-Heres versus Come-Heres: Negotiating Conflicting Community Identities," *Journal of the American Planning Association* 59 (1993): 156–171. And the gay enclave-making that shaped Provincetown resembled that in urban and suburban places like Park Slope in Brooklyn, the Castro in San Francisco, Greenwich Village and Chelsea in Manhattan, and New Orleans in Louisiana; and in resort areas such as Cherry Grove on Fire Island, Miami Beach in Florida, Palm Springs in California, and Rehoboth Beach in Delaware. See Boyd, 2003; Simon; Laurence Knopp, "Some Theoretical Implications of Gay Involvement in an Urban Land Market," *Political Geography Quarterly* 9 (1990): 337–352; Newton, 1993; Sy Adler and Johanna Brenner, "Gender and Space: Lesbians and Gay Men in the City," *International Journal of Urban and Regional Research* 16 (1992): 24–34; Tim Davis, "The Diversity of Queer Politics and the Redefinition of Sexual Identity and Community in Urban Spaces," in *Mapping Desire: Geographies of Sexuality*, ed. David Bell and Gill Valentine (New York: Routledge, 1995); M. Lauria and Laurence Knopp, "Toward an Analysis of the Role of Gay Communities in Urban Renaissance," *Urban Geography* 6 (1985): 152–169; Tamar Rothenberg, "'And She Told Two Friends': Lesbians Creating Urban Social Space," in Bell and Valentine, 165–181; Gill Valentine, "Out and About: Geographies of Lesbian Landscapes," *International Journal of Urban and Regional Research* (1995): 96–111.

    10. Cohen, 9. Cohen's analyzes niche or identity-based marketing as a historical process of "market segmentation." See chapters 7 and 8 in particular, pp. 292–344.

NOTES TO CHAPTER 6

1. See Debra Michals, "Liberation through the Marketplace: Second Wave Feminism and the Politics of Women's Small Business Ownership" (paper, Berkshire Conference, Rochester, N.Y., June 5, 1999).

2. Moffett, 25. For information on Harriet Adams see Frank Crotty, "Around These Parts"; "The Captains Vittles"; "Country Store Draws Crowds," *The New Beacon*; Marion B. Haymaker, "Books at the Library"; Evelyn Lawon, "Dateline: Cape Cod"; and *Provincetown Advocate*, December 15, 1962, all from her grandson's (Daniel Towler) local history collection. For guesthouse owners see Automobile Legal Association, *Automobile Green Book*, 125; and Provincetown Art Association and Museum, *The Guide Book*, 72–83. Other rooming house keepers included Mrs. Charles Robsham, proprietor of the Vernon Inn and Cottages; Mrs. H. S. Cook, Mrs. A. F. Davis, Mrs. William Enos, Mrs. E. M. Gibbs, Mrs. Sarah C. Holmes, Mrs. Levi A. Kelley, Mrs. Nellie G. Lewis, Mrs. Frank L. Mayo, Misses Rich, Mrs. Fred H. Roe, and Mrs. Joseph L. Silva. Also listed in *The Guide Book* were Hannah Curran, milliner; Sara Johnson and Beatrice Welch, piano teachers; and Mrs. John R. Manta, a singing teacher. See also Florence Alexander, interview; Ursula Silva, interview; Hall, interview; Matta, interview.

3. See License Records, Innholders, 1966, 1973; Selectmen's Meeting Minutes on Club Licenses, 1950–1975; and Assessor's Records, 1950–1975, PTHA. See also Hand, interview; Richtman, interview.

4. See Maltby, 186, on women's difficulties getting access to capital and being taken seriously as entrepreneurs.

5. See License Records, Innholders, 1966, 1973; Selectmen's Meeting Minutes on Club Licenses, 1950–1975; and Assessor's Records, 1950–1975, PTHA.

6. On the founding of the Provincetown Business Guild (PBG) see *Provincetown Advocate*, August 24, 1978. On Marvin Coble's victory, see *Provincetown Advocate*, April 19, 1979; and Gregory Katz, "Gay-Straight Integration Succeeds in Provincetown," *Cape Cod Times*, May 13, 1979. While 60 percent of all voters voted for Coble over a Provincetown native, on election day some disgruntled residents poured sand into the gas tank of his car.

7. "America the Beautiful . . . Nevertheless," *Inside Provincetown* magazine, 1966, PPL.

8. Ross, interview.

9. Shultz, interview.

10. Garfield, interview; Stevens, interview; Foley, interview.

11. Spencer, interview.

12. Ross, interview

13. Shultz, interview.

14. See *Provincetown Magazine*, 1977, PPL.

15. Ibid.

16. Joy McNulty, interview by author, audiotape recording, Provincetown, Mass., October 28, 1997, POHP, PPL.

17. Corbo, interview.

18. Denise Chamberlin, telephone interview by author, audiotape recording, Belmont, Mass., January 17, 1999.

19. Ross and Shultz, interview.

20. Corbo, interview.

21. Stan Sorrentino, letter to the editor, *Provincetown Advocate*, January 9, 1975.

22. *Provincetown Advocate*, letter to the editor, January 16, 1975.

23. See Foley, interview; Stevens, interview; Corbo, interview; and Gabriel Brooke, interview by author, audiotape recording, Provincetown, Mass., February 12, 1998, POHP, PPL.

24. Carol Karlson, telephone conversation with author, Provincetown, Mass., October, 1997.

25. For discussions of the emerging gay market see Sean Strub, "The Growth of the Gay and Lesbian Market," in Duberman, 514–518; Amy Gluckman and Betsy Reed, "The Gay Marketing Moment," in Duberman, 519–525; J. Ridgon, "Overcoming a Deep-Rooted Reluctance, More Firms Advertise to Gay Community," *Wall Street Journal*, July 18, 1991; Jane Renee Ballinger, "Marketing a Movement: Media Relations Strategies of the Gay and Lesbian Movement" (Ph.D. diss., University of Texas, 1998); S. Elliot, "A Sharper View of Gay Consumers," *New York Times*, June 6, 1994, Section C, 7; Grant Lukenbill, *Untold Millions: The Gay and Lesbian Market in America* (New York: HarperCollins, 1995); John D'Emilio, "Capitalism and Gay Identity," in *Powers of Desire*, ed. Ann Snitow, Christine Stansell, and Sharon Thompson (New York: Monthly Review Press, 1983), 100–117; Ronald Alsop, "In Marketing to Gays, Lesbians Are Often Left Out," *Wall Street Journal*, November 11, 1999. Alsop reported that only 27 percent of advertising outreach targets lesbians. Alsop did not mention how the gay and lesbian market panders to white, middle- and upper-class gays and lesbians. See especially M. V. Lee Badgett, "Thinking Homo/Economically," in Duberman, 467–476.

26. Anonymous, letter to Womencrafts, September 6, 1991. I am grateful to Carol Karlson and Jo Deall for providing this letter.

27. Badgett, "Thinking Homo/Economically," in Duberman. On consumption shaping identity see Shaffer, 6.

28. See Corbo, interview; Michael Wright, interview by author, audiotape recording, Provincetown, Mass., September 18, 1997, POHP, PPL.

29. Brooke, interview; Gabriel Brooke, panelist at Provincetown Heritage Museum, Women's Week, October 1997.

30. Michael Wright's parents decided to name their first-born child Michael regardless of its sex or gender. See Wright, interview.

31. Virginia Allen, telephone interview by author, Durham, N.C., September 1, 2004.

32. Helen Caddie-Larcenia, telephone interview by author, audiotape recording, Durham, N.C., August 3, 2000.

33. On the history of Women Innkeepers see Wright, interview; Brooke, interview; Corbo, interview; Jackie Verna Kelly, telephone interview by author, audiotape recording, Durham, N.C., August 15, 2004. See also WIP guides, 1985–1997. I am grateful to Michael Wright for providing written materials on the Women Innkeepers.

34. Provincetown's board of selectmen recognized the Women Innkeepers publicly for their efforts in extending Provincetown's economic season. See Corbo, interview.

35. For comments and discussion of Provincetown's transgendered populations see *Provincetown Advocate*, October 30, 1975; Transgender Symposium, Provincetown, Mass., October 22 and 23, 1999. For reasons of space and scope, a more complete history of Provincetown regarding transgendered persons and bisexuals will not appear in this book.

36. Sherry Dranch, Randy Turoff, Jackie Lapidus, Linda Weinstein, Michael Wright, and Roslyn Garfield pooled their literary, graphic, and legal skills and published *Womantide: The Lesbian Magazine of Provincetown* from at least 1982 to 1985. Susan Mitchell provided me with a nearly complete set of *Womantide* magazines and Jackie Lapidus kindly offered more information.

37. Susan Areson, "Selectmen Seeking Behavior Rules," *Provincetown Advocate*, August 21, 1980.

38. During the summer of 1998, Ogunquit, Maine, another gay resort town, faced severe economic and political problems because of a discernable degree of homophobia within their board of selectmen. See *InNewsweekly*, January 1, 1999, 11.

39. See Gleason, 143.

40. McNulty, interview.

41. Caddie-Larcenia, interview.

42. Susan E. Cayleff, Susan J. Passino, S. Lynn Rubin, letter to the editor, *Provincetown Advocate*, July 25, 1974.

43. Ibid.

44. "Rift between the Gay Sexes," editorial in *Provincetown Advocate*, March 6, 1975. See also Corbo, interview; Gleason.

45. Two examples of women who sold their guesthouses during the late 1990s are Michael Wright of Plums and Carol Whitman of the Dusty Miller Inn. Whitman said she sold simply because she was tired of being in the business and a gay man approached her at the right time with the right price ($600,000+). She did not advertise, and she had no other offers on the table. The new owners bought the house next door, and their "complex" is now called Crowne Point, "a historic Provincetown inn." The Gull Walk Inn was purchased in 2003 by a mother-son team and is now the Secret Garden Inn, and Brooke started selling her guesthouse room-by-room as "luxury condominiums" beginning in 2004. Diane Corbo, telephone conversation with author, May 10, 2004.

46. See Helaine R. Zimmerman, letter to the editor, *Provincetown Advocate*, September 18, 1986.

NOTES TO CHAPTER 7

1. See R. D. Skillings, "Demography," in *P-Town Stories: Or, the Meatrack* (Newton/Cambridge, MA: Applewood Press, 1980).

2. See "Selectmen Order Removal of Town Hall Benches," *Provincetown Advocate*, July 1, 1971; "Selectmen Vote to Return Benches in Response to Throng at Hearing," *Provincetown Advocate*, July 22, 1971.

3. See Frank Reeves and Peter Steele, "Police Confront Angry Spiritus Crowd," *Provincetown Advocate*, August 21, 1986, where Police Chief James P. Meads finally admits that the benches decision was an "anti-gay" act. For memories of the benches controversy as an anti-hippie act, see Bernard "Sonny" Roderick, interview with author; and Peter Macara, interview with author. For official meeting minutes, see Selectmen's Meeting Minutes, June 28, 1971, and July 19, 1971, PTHA.

4. Clifton S. Perry, letter to editor, *Provincetown Advocate*, July 15, 1971; "Selectmen Vote to Return Benches," *Provincetown Advocate*, July 22, 1971.

5. "Selectmen Order Removal of the Town Hall Benches," *Provincetown Advocate*, July 1, 1971. See also Mary Hackett, interview by Jay Critchley, audiotape recording, n.d., PPL.

6. "Property Owners and the 'Riff-raff," *Provincetown Advocate*, July 22, 1971.

7. Sylvia S. Lazerow, letter to the editor, *Provincetown Advocate*, July 29, 1971.

8. See, for example, Coleman; Mark David Spence, "Get Off My Wave! Surfing, Tourism, and Consuming the California Dream" (paper, American Historical Association's Annual Meeting, New York City, January 4, 1997); Jackle; Eadington and Smith. On gay tourist studies see Debra L. Kuffner, "Gay Space and Tourism: A Semiotic Content Analysis of Destination Brochure Images" (master's thesis, Arizona State University, 2002); Howard L. Hughes, "Marketing Gay Tourism in Manchester: New Market for Urban Tourism or Destruction of 'Gay Space'?" *Journal of Vacation Marketing* (March 2003): 152–163; Alyssa Cymene Howe, "Queer Pilgrimage: The San Francisco Homeland and Identity Tourism," *Cultural Anthropology* (February 2001): 35–61; Simon.

9. See *Assessor's Valuation of the Town of Provincetown*: 1916, 1946, 1951, 1961, 1970, 1978. (These were the only reports archived at the CCPMA, PPL, THA, and PHA.) *Real Estate Commitment for Town of Provincetown, 1983, 1989, 1994, 1999*, at the Provincetown Town Hall Assessors Office. See Cape Cod Commission, *Cape Trends*, 1998, at www.capecodcommission.org (accessed September 3, 2004), which states, among other things, that Provincetown led Cape towns regarding increases in the price of home sales. In 1997, while the median price of home sales on Cape Cod was $129,900 (compared with $148,000 statewide), in Provincetown it was set at $220,000 for 105 sales. For more recent median sales price indexes, see *City and Town*, July/August, Massachusetts Department of Revenue Division of Local Services; U.S. Bureau of the Census (annual), *Characteristics of New Housing*, Current Construction Reports, ser. C25 (Washington, DC: U.S. Department of Commerce); for median sales prices of existing single-family homes by region and metropolitan areas, see National Association of Realtors, *Real Estate Outlook and Home Sales Yearbook*. See also James W. Hughes, "Economic Shifts and the Changing Homeownership Trajectory," *Housing Policy Debate* 7 (2) 1996. The Warren Group, a real estate and financial information service, lists slightly different figures (a combination of new and existing home sales) on their Web site, www.thewarrengroup.com (accessed September 3, 2004), a median sales price in 1995 of $155,229, and in 2001 of $375,000.

10. See articles 29 and 30 of Provincetown annual meeting, April 7, 1997, PTHA.

11. See John Ruggieri, letter to the editor, *Provincetown Advocate*, July 27, 1989.

12. Because of the sensitive nature of youth prostitution in Provincetown, not one of my narrators was willing to go on the record. Off the record, however, many

pointed to instances when young boys from working-class families would go out "on the town" with no money but come home with items like a new pair of sneakers or a shiny new belt.

13. Kathe Izzo, ed., *Flicker* (Provincetown: Provincetown Arts Press, 1997); and Kathe Izzo, ed., *Flicker II: Fuel* (Provincetown: Provincetown Arts Press, 1998).

14. "Carmen," ed., *The Effects: Of Living on a Sandbar* (n.p., ca. 1998): 2.

15. Linsey Smith, "Unity, Equality, Where'd They Go?" in *The Effects*, 18.

16. See Peter Macara, interview; and Pat Cordeiro and Jane Rowe, *Students of Provincetown Elementary School, An Elementary View of Provincetown* (n.p., 1988), CCPMA, where one student writes about the gay Carnival parade under the general heading of "holidays."

17. See Leonard, interview; Louise Meads, interview with author, audiotape recording, Provincetown, Mass., February 5, 1998; James F. Meads, interview with author, audiotape recording, Provincetown, Mass., February 5, 1998; "Students Suffer Anti-Gay Slurs," *Provincetown Advocate*, April 2, 1987. See also editorial, "Strike a Blow against Homophobia," *Provincetown Advocate*, January 19, 1987.

18. On townspeople who disappear come July and August, see Cy Fried, interview by author, videotape recording, Provincetown, Mass., February 12, 1997; Miriam Fried, interview by author, tape recording, Provincetown, Mass., February 12, 1997; Howard Schneider, interview by author, videotape recording, Provincetown, Mass., November 26, 1996; Shultz, interview; Ross, interview; Goveia, interview.

19. Joe Scascitelli (CCNS Lifeguard), conversation with author, Herring Cove Beach, Provincetown, Mass., summer 1996; Roger Brunelle (CCNS Lifeguard), conversation with author, Herring Cove Beach, Provincetown, Mass., summer 1994.

20. Costa, interview. See also Erin K. Thomas, interview by author, audiotape recording, Provincetown, Mass., March 13, 1997. Also see Marilyn Miller, "Provincetown's Tired, Hungry and Poor Look to Truro: Gentrification, Loss of Diversity Hasten Outflow," *Provincetown Advocate*, January 1, 1998; Ed Bilodeau, "Truro Feels Threatened by Provincetown Influx: Residents Aghast at Possible Rising Costs," *Provincetown Advocate*, November 6, 1997; Marilyn Fifield, *Demographic and Economic Characteristics and Trends, Barnstable County—Cape Cod* (Barnstable, MA: Cape Cod Commission, 1998), 54. I am grateful to Marilyn for providing as much statistical information as possible for this project. See "Gays Affect Land Values, Brief Study Shows," *Inside Provincetown* 1 (3) 1997.

21. Sue Harrison, "Rilleau Sandal Tradition Moves On after 60 Years," *Provincetown Banner*, September 4, 1997; Gilman, interview.

22. Frank Reeves, "Videotape Blames Art Decline on Gays," *Provincetown Advocate*, May 7, 1987.

23. See Peter Coes, interview by author, videotape recording, Provincetown, Mass., December, 1996; and Harvey Dodd, interview. On the Fine Arts Work Center, see "A Winter Community for Young Artists and Writers," *Provincetown Advocate*, October 1, 1971. See also "Fine Arts Work Center," PPL Vertical File.

24. See the Warren Group; Hughes, "Economic Shifts."

25. Cliff Amlung, interview by author, tape recording, Provincetown, Mass., April 4, 1998.

26. John Caruso, "Provincetown and Racism: The Problems Faced by Seasonal Workers of Color," *In Other Words*, March/April 1995.

27. While this trend has yet to take hold in Provincetown, elsewhere on Cape Cod Jamaican workers have been advancing slowly as business and property owners. See *In Other Words: A Publication by Cape Codders against Racism*, 1996–98. See also Provincetown town meeting, April 7, 1997, article 13 and discussion; and McNulty, interview.

28. Ethan Zindler, "Coalition Seeks Aid in Visa Cutoff," *Cape Cod Times*, April 29, 2004; nl.newsbank.com (accessed April 29, 2004); conversation with Christian (pseud.), Provincetown, Mass., August 1997.

29. Eadington and Smith, 9.

30. For instances where there was almost total native displacement or where nearly all financial winners were newcomers, see Norkunas; and on mining towns that are now ski resort villages in Colorado, such as Vail and Aspen, see Coleman.

31. Although quantifying the number of straight-owned versus gay-owned businesses in town is impossible at this point, since no official records track sexual identity and ownership patterns, when cross-listing Provincetown's licensing records and the PBG's membership list, approximate figures do emerge. According to these lists, in 1990, for example, out of approximately 120 businesses offering accommodations, fewer than half were gay owned. Examples of successful native business owners include Chuck Silva, who runs the concession stand at Herring Cove Beach and owns a substantial amount of property in town; Donald Edwards who has owned, among other things, the Governor Bradford Bar and Restaurant and the Pilgrim House Hotel and Bar; and Clement Silva Jr., a gay-identified native who is the co-owner of Clem and Ursie's Seafood Restaurant and Market.

32. See Napi Van Derek, interview; Jerome Lee Costa, interview; "PBG Meets with Police about Gay Harassers," *Provincetown Advocate*, January 9, 1986; "Cops Arrest 2 in Beating," *Provincetown Advocate*, July 18, 1974; E. Robinson, letter to the editor, *Provincetown Advocate*, July 26, 1976; Marilyn Miller, "Teenagers Attack Two Men on Street," *Provincetown Advocate*, November 24, 1982; Laura J. MacKay, "Provincetown Has Anti-Gay Problem, Police Say," *Cape Codder*, June 28, 1993, and May 21, 1993; "Police Break Up Gang Crime Wave," *Provincetown Advocate*, August 14, 1949; Laurel Brooke, letter to the editor, *Provincetown Advocate*, May 7, 1987, where she argues that harassment toward gays was up 150 percent from 1985.

33. "I Did Not Come Here to Be Beaten," letter to the editor, *Provincetown Advocate*, June 18, 1971.

34. Name withheld by request, letter to the editor, *Provincetown Advocate*, June 24, 1971.

35. "In Praise of Thugs," editorial in *Provincetown Advocate*, June 24, 1971.

36. Name withheld by request, letter to the editor, *Provincetown Advocate*, July 1, 1971; William F. Damon and William F. Roberts, associate directors, Homophile Assistance League of Provincetown, letter to the editor, *Provincetown Advocate*, July 1, 1971; Mrs. May McClintock, letter to the editor, *Provincetown Advocate*, July 1, 1971. See also R. Bourguin, Wyoming, letter to the editor, *Provincetown Advocate*, July 22, 1971; P. H. Goss, letter to the editor, *Provincetown Advocate*, July 8, 1971; and Bernard C. Meyers, M.D., letter to editor, *Provincetown Advocate*, July 8, 1971.

37. For information regarding Provincetown's Community Policing Program, see Keith Bergman, "'Implementing the Philosophy of Community-Oriented Policing in the Town of Provincetown': A Report to the Massachusetts Executive Office of Communities and Development under the FY 1993 Municipal Incentive Grant Program," 1993, PPL; "Public Safety Program Excellence Award in Memory of William H. Hansell, Jr.," article in ICMA Annual Awards 1995 Brochure, PPL. See also *Overcoming Hate Crimes, a Success Story in Community-Oriented Policing*, special collection, videotape cassette, PPL.

38. *In Other Words: A Publication by Cape Codders against Racism*, fall 1996; Laura J. MacKay, "Retaining Order Issued after Racial Attack in Provincetown," *Cape Codder*, June 22, 1993.

39. Josephine Johnson, letter to the editor, *Provincetown Advocate*, August 2, 1979.

40. Russell Pagliaro, letter to the editor, *Provincetown Advocate*, December 23, 1982.

41. See E. Margaret Spooner, letter to the editor, *Provincetown Advocate*, November 20, 1980; and Michael P. Ahern, letter to the editor, *Provincetown Advocate*, July 11, 1974.

42. Marilyn Miller, "Parker Complains to State about Discrimination: Claims He Was Punished for Being Heterosexual," *Provincetown Advocate*, June 29, 1996.

43. Police raided the A-House numerous times. See Selectmen's Meeting Minutes, July 22, 1955, August 19, 1955, July 21, 1960, and October 10, 1960. See also Steven Schwadron, "Selectmen Revoke A-House License," *Provincetown Advocate*, August 25, 1977.

44. See "Police Arrest 21 Nude Men in Herring Cove Beach Raid," *Provincetown Advocate*, August 6, 1970; Peter Steele, "Seashore Gets Tough on Sex Acts," *Provincetown Advocate*, October 5, 1989; Eric Raymond Van Horn, letter to the editor, *Provincetown Advocate*, July 24, 1975; Howard Wolbarsht, letter to the editor, *Provincetown Advocate*, July 15, 1982; and Selectmen's Meeting Minutes, July 27, 1970, where Police Chief James P. Meads requests fencing, and Selectman Ernest Irmer suggests barbed wire.

45. On bas-relief incidents, see "Cops Bust Eight for Sex by Bas-Relief," *Provincetown Advocate*, July 11, 1974; "Board Lights Up Bas-Relief Area," *Provincetown Advocate*, July 25, 1974; Dan Boynton, editorial, "Unnatural Acts," *Provincetown Advocate*, July 18, 1974.

46. See Lisa Duggan, "Prologue," in *Policing Public Sex*, ed. Dangerous Bedfellows (Boston: South End Press, 1996); and Allan Bérubé, "History of the Gay Bathhouse," in *Policing Public Sex*, 185.

47. According to the written and verbal record, one of the last times gay male cross-dressing was questioned in Provincetown was in 1970 at a meeting during which the board of selectmen were considering whether or not to allow a gay pride parade to march down Commercial Street. Selectman Marion Taves and others questioned parade organizers as to the amount of "mummery" or cross-dressing that might take place. See "Homosexuals Plan March Despite Selectmen's Ruling," *Provincetown Advocate*, June 25, 1970.

48. See Gayle Rubin, "Thinking Sex: Notes for a Radical Theory of the Politics

of Sexuality," in *The Lesbian and Gay Studies Reader,* ed. Henry Abelove, Michele Aina Barale, and David Halperin (New York: Routledge, 1993), 3–45.

49. Peter R. Hardaway, letter to the editor, *Provincetown Advocate,* August 22, 1985.

50. Editorial, "Humiliating," *Provincetown Advocate,* July 28, 1977; editorial, "Harsh Words," *Provincetown Advocate,* August 4, 1977.

51. Char Priolo, letter to the editor, *Provincetown Advocate,* August 3, 1989.

52. Philippe D'Auteuil, letter to the editor, *Provincetown Advocate,* August 3, 1989.

53. James Bella, letter to the editor, *Provincetown Advocate,* August 3, 1989; Rene LeBlanc, letter to the editor, *Provincetown Advocate,* August 3, 1989.

54. William T. Henderson, letter to the editor, *Provincetown Advocate,* August 3, 1989; Vida Wongola, letter to the editor, *Provincetown Advocate,* August 3, 1989; A. J. Souza, letter to the editor, *Provincetown Advocate,* August 3, 1989. Souza earlier in the letter explained that children observed the parade and were then inquiring about the meaning of the sign.

55. Helen Souza, letter to the editor, *Provincetown Advocate,* August 24, 1978. See also Dr. Daniel L. Ogden, letter to the editor, *Provincetown Advocate,* March 8, 1979.

56. Dolores M. deSousa, letter to the editor, *Provincetown Advocate,* June 10, 1976.

57. Marjorie Osborne Whorf, letter to the editor, *Provincetown Advocate,* April 16, 1979.

58. Albert S. Johnson, letter to the editor, *Provincetown Advocate,* July 31, 1986.

59. Kate Barnett, letter to the editor, *Provincetown Advocate,* January 16, 1986; Anette Dalpe, letter to the editor, *Provincetown Advocate,* September 25, 1986.

60. Will Walker, letter to the editor, *Provincetown Advocate,* October 9, 1986; Sally Price, letter to the editor, *Provincetown Advocate,* August 28, 1986; Mrs. Henry Morgan, letter to the editor, *Provincetown Advocate,* September 4, 1986.

61. Catherine B. Cadose, letter to the editor, *Provincetown Advocate,* October 5, 1972; Frank W. Adams, letter to the editor, *Provincetown Advocate,* September 17, 1981.

62. Danny Barillo, letter to the editor, *Provincetown Advocate,* January 23, 1986. See also Jack Winslow, letter to the editor, *Provincetown Advocate,* August 22, 1974.

63. Sidney Wordell, letter to the editor, *Provincetown Advocate,* February 5, 1987.

64. Provincetown's wastewater management problem has been on the table at nearly every town meeting for at least the past decade and is still, in 2004, not resolved. See, for example, article 3, line 6, special town meeting, April 3, 1995; and Department of Environmental Protection, in Town of Provincetown, *Annual Report, 1995,* 65.

65. Ronald White, interview by Justin White, audiotape recording, Provincetown, Mass., November 1997; Michael Travota, interview by Justin White, audiotape recording, Provincetown, Mass., November 1997.

66. See "PHS Enrollment Declines by 71," *Provincetown Advocate,* September 18, 1975. See also school reports in annual town reports that chart school enrollment each year.

67. Editorial, "Town without Children," *Provincetown Banner,* February 13, 1997; on school enrollment from 1951 to 1997 see Gleason, 82.

68. "Unemployment, the Winter Line," *Provincetown Advocate*, November 8, 1973; "Unemployment Claims Rocketing," *Provincetown Advocate*, November 21, 1974. On unemployment percentages and changes over time, see "Unemployment Rate Extremes and Annual Average, 1975–1997 (graph)," in Marilyn Fifield and Cape Cod Commission, *Cape Trends: Demographic and Economic Characteristics and Trends, Barnstable Country—Cape Cod*, 5th ed. (Barnstable, MA: Cape Cod Commission, 1998), 77, which shows that percentages peaked in the mid-1970s and early 1990s. For an excellent graph on monthly unemployment rates for 1981, 1990, 1995, see Gleason, 85. On increases in drug trafficking, see "Police Pick Up 11 for Dope, Seek 20," *Provincetown Advocate*, November 30, 1972; "5 Local Fishermen Caught off Jamaica with 7 Tons of Marijuana," *Provincetown Advocate*, November 30, 1972. On alcohol problems, see Jim Gilbert, "Alcoholism Serious Cape Problem," *Provincetown Advocate*, March 11, 1976. Regarding cases of alcoholism in the state, Gilbert reported on Cape Cod's status as being ranked second, behind Boston. See also Margaret Ryan, "Alcoholism Statistics Are Sobering," *Provincetown Advocate*, January 21, 1982, where she reports that Barnstable Country had more registered alcoholics than any other county in the state. On Provincetown as a place that fosters alcoholics and as a place of "recovery" for alcoholics, see K. C. Myers, "End of the Road, Beginning of the World: Provincetown Can Help with Troubles, or Make Them Worse," *Cape Codder*, February 4, 1994.

69. The Crown and Anchor fire in 1998, Hurricane Bob in 1991, and the unexpected and unsolved murder of native Linda Silva in 1997 are but a few of Provincetown's more recent townwide tragedies.

70. "When Tragedy Hits," *Provincetown Advocate*, May 31, 1956; "$75,000 Fire Destroys Moors Club, Work Is Started on New Structure," *Provincetown Advocate*, May 31, 1956; "Police, Fireman, Plunge into Smoky Blaze to Save Residents: Firefighters Driven by Fear for Occupants," *Provincetown Advocate*, November 21, 1996; "Residents Rousted by Alarm, Smoke, Neighbors and Firefighters," *Provincetown Advocate*, November 21, 1996.

71. See "Gay Carnival Bigger Than Last Year," *Provincetown Advocate*, August 22, 1985.

72. Constance Black, letter to the editor, *Provincetown Advocate*, April 21, 1988.

NOTES TO THE CONCLUSION

1. Jennifer Longley, "Wanted: Foreign Help [Kennedy-Sponsored 40K Emergency Visas for Cape Cod, Boat Builders, MA Ski Resorts]," *Boston Globe*, April 1, 2004; http://www.libertypost.org/cgi-bin/readart.cgi?ArtNum=43448 (accessed April 28, 2004).

2. "Homeland Security Could Hamper Maine's Tourism Industry," *USA Today*, March 23, 2004. See www.usatoday.com/travel/news/2004-03-23-tourism-security_x.htm (accessed April 28, 2004); on Massachusetts labor statistics, see Massachusetts Division of Unemployment Assistance and Massachusetts Labor Force Data, www.detma.org (accessed May 4, 2004).

3. Robin Beck, "Local Tourist Businesses Threatened with Major Labor Shortage," *Boothbay Register*, March 25, 2004.

4. See David Borges, "Endnotes: Foreign Workers Keep the Massachusetts Economy Rolling," *Massachusetts Benchmarks* 4 (summer 2001); www.massbenchmarks.org (accessed April 28, 2004).

5. Ethan Zindler, "Coalition Seeks Aid in Visa Cutoff," *Cape Cod Times*, April 29, 2004; nl.newsbank.com accessed April 29, 2004); Beck, "Local Tourist Businesses Threatened." In this article, Dick Grotton of the Maine Restaurant Association called the labor shortage "a crisis situation."

6. Longley.

7. Sally Rose, "Visa Limit Vexes Local Businesses," *Provincetown Banner* and *Provincetown Advocate*, March 18, 2004.

8. To: glc1173 from Beermaven, in Longley.

9. Mandy Locke, "Summer Visa Changes Will Leave Vineyarders Short on Foreign Help," *Vineyard Gazette*, April 28, 2004, www.mvgazette.com (accessed April 28, 2004).

10. Longley. See also Ethan Zindler and Susan Moeller, "Cape Taps New Source for Workers," *Cape Cod Times*, April 21, 2004, nl.newsbank.com (accessed April 29, 2004).

11. Zindler and Moeller. See also Jay Davis, "Tourist Businesses Now Eye Virgin Islands Workers," April 21, 2004; http://rockland.villagesoup.com (accessed April 28, 2004).

12. Beck.

13. Philip Dinham, "Temporary H-2B Worker, Is Jamaica's Remitted Salvation under Threat?" www.jamaicans.com (accessed April 28, 2004).

14. On gender, race, and global capitalism see Christine G. T. Ho, "Caribbean Transnationalism as a Gendered Process," *Latin American Perspectives* 26 (September 1999): 34–54; C. Katz, "On the Grounds of Globalization: A Topography for Feminist Political Engagement," *Signs* 26, 1213–1237; and Karen Brodkin, "Global Capitalism: What's Race Got to Do with It?" *American Ethnologist* 27 (2000): 237–256.

15. Laura Bly, "Localities Cashing in on Same-Sex Marriages," *USA Today*, February 27, 2004, D1; Fred Bayles, "Provincetown Plans Marriage Licenses for Non-Mass. Gays," *USA Today*, April 13, 2004, A3.

16. Douglas Belkin, "Massachusetts Tourism, Marriage Industry Foresees Boom in Same-Sex Nuptial," *Knight Ridder Tribune Business News*, February 26, 2004; Conor Berry, "Restaurants Busy, Bookings Up as Gay Marriage Boosts Provincetown," *Knight Ridder Tribune Business News*, May 11, 2004; Sarah Schweitzer, "Provincetown, Mass., Prepares for Gay Wedding Celebration," *Knight Ridder Tribune Business News*, May 14, 2004; Warren St. John, "Provincetown's Days in the Sun Are Coming Early This Year," *New York Times*, May 17, 2004, A17.

17. Mary Wittenburg, "Amid Roses and Camera Clicks, Day of Vows: From Provincetown to Springfield, Gays Apply for Marriage Licenses as Media Chronicle Historic Moment," *Christian Science Monitor*, May 18, 2004. For online instructions on how, where, and when to get married in Provincetown, see also www.provincetown.com/plan/marriages/ (accessed April 28, 2004). It offers a list of ministers and officials who are eligible to perform ceremonies, a list of restaurants and caterers, and a list of photographers and videographers.

18. John D'Emilio was one of the first scholars to make a connection between

homosexuality and capitalism, in his groundbreaking essay "Capitalism and Gay Identity."

19. For a list of committees, see www.provincetowngov.org (accessed April 28, 2004).

20. See Michael Cunningham, "The Secret of Provincetown: Cape Cod's Rainbow Colony," *Our World*, July/August 1991, 24.

21. Dan Scroggins, conversation.

22. Amelia Carlos, interview.

23. Gordon Wood, "Faux Populism," review of *Self Rule: A Cultural History of American Democracy,* by Robert H. Wiebe, *New Republic* (October 1995): 39.

NOTES ON SOURCES AND HISTORIOGRAPHY

See Karen C. Krahulik, "Cape Queer: The Politics of Sex, Class and Race in Provincetown, Massachussetts, 1859–1999" (Ph.D. diss., New York University, 2000), 2–3, 8–10, 15–18, for notes on sources see 405–414; and Karen C. Krahulik, "Cape Queer?: Space-taking Politics in Provincetown, Massachussetts," *Journal of Homosexuality,* forthcoming.

Index

AMERICAN HISTORY AND CULTURE

General Editors: Neil Foley, Kevin Gaines, Martha Hodes, and Scott Sandage

Guess Who's Coming to Dinner Now? Multicultural Conservatism in America
Angela D. Dillard

One Nation Underground: A History of the Fallout Shelter
Kenneth D. Rose

The Body Electric: How Strange Machines Built the Modern American
Carolyn Thomas de la Peña

Black and Brown: African Americans and the Mexican Revolution, 1910–1920
Gerald Horne

Impossible to Hold: Women and Culture in the 1960s
Edited by Avital H. Bloch and Lauri Umansky

Provincetown: From Pilgrim Landing to Gay Resort
Karen Christel Krahulik

About the Author

KAREN CHRISTEL KRAHULIK received her bachelor's degree in religion from Princeton University in 1991 and her doctorate in American history from New York University in 2000. She has received grants from New York University, Harvard University, the Massachusetts Foundation for the Humanities, and the Bay State Historical League. After living in Provincetown for three years, she moved to Duke University, where she directs the Center for LGBT Life and teaches in the Women's Studies Program.